CONVERGENCE

ISBN 978-1-119-25621-2 (hardback)
ISBN 978-1-119-25623-6 (ePDF)
ISBN 978-1-119-25628-1 (ePub)
ISBN 978-1-119-25626-7 (O-BK)

Executive Commissioning Editor: Helen Castle
Project Editor: Miriam Murphy
Assistant Editor: Calver Lezama

Page design by Emily Chicken
Cover image by Aaron Laniosz
Cover design and page layouts by Karen Willcox, www.karenwillcox.com
Printed in Italy by Printer Trento Srl

CONVERGENCE: THE REDESIGN OF DESIGN

WILEY

Randy Deutsch

CONTENTS

DEDICATION

To my daughter, Michol:

May your curiosity, multivarious interests and passion for learning converge into a fulfilling lifetime of self-expression, service, and exploration.

ACKNOWLEDGEMENTS

We often think of reading and writing as a solitary acts, but they can also be common acts of convergence. Salman Rushdie once explained, "a different kind of identity is produced 'as reader and writer merge, through the medium of the text, to become a collective being that both writes as it reads and reads as it writes.' For Rushdie, this is the greatest and most subversive gift offered by a book."[1]

I would like to thank my team at Wiley for the opportunity to write for AD, and for their guidance, support, and encouragement throughout the writing of this book. Special thanks to Amanda Miller, vice president and publisher; Dr. Paul Sayer, publisher; Miriam Murphy, project editor; Amy Odum, senior production editor; Justin Mayhew, associate marketing director; and Calver Lezama, who has now worked with me on several books.

A hearty thank you to Helen Castle for recognizing the promise of the book from the very beginning and for helping to shepherd the initial idea for the book into its present state.

Also special thanks to my contributors Brian Ringley, Nathan Miller, Toru Hasegawa, Robert Yori, Robert Vierlinger, Sam Miller, Anthony Buckley-Thorp, the folks at PARTISANS, Philip Beesley, Markku Allison, Yun Kyu Yi, Mani Golparvar Fard, Jamie Farrell, Nels Long, M A Greenstein, Jose Sanchez, Carin Whitney, and Matthew Krissel for their generosity of time, and sharing of their experience and insights.

Lastly, my thanks to Aaron Lanoisz, who not only rendered the expert, colorful diagrams throughout the book, but also provided the inspiration for the cover. Aaron proved to be a gifted, trusted and creative collaborator and always-reliable sounding board throughout the writing of the book, and for that—and his wisdom and patience—I am grateful. I am confident that he is on his way to become a leading architect.

ENDNOTES

1 Les Back, *Academic Diary*, MIT Press, Cambridge MA, 2016, p. 123.

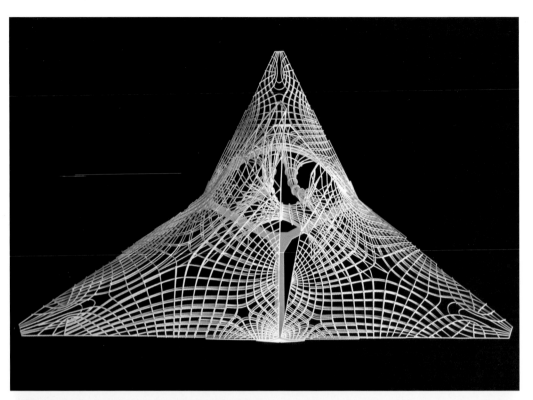

2

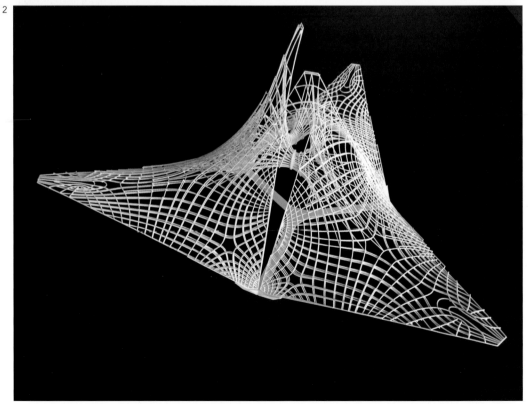

INTRODUCTION
DESIGN IN A TIME OF SIMULTANEITY, SUPERINTEGRATION, AND CONVERGENCE

*This convergence will be recognized as the largest, most complex,
and most surprising event on the planet up until this time.*
—Kevin Kelly[1]

There is today a pronounced and accelerated convergence in architecture. This convergence is occurring in building design, fabrication, and construction because of doers, not thinkers, and in practice, not academia. It is about solution-centric individuals engaging in real-time problem solving, not in abstractions. The nature of this convergence, where things are converging, and what that convergence means for architecture is the subject of this book.

The emergent forces and technologies that have come together in the second decade of the twenty-first century have developed to the point where real-time integration of all facets of the design and construction process is now possible. Computational tools, collaborative work processes, and the cloud make real-time/right-time convergence today a reality. However, tools aren't the only things causing this convergence: it's also due to the maturity of the design community. Those who have been at this for a while, as they attest throughout this book, recognize a convergence of forces, technologies, and workflows not only in their own work, but throughout the profession and industry.

There is even another force at work: millennials. No longer restricted to use of the tools created and distributed by software manufacturers, and impatient with the old guard, standard procedures, business as usual, and the status quo, young and emerging professionals are driving this movement toward convergence by taking matters into their own hands via employee-created and freely disseminated software plug-ins and add-ons, along with user-empowered scripting and visual programming, thereby improving workflows and increasing efficiencies.

CONVERGENCE DEFINED
Design professionals today recognize that technology and work processes are converging in their area of practice or expertise. *Convergence* refers to two or more things coming together, joining together, or evolving into one. It is manifested in such things as building information modeling (BIM) and computation; gaming and spatial analysis that join in virtual reality; design optimization and fabrication; and reality capture co-joining in photogrammetry, visual sensing laser scanning, drones, and robotics. What design professionals don't realize is that these convergences are taking place in all facets of the design professions and construction industry. Moreover, they don't have a thorough understanding of

1 and 2 Robert Vierlinger with Bollinger+Grohmann Engineers and Zaha Hadid Architects (ZHA), 3D print of the Pavilion for the CIAB, 2013.
The project development of expressive structural logics with Karamba3d demanded an extraordinary level of interdisciplinary collaboration in the design and development of the structure.

how the pieces fit together, what the potential impacts are, or—most importantly for their practices—where all of this is heading. The convergence referred to in the book title has both practical and emergent antecedents. Architecture is a complex undertaking requiring the input of many individuals with varying interests, backgrounds, and expertise. This has not changed—and will not change. What *is* changing is the way these individuals are working, communicating, and collaborating. Their individual contributions—and the tools they are using—are converging. To meet today's demands for speed, affordability, and quality, they are integrating their efforts. With increasing demands to make decisions in real time, design professionals—having met the challenges and opportunities of this moment—are moving beyond the linearity metaphor and thinking in terms of simultaneity, superintegration, and convergence.

Architects and other design professionals today are expected to design and construct in a manner that uses fewer resources, while still innovating, adding value, and reducing waste. Deliverables

3 Deutsch Insights, role convergence diagram, 2017. The comprehensive body of convergence is made up of individual converging chromosomes.

3

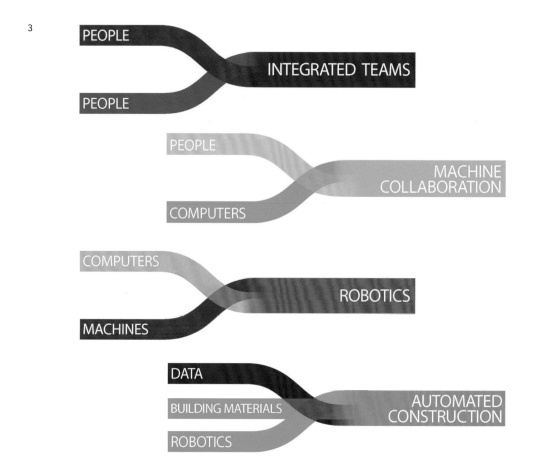

have to take less time and cost less money to produce, while not compromising on quality—expectations that many feel are unrealistic at best, and often result in a negative impact on outcomes, working relationships, and experiences. Old paradigms such as "Quality, speed, and price: pick any two" no longer apply. Owners expect all three—perfect, now, and free—on almost every project.

Traditional linear thinking no longer works in this converged-upon world. At the same time, the emergent forces and technologies that have come together in the second decade of the twenty-first century have developed to the point where they make real-time integration of all facets of the design and construction process possible. Computational tools, work processes, and the cloud make real-time convergence today a reality.

Architects in particular are about to go through a period of intense change, a transformation brought about due to convergence. An understanding of the convergence that is taking place is pivotal to practice and how architects will work in the years ahead; it is critical to education and how architects are trained and educated; and it is central in the reappraisal of the architecture that this transformation will bring about.

4 Deutsch Insights, circle flow diagram, 2017.
Emergent forces and technologies have developed to the point where real-time integration of all facets of the design and construction process is now possible.

4

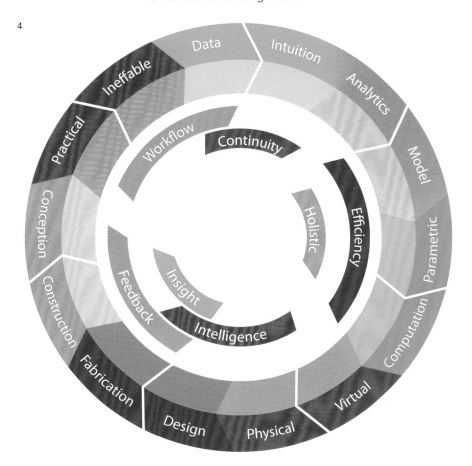

5 Deutsch Insights, Practical and Ineffable Convergence, 2017.
Design professionals are increasingly challenged to realize meaning and agency within the constraints of computational tools.

Whereas convergence is marked by a blurring of lines, disciplines, and roles brought about by interdisciplinary collaboration, until recently architects have tended to innovate only in their own sector. Today, for example, contractors often are at the table with the owner and architect from day one—something architects didn't have to consider even a generation ago. "Architects and general contractors don't always involve subcontractors in early phases of design and preconstruction. But if they want to prevent time and money from trickling down the drain, they should."[2]

In the past, architects had a tendency and preference to study and address each subject separately. Some people in our industry address BIM, some address computational tools … but few address both combined. BIM has enabled architects to include means and methods in their models, enabling them to venture into design-build delivery methods, fabrication, and direct-to-fabrication projects from their models. Who is tracking that movement? Like the Internet, convergence exists despite isolated, disconnected, or unconnected efforts and focus.

It is hard to address a tool or process that is in motion, especially one that is moving toward, or merging with, another. When something moves, it has a trajectory: It moves toward or away from something, whether by means of push or pull. If everything converges, what is it converging toward? What is the end point? The meeting point? What are we working toward?

Is that meeting point nothing more than increased efficiency? Today's architecture, engineering, construction, and operations (AECO) industry is marked by productivity, innovation, affordability, and speed. It's not just that things are speeding up, but that they are moving *toward* each other: they're converging. If the vocabulary we use to explain our work is any indication, we as an industry have spent the past decade leveraging the language of performance to get work approved that aims at—if never quite achieving—the nexus of perfect, now, and free.

CONVERGENCE PARADIGMS

Because so many innovations appear to be disconnected and disparate, there's a temptation, when looking for a guiding theory or justification, to tie them together into a convenient framework. Does doing so conclusively capture the trajectory of convergence? Three convergence models represent lenses by which to see what is occurring in our industry: Software of Everything, Master Algorithm, and Total Architecture.

There have been numerous attempts to create a Software of Everything. Specific tools such as Kimon Onuma's Onuma System address the entire building lifecycle from planning through operations, and (in a more limited way) Tekla's Structural Designer combines structural analysis and design into a single application. However, a more general look at how BIM itself represents a convergence of all facets of design, construction, and beyond will serve as an illustration of what the Software of Everything might look like.

As will be explored in a later chapter, purpose-built BIM models are being used today for code compliance, cost estimating/quantity take-offs, coordination and fabrication, scheduling, and on-site production control. But that is not all. In current applications of BIM, in addition to design authoring you can model existing conditions, conduct a site analysis, undertake programming, do engineering analysis, evaluate for LEED status, conduct a design review, do clash detection, validate for code compliance, undertake digital fabrication, oversee asset management, and record modeling of construction and conditions

6 Deutsch Insights, Venn diagram, 2017
Diagram representing the convergence of design, structural analysis, and the cloud.

6

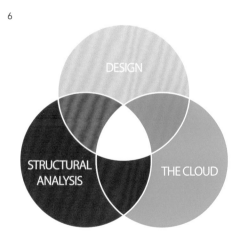

over time via machine vision. Without purporting to be everything for and to everyone, BIM stands as an exemplar of the Software-of-Everything approach to convergence. More on the Software of Everything can be found in the epilogue.

The Master Algorithm framework is represented by Flux's Metro software; Aditazz's competition-winning, computer-generated process; and other pervasive computing and generative design-by-algorithm approaches. The Algorithm of Everything is discussed in Chapter 4. Total Architecture represents a gestalt approach, a comprehensive high-tech/high-touch design process practiced by such hybrid firms as PARTISANS' partners and Assemble. Further discussion of Total Architecture, or the Architecture of Everything, can be found in Chapter 7.

Nevertheless, as convenient as these frameworks are, they don't tell the whole story of the convergence that is occurring today. At best, they distill a single strand of the converging branches, but leave out a great deal, not the least of which is the human element—creativity, intuition, insights, the human override—that cannot be accounted for in singular explanations. You might argue that it's all human generated—including, if not especially, algorithms—and that we're fooling ourselves when we discount the human effort and, yes, creativity behind the computational rule-making. We start to split hairs when through machine learning robots and drones start to teach themselves—and each other. (Where is the human element in that scenario?) *Convergence*, as the word implies, doesn't distinguish between what is man-made and what is machine-made, as it is interested in where the two meet.

These frameworks call attention to the challenges that convergence raises, forcing us to reckon with and overcome them. Where in the design process is human input needed and where is it redundant? What role will our legacy tools play and to what extent are they holding us back? How much depends on our industry's ability to learn new skillsets (our technology readiness) or on our acquiring the mindsets necessary to keep up and avoid creating workflow bottlenecks? "The problem with architecture and construction," says Petr Novikov, "is that we design digitally and then construct manually."[3]

This book, as an investigation and meditation on the impact of technology on the education and making of design professionals, sees convergence as a way to explain and illustrate what is happening now in the world of architectural design, as well as to discuss the implications for the future of education, training, and practice. There is a need to clarify and make concrete what is happening at this moment in time for those who want to stay relevant but may be too close to connect the dots for themselves.

Books—whether physical, digital, audio, or whatever new as-yet-introduced format—are seen by some as antiquated technology. In the middle of the second decade of the third millennium, though,

7 Deutsch Insights, Venn diagram, 2017
Diagram representing the convergence of what is designed, how it is constructed, and how it operates.

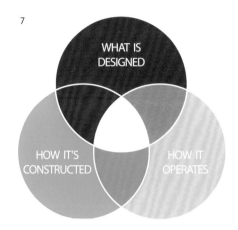

7

WHAT IS
DESIGNED

HOW IT'S
CONSTRUCTED

HOW IT
OPERATES

books are still the best means we have for synthesizing moments and movements; giving them a name; and, as importantly, using a language that can be understood, shared, and discussed by others. The purpose of this book is to bring a trend to the fore, give it a name, and start a dialogue. Although we cannot stop the rise of technology, we can seek to understand where this trend is headed—and in so doing devise a new model that helps the profession and industry move forward.

Along with a name, this book sets out to give this industry-wide transformation a direction and a sense of clarity, by shining a light on the factors that have given rise to it. This is so we can recognize where it is occurring, more readily adapt to and prepare for it, and anticipate where it is going to occur—but also to make it less threatening and more manageable. As this book is about the firms, individuals, and teams who have innovated to thrive in this environment, it sets out to provide design professionals working today with a better understanding of what is occurring in their field.

A note on the diagrams interspersed in the pages that follow: They are intended to provide a snapshot of what technologies and work processes are coming together, and what this coming-together means in terms of workflows, work outcomes, and the way we practice. When combined, they begin to form a design ecology—a design ecosystem—that points to a direction where the industry is headed. These snapshots, collectively, form the start of a roadmap for things to come. You—the reader, designer, design technologist—get to complete this story.

The convergences explored in this book have implications for both education and practice. The topic of convergences will be at once familiar, and of especially urgent interest, to emerging design professionals and academics, a readership that is knee-deep in the technology but is unable to articulate on a higher plane how what they do fits into the bigger scheme of things. They were members of the online crowdsourced library of applications AEC-APPs, and more recently of SmartGeometry, of the Association for Computer Aided Design in Architecture (ACADIA) (but not necessarily the American Institute of Architects [AIA] or the Royal Institute of British Architects [RIBA]), and represent the future of the new architecture, engineering, and construction (AEC). They are voracious readers, learners, and makers, and have figured out how to move a piece of the profession and industry forward, yet are keenly interested in learning how their individual efforts fit into a larger framework.

Convergence is the natural succession in the research that aligns with, grows out of, and builds on my previous two books on collaborative building information modeling (BIM) and data analytics in the AEC industry. Convergence hints at what the future of architectural practice might look like and where architectural design is heading.

Convergence helps identify the future for architects as digital knowledge workers who bring not only skills supported by the

8 Philip Beesley, PBAI, Hylozoic Ground, Canadian Pavilion, Venice Biennale, Venice, Italy, 2010.
Following page: Hylozoic Ground, where tens of thousands of lightweight, digitally fabricated components were fitted with microprocessors and proximity sensors that reacted to human presence. Photograph by Philip Beesley.

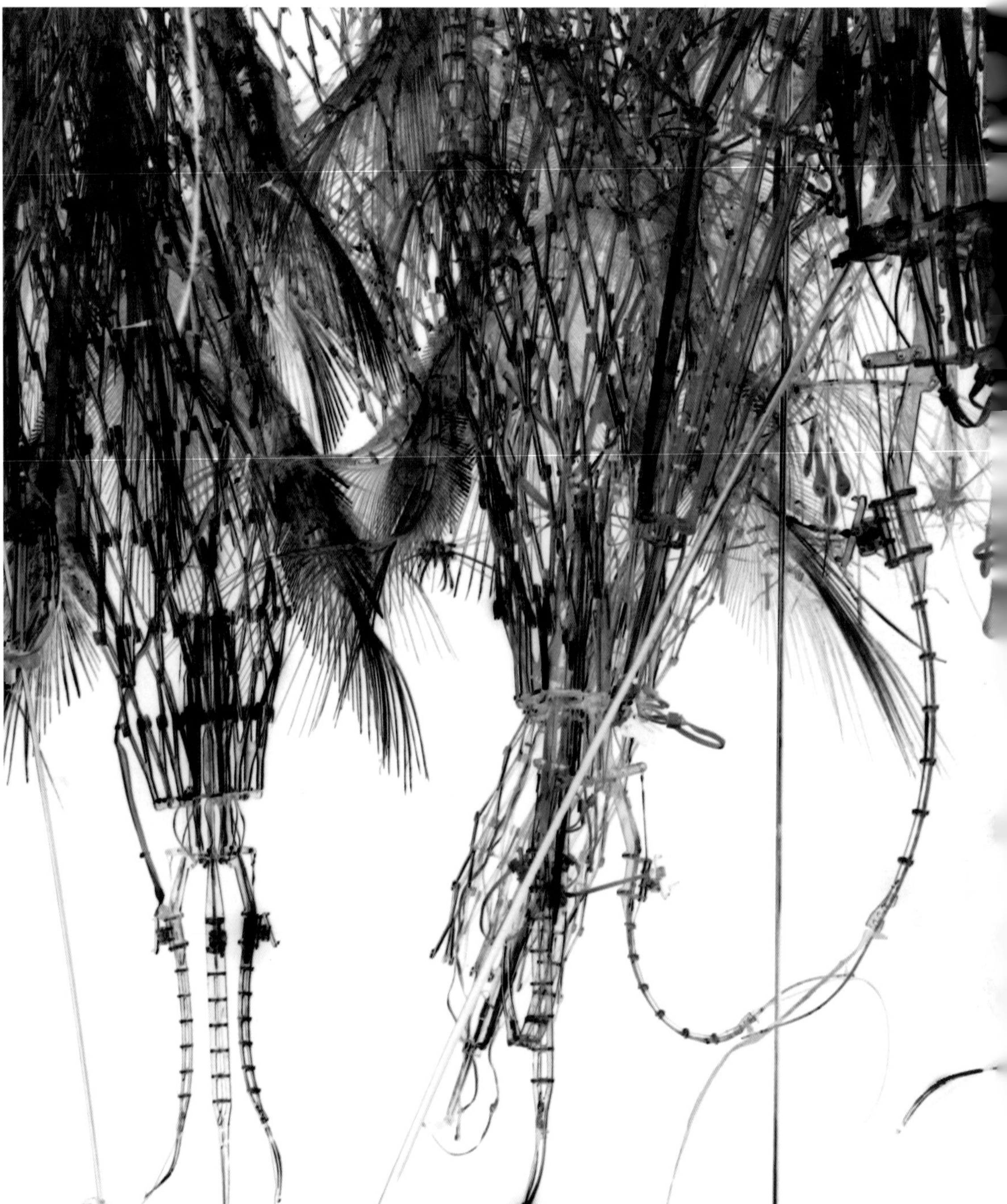

continued development of technology and digital processes, but also (and importantly) any creative skills they may possess. More importantly, it helps the reader adapt to the new reality of work. Adapting to the new world of work requires learning to think simultaneously on several fronts and from several points of view. This is the world of convergence.

CONVERGENCE QUESTIONS

Convergence raises as many questions as it sets out to answer. Are things in our industry converging? If so, what is converging and how is this convergence coming about? In other words, what is fueling this convergence? In what ways is convergence part of the transformation and change the industry is going through? Where is convergence headed? How far can it go? Is any part of the convergence that is currently occurring in design and construction unique to our industry? If so, what part(s)? Why is this convergence happening now? What do we hope to gain by converging our tools and work processes? What specific challenges does convergence present to the designer?

Sophisticated tools for modeling and representing buildings already exist. How we use those tools, and how they dictate what the outcomes will be, is a design challenge. What specifically are the tools and work processes that are converging? How are individuals and organizations converging their tools and work processes? What benefits are they seeing? What is the ultimate endgame in the convergence of our tools and work processes? What specific skillsets would someone need to develop to work effectively as tools and work processes continue to converge? What are the implications of convergence for the role of the designer, and for aesthetics? For how we design, build, fabricate, and construct? In other words, for how we work?

Convergence improves the flow of data, information, and knowledge. Convergence improves the ease of use and accessibility of our tools. Convergence addresses emergence and complexity by rejecting a piecemeal approach in favor of holistic, integrated solutions. Brian Ringley, educator and design technology platform specialist at Woods Bagot, juggles a number of digital tools and work processes. "If we make the base assumption that convergence makes our lives easier, makes delivery more efficient, and makes the world a better place, the questions become: What are we sacrificing for that convergence to happen?" asks Ringley. "And, knowing what we're sacrificing, does it matter? Awareness is the first step. Then, once we're aware of what is being sacrificed, does that matter to us?"[4]

Convergence makes our lives easier, and our work more productive and efficient. But what are we sacrificing? This book, *Convergence*, addresses this question, painting a picture of what practice and education will look like once we've found a solution. As the convergence of computing and telecommunications resulted in modern telephony, what factors exist today to make convergence a reality and likely to continue, given how systems have evolved to converge at this point in time? Chapter 1 looks at other fields that have experienced convergence, and explains how convergence relates to, but ultimately differs from, integration, consolidation, multitasking, automation, and other forms of optimization—symptoms that do not on their own explain the rise of convergence.

Chapters 2 through 8 explore convergences in contemporary design practice that now occur at the meeting of two seemingly opposite forces: data and intuition; analytics and model; parametrics and computation; virtual and physical; design and fabrication; conception and construction; and practical and ineffable. Each chapter builds upon the preceding chapters.

This book is an attempt to understand what is happening in the design professions and building industry as it is happening; thus, it cannot claim to provide a comprehensive picture. The epilogue explores what the future holds for convergence, and whether it will ultimately result in a single unified platform.

ENDNOTES

1 Kevin Kelly, The Inevitable: Understanding the 12 Technological Forces That Will Shape Our Future (New York: Viking, 2016), 291.
2 Angus W. Stocking, "Want More Time for Design? It's All About Prefabrication and Lean Manufacturing in Construction," September 2, 2015, https://redshift. autodesk.com/prefabrication-and-lean-manufacturing-in-construction/
3 Quoted in Zach Mortice, "4 Ways a Robot or Drone 3D Printer Will Change Architecture and Construction," September 1, 2015, https://redshift.autodesk.com/drone-3d-printer/
4 Brian Ringley, interview with author, January 5, 2016.

IMAGE

Figures 1 and 2 © Robert Vierlinger; figures 3–7 © Deutsch Insights; figure 8 © PBAI, Philip Beesley photographer

CHAPTER 1
10 FACTORS LEADING TOWARD CONVERGENCE

There will be a stronger connection between what's designed, built, and how it operates.
—Philip Bernstein[1]

This chapter is intended to provide a high-level overview of a trend in the profession and industry. Before exploring specific examples of convergence in our industry, it is important to understand the factors that lead to convergence, to place convergence into a larger context, and to address challenges brought about by convergence. In this chapter we'll explore what convergence is—and isn't; what factors enable convergence; how convergence relates to and differs from integrated design, lean, and other industry trends; and what, if anything, are the distinguishing factors of an AEC convergence.

In the introduction *convergence* was defined as two or more things coming together, joining or evolving into one. Two concurrent forces focus the topic. Today nearly everyone in AE firms feels pressure to work faster, at lower expense, while maintaining a high level of innovation and quality. One explanation for this pressure can be traced back to the most recent economic downturn: since 2008, architects and other design professionals have been expected to design and construct in a manner that uses fewer resources while still innovating, adding value while reducing waste. Deliverables have to take less time and cost less money to produce, while not compromising on quality. However, these expectations are unrealistic at best, and often have a negative impact on outcomes, working relationships, and experiences.

Especially since the most recent economic downturn, architects have had to economize and work more efficiently—not only to become more productive, but also to measure and demonstrate their effectiveness. This pressure is compounded by a shrinking workforce, within which design professionals are expected to make do with less. "During and after the recession, construction capacity was destroyed due to job loss as millions of construction workers were out of work," says one account. "In 2010, the number of people working in U.S. architectural firms plummeted. In turn, clients used the crisis to drive prices down further, taking advantage of the marketplace in crisis. Construction was buying at rock bottom, and architects were working at below-breakeven

1 Deutsch Insights, 2017.
A convergence is occurring
as traditional design and
construction phases blur.

cost just to keep the lights on. Many in the construction industry retired or departed. Five years after the recession, as design and construction vitality returns, the capacity to support it no longer exists in its previous form."[2] The situation is exacerbated by a reduction in the number of students pursuing careers in architecture; by firms not replacing those who have been laid off, because they were found to be redundant; by higher expectations for new hires due to advances in digital technology; and by the fact that there is a smaller pool of talented design professionals to hire from. Thus, architects feel pressure to perform in ways that are smarter, faster, and require fewer resources.

CONVERGENCE AND INTEGRATION

To meet today's demands for speed, affordability, and quality, design professionals are integrating their efforts—and yet integration alone is not enough. Convergence relates to, but ultimately differs from, integration, integrated design, and integrated project delivery (IPD). Convergence ignores boundaries, whereas integration just moves them. This becomes apparent when looking at the Macleamy Curve or participating on an IPD project team. Convergence bypasses integration as a method for bringing two or more things together. Integration is about meeting earlier, and so reflects linear thinking. Integration is about breaking out of silos. With convergence, there are no silos.

With increasing demands to make decisions in real time, design professionals—having met the challenges and opportunities of this moment—are moving beyond the linearity metaphor and thinking in terms of simultaneity, superintegration, and convergence. At the same time, emergent tools and processes have arrived in time to make this possible. Nevertheless, *convergence* is incorrectly used as a substitute for related terms.

CONVERGENCE AND CONSOLIDATION

As with integration, convergence differs from but is informed by consolidation. As an industry, we're too loose and subjective in our substitutions, solipsistically comparing convergence with mergers, acquisitions, overlaps, synergy, and consolidations.

Convergence goes beyond the simple combining of two entities. Still, it is easy to see why design professionals confuse

2

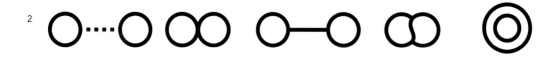

REMOTE   TOUCHING   CONNECTED   MESHED   UNIFIED

convergence with consolidation. No sooner does one learn a new tool—think Ecotect or Sefaira—than it is usurped by a conglomerate's even larger tool. Whether in school or practice, it is no longer enough to know individual topics, technologies, or tools: our new tools and work processes only have meaning in relation to other technologies and workflows. Mergers and acquisitions are a form of integration[3] where boundaries or moved, not obliterated.

While convergence is separate and different from consolidation, because many architecture firms are considering mergers or acquisitions, it is important to point out that mergers and acquisitions inform one another and therefore serve as a factor that brings about convergence, in that they ease access to information and resources ("We've been able to make connections neither of us could have made individually"[4]). The mergers and acquisitions of architecture firms are a consequence of the economic downturn[5]—a symptom, but not interchangeable with convergence.

Convergence, in other words, comprises even more than compression, in which everything in the building process becomes condensed. "'Building construction could become an incredibly fast and bespoke process,' … . 'Everything will get compressed.'"[6] Stuart-Smith imagines that constructing a building will be like using a desktop 3D printer: "You can make variety at no additional cost, and you can do it very quickly."[7] He envisions a near-future world where "drones troubleshoot … their designs as they go along, smoothing out errors and imperfections and planning ahead, building structures without any need for human supervision. … [T]his level of automation will bring increased accuracy, as well as material and energy efficiency."[8] Consolidation is more about reducing gaps—and therefore remaining in the linear paradigm—than collapsing gaps altogether.

What forces are propelling convergence forward? To take just one example, what role does the owner's demand for a decrease in finger-pointing—one-stop shopping for a single source of responsibility—and consolidation of building components play?

CONVERGENCE AND AUTOMATION
Convergence also differs from—but is informed by—automation, simulation, multitasking, lean, scrum, and other forms of optimization. By most accounts, a fully automated architectural

2 Relationship Types Diagram, 2017. Individual technologies, tools, and work processes have multiple ways in which they can interact. (Diagram after five levels of system integration, Richard Rush, *The Building Systems Integration Handbook*, 1986.)

process is still a long way off—or unlikely ever to substantially replace design as an activity.

Automating code compliance in architecture, engineering, and construction is one such area informing convergence in architecture. In a later chapter, we'll look at research in this area as it relates to convergence. For now, suffice it to say that researchers have attempted to develop methods for automated code checking going as far back as the 1980s, and in the years since we've seen tools such as Solibri Model Checker, AutoCodes, and Singapore's CORENET program attempting to automate this portion of the process. Another take on automation and convergence is where the computer is the designer,[9] or when buildings design themselves.[10]

While the topic of automating design will be addressed in a later chapter, one doesn't need to look to extremes, as custom tools can automate one's work process. There are many things in society today that are diverging rather than converging, such as the richer-vs.-poorer divide. The opposite of convergence isn't divergence, it's duplication and redundancy. Why do something over and over when it can be automated?

CONVERGENCE AND EFFICIENCY

Even more than automation alone, convergence is a strategy for increasing efficiency in design/fabrication/construction/operations. In this sense convergence serves as the answer to AECO productivity problems. Forget Moore's Law: under "Koomey's law," it's efficiency, not power, that doubles every year and a half.[11] Architects no longer need to work inefficiently: A change anywhere in BIM is a change everywhere, and they can apply the latest trends from Silicon Valley and the information technology (IT) industry in agile project management (scrum) and streamlining work processes in the automotive industry (lean) to their next building project. There is no question that the convergence that is now taking place in architecture is making design and construction more efficient, and creating opportunities—whether workarounds, just-in-time training, modularization, or automation of repetitive design actions—for design professionals to work smarter. Lean construction planning software such as BIM 360 Plan, for example, helps "reduce waste associated with overproduction, excess inventory, and task rework."[12] Increasingly, there are synergies between BIM and agile project management and lean construction— and here the operative word, *synergy*, is code for *convergence*.

With the industry's current interest in productivity and demonstrating outcomes, it would seem that efficiency is the *raison d'être* of convergence. It certainly is the case with BIM. How can everything be faster/better/cheaper/smarter/lighter/denser/greener?

Start with faster: Critical path items, such as room labeling in CodeBook and DRofus, not only assure program validation but also help tighten bloated schedules. Nathan Miller and

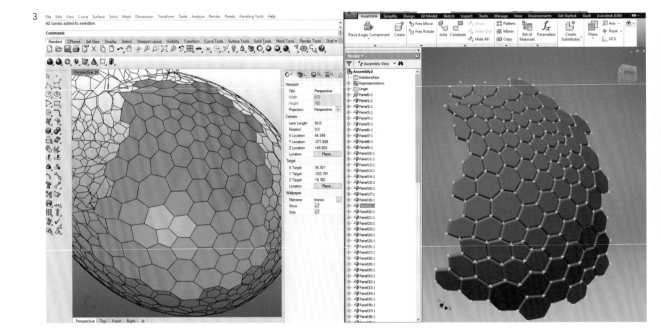

3 Proving Ground, Grasshopper-Inventor
Interoperability Design, 2016.
Design for manufacturing and mass
customization, enabled by making new data
connections between tools in the larger industry
supply chain.

4

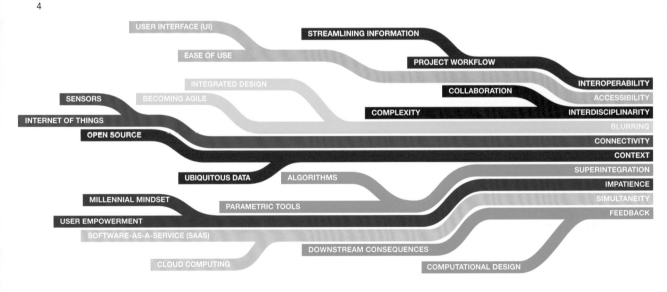

Proving Ground promise that they can help you, as a design professional, "plan your project for a better workflow by helping you define strategies that reduce the duplication of modeling work, expedite data transfer, and enable the ability to adapt to change."[13] What AECO consultants are selling is speed. Mies van der Rohe's dictum *Less is More* has become today's need to *Do More with Less*.

CONVERGENCE TRIGGERS

Whether brought about by, or compared with the four drivers—integration, consolidation, automation, and efficiency—the convergence we are seeing in the AECO industry is ubiquitous, taking place in all facets of the design professions and construction industry. The industry, as a whole, is just now beginning to realize this convergence, and yes, there is a struggle. Here, we'll look at the specific factors—the components and characteristics—that enable convergence in design, fabrication, and construction.

Why is convergence happening now? What is fueling or driving this convergence?

Convergences are triggered today by the changes brought about by computational tools, shifting work processes, the ubiquity of the cloud, and technological disruption. Some convergence factors are specific to the AECO industry, while other triggers are seen in other sectors or markets as well. What convergence factors—including the cloud, Internet, and digitization/digitalization—are general to other fields?

As with architecture, the field of journalism leverages digital technology, "with its flexibility, speed, boundless capacity, and ease of interactivity."[14] Digitalization, digitizing, or digitization, found in all convergence, is the "representation of an object, image, sound, document or signal (usually an analog signal) by generating a series of numbers that describe a discrete set of its points or samples."[15]

In a later chapter, we'll explore the reconciliation between digital and reality within convergence. Admittedly, for convergence to take place, additional factors (e.g., economic and cultural forces) beyond the purview of this book come into play, filling significant roles in the streamlining of technology and work processes that we are currently experiencing. The AECO industry faces incredible shifts—in digital tools, in data-driven design and construction, and in advanced computation—that dramatically alter contemporary workflows.

4 Deutsch Insights, Convergence Drivers Sankey diagram, 2017.
Convergence comprises more than compression and consolidation, where everything in the building process becomes condensed.

10 FACTORS BRINGING ABOUT CONVERGENCE

Central to our understanding here are 10 factors and forces leading to, or contributing to, or fostering convergence in the AECO industry: (1) accessibility, (2) blurring, (3) context, (4) connectivity, (5) feedback, (6) impatience, (7) interdisciplinarity, (8) interoperability, (9) simultaneity, and (10) superintegration.

ACCESSIBILITY

At first glance, it might be hard to see the connection between user interface (UI), ease of use of digital tools, accessibility of other industries' workflow and data and access to a larger amount of the AEC industry workflow, and convergence. However, looking at how designers work today versus in the recent past, the connection between the two becomes clear. "It can be anything from I now have access, as a designer, to material information through a tool like KieranTimberlake's Tally in the realm of material science," suggests Brian Ringley, design technologist at Woods Bagot.[16] "To something where I now have access to Karamba Grasshopper workflow where my design is being directly driven by structural knowledge, which is typically outside of my field, which is directly controlling a robot, which is also not necessarily central [to my field]. This kind of control, openness and connectivity to the traditional design model is largely due to big data, interoperability, more accessible algorithms through user-friendly software, and computational power through contemporary hardware."[17]

"What we are working towards is that everyone has an access point to the model," adds Ringley. This is where defining accessibility in terms of ease of use becomes critical. "One important distinction to make is that by *easier* I mean accessibility—that more people can access something because it requires less specialized knowledge."[18]

It is a fundamental tenet of technology that if software is overly complex and difficult to work with, no one is going to use it. Examples in our industry are legion. For some, Revit's user interface can be nonintuitive and tedious. To increase its ease of use, some suggest incorporating the use of Dynamo in workflows. The free plug-in Human UI for Grasshopper creates a user-friendly interface for nonprogrammers to modify designs in Rhino. Both CodeBook and DRofus fill in gaps in the critical path, making the complex that much simpler and easier.[19]

With time, our tools—both hardware and software—are becoming easier to navigate and work with. No further evidence is needed than the fact that we can today talk hands-free with computers (e.g., Siri[20]). And with accessibility to otherwise complex and proprietary tools comes convergence.

"In terms of accessibility, and integrating these tools into our daily life, how many people didn't embrace BIM because they couldn't get it installed on their computer?" asks Anthony Buckley-Thorp of Flux. "Or their system crashed because they tried to do it on a laptop and their graphics card? If we can start providing access to this data in the web browser. Even my dad uses Facebook now, and he would not use other digital tools. It is so easy today to get direct access. There's the deluge right there."

BLURRING

The blurring of boundaries, phases, and roles brought about by the implementation of integrated design, and by working

5

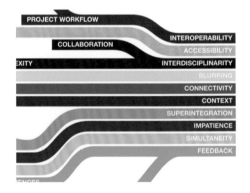

PROJECT WORKFLOW

COLLABORATION

EXITY

INTEROPERABILITY

ACCESSIBILITY

INTERDISCIPLINARITY

BLURRING

CONNECTIVITY

CONTEXT

SUPERINTEGRATION

IMPATIENCE

SIMULTANEITY

FEEDBACK

IENCES

collaboratively on integrated teams, has encouraged convergence in the profession and industry. Organizations have flattened, becoming more adaptive and agile, in response to economy demands, and with that flattening there has been a decrease in the importance of titles and an increase in the removal of silos. Professional identities, roles, and attendant responsibilities have followed suit. Blurring takes place not only within organizations, but also between organizations. "The convergence phenomenon implies the deconstruction of existing value chains, transforming industry boundaries and creating new competitive spaces."[21]

Roles within organizations have evolved in recent years due to the advent of new digital technologies and work processes. The rise of the design technologist—who can add (billable) value to teams while working or researching independently (overhead) when required—and the attendant diminished role of the IT professional within architecture firms is one such example. Usually an architect (as opposed to strictly a technology expert), a design technologist provides digital design leadership while directly contributing to the production of the design, visualizations, and building delivery solutions. Although the position differs from firm to firm, *design technologist* is a leadership position, one that is not normally filled by recent architecture school graduates, but instead by licensed architects. Design technologists—and their digital technologist brethren—have been taking IT away from the IT folks, just as BIM managers have been doing for CAD managers. In fact, the introduction of technologies and workflows in the industry has required new roles from the lowest rungs of the organization chart to the highest tiers (CIOs and CEOs), where the role of the architect is increasingly requiring not only the delivery of design intent but also the orchestration of information.

The blurring of roles and boundaries is not confined to other industries (e.g., New Industrial Convergence refers to a blurring in the boundaries between manufacturing, medicine, and media). As will be explored in the chapters that follow, convergence has brought about hybrid firms that include fabrication and manufacturing in their nontraditional workflows. Indeed, some are calling for an industry-wide overhaul of how architects define what they do in the 21st century, by not merely blurring but obliterating the lines between architecture, engineering, and construction.[22]

CONTEXT
With convergence, we're rewriting the very definition of what we mean by a building being *contextual*. With available open source data, there is no excuse for buildings not to be informed by their surroundings. The days of the iconic object designed in spite of, rather than in concert with, its surroundings are over.[23]

CONNECTIVITY
While convergence leverages the input of individuals from diverse backgrounds on collaborative teams, the operative word is *connection:* the connecting of experts to move projects forward faster. According to Scott Simpson, Senior Fellow of

5 Deutsch Insights, Convergence Drivers enlarged diagram, 2017.
It is important to understand the factors that lead to convergence, and to place convergence into a larger context, to see where the industry is headed.

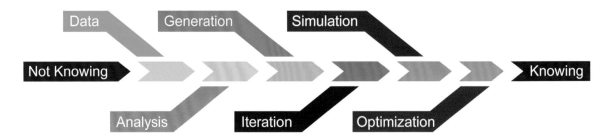

6

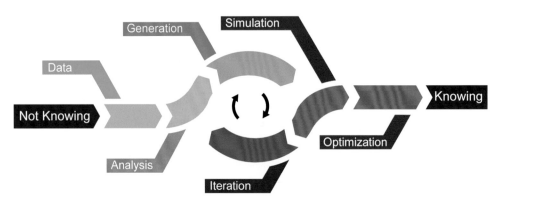

7

6 Deutsch Insights, linear decision knowing flow diagram,
2017.
Design professionals infrequently happen upon decisions
that "stick" by means of a linear process.

7 Deutsch Insights, iterative decision knowing flow
diagram, 2017.
More often, design professionals move from not knowing
to knowing by means of an iterative feedback loop,
converging in on a decision.

the Design Futures Council, "A key concept of this brave new world is 'convergence'—finding ways to connect experts from disparate disciplines to devise truly new solutions to problems."[24] As Marc Benioff wrote in his foreword to Scoble and Israel's *The Age of Context*, "Today … the world is being reshaped by the convergence of social and mobile cloud technologies. The combination of these technologies enables us to connect everything together in a new way and is dramatically transforming the way we live and work."[25]

One can also see the impact that connectivity and the Internet of Things (IoT) will have on convergence: buildings, structures with embedded sensors, and objects will all be connected. The connection between and among things implies a relationship between objects that provides opportunities to be exploited by the industry. One such connection is between BIM tools and the IoT to address a building's power consumption[26] and energy management. The IoT also provides architects with the opportunity to validate/invalidate their assumptions, such as when sensor technology generates feedback (see the next factor) on a design direction virtually before the design team—and importantly, the client—commits to a particular course of action.[27] The operative word for the IoT is *connectivity*.

FEEDBACK
Our architectural decisions have very real consequences. The ability to think of potential impacts and downstream consequences for our architectural acts is increased when presented with a feedback loop. Some of our more nuanced computational design tools have the model turn green when the design is well within constraints and red when we exceed them. Similarly, we can hold a smartphone camera up at the jobsite and observe where construction is ahead of schedule (the model on your phone turns green) and behind schedule (red). Most feedback loops are limited in scope. Feedback loops that take the entire building lifecycle into consideration, where current decisions are based on anticipated results or outcomes reported from the future, may not be far off. On February 17, 2016, I tweeted (with tongue positioned securely in cheek):

> *New tool performs post-occupancy evaluation before commencing design so you can revise before you begin.*

A few hours later, Professor of Construction Management at the University of Brescia, Italy, Angelo Ciribini, reply-tweeted from Milan, Italy:

> @randydeutsch We are investigating such a topic at @polimi with @s_mastrolembo @ThePhilpster

It appears that we'll soon be making decisions early on in conceptual design based on and informed by events in the future that haven't happened yet.

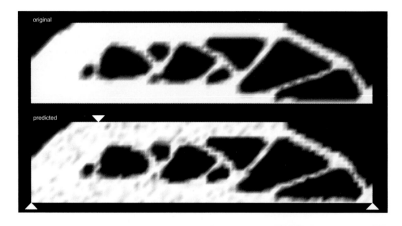

8

9

8 Robert Vierlinger, Truss Optimization, 2016.
Machine learning applied to the topological
optimization of a truss.

9 Robert Vierlinger, Human-Machine
Convergence in Architecture, 2016.
Patterns of façade openings evolved with
Octopus Machine Learning Tools.

IMPATIENCE

Impatience … the millennial generation wants it now, and doesn't understand why they have to wait. For this reason, millennials are a driving force behind convergence, a sentiment shared in a recent tweet by architect and educator Hiroshi Jacobs:

> Generation Z, Digital Natives, will demand control
> of their tools … @roshiJacobs #AIABCC16

As mentioned in the introduction, millennials are impatient with the old guard, standard procedures, business as usual, and the status quo. Emerging professionals are taking matters into their own hands via employee-created and freely disseminated plug-ins and add-ons, along with user-empowered scripting and visual programming, thereby improving workflows and increasing efficiencies. "Millennials have always had immediate access to a lot of things. They would never have used the Dewey Decimal system to find resources," says Ringley. "They would never have used hand-written citations on note cards to laboriously construct an outline for a research paper. Those are exercises we [older persons] went through." Ringley continues, "There was a bit of tedium involved. Sometimes tedium begets richer engagement with content. There is an impatience—and intolerance—with that tedium."[28]

With so many digital tools and apps already available, why author new tools? What triggers the need to create a new tool such as Octopus for gh3d? Is it just one thing, or are there multiple triggers? One way to reframe the making of digital tools is as applied research, says Robert Vierlinger of Bollinger+Grohmann Engineers. "The limits to the practically possible are a key driver to research, to create something which is justified by a real-world, full-scale application," said Vierlinger. "Needs and problems from practice provide research questions and ultimate testing grounds for the hypothesis and methods developed. What is created? For which problems? On what level has it been, what will be the future? Our research group creates tools which are tested and used at Bollinger+Grohmann Engineers, but further many people around the world. This ensures relevance and provides context. A sometimes criticized split of focus between academia and building industry can be easily outweighed by the matter of relevance. The idea for the original Octopus plug-in for gh3d was to intensify the ways in which a human designer could interact with a digital design aid to solve problems, and was inspired by issues of little control we ran into with existing tools like Galapagos. Karamba3d by my colleague Clemens Preisinger was made for high-performance integrated structural analysis, and similarly the recent machine learning tools in Octopus come from different needs regarding digital design communication, formation, representation, and performance."

INTERDISCIPLINARITY

As both an art and a science, architecture requires interdisciplinary, multidisciplinary, and transdisciplinary participation, merging

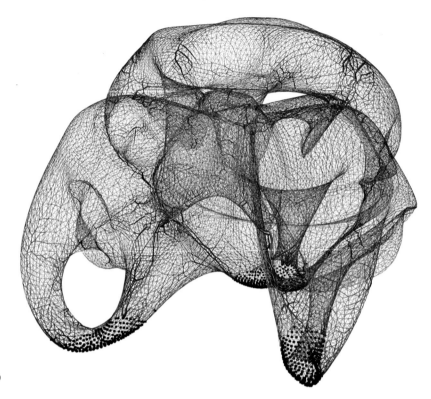

10

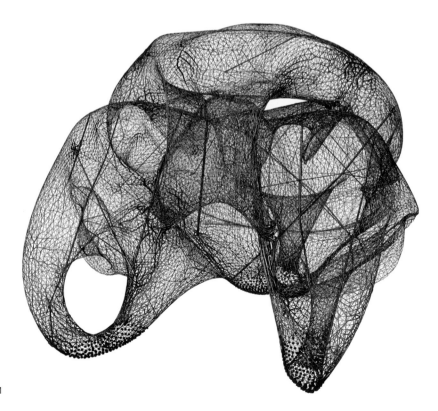

11

systems thinking and STEM subjects with those in design and the arts. For this reason, schools need to educate designers to work compatibly and effectively with those from across different units, domains, and fields. Like it or not, this is where design practice is heading; we need to understand the implications for education and training, research, and development. Tim Brown of IDEO could have been speaking for the architecture profession when he wrote that "the interdisciplinary path opens up a host of purposeful challenges that can be approached through the lenses of science, the arts, business or non-profit and, of course, some combination of all of them."[29] Brown continues: "Going wide … is about making connections between what you already know and what you're curious about discovering. It requires systems thinking in order for the whole to be greater than the sum of the parts. It means developing the skills to collaborate for the purpose of learning. It's about seeing the creative possibilities in breaking down boundaries and describing the world, your organization, the problem in new ways. It probably means having a difficult time describing to your parents what you do."[30]

Firms themselves—referred to as *hybrid firms*, such as the Turner Prize-winning collective, Assemble—are becoming interdisciplinary. Managing technological partnerships and competencies across and within industries requires a redefinition of what it means to be a firm, as well as a rethinking of firm boundaries: "The convergence phenomenon is driven by a global dispersion of involved resources, an increasing amount of technological intersections and unifying disciplines, resulting business opportunities for collaborative design and innovation, as well as the sustained customer demand for full solutions and service provisioning. As a result, the convergence phenomenon implies the deconstruction of existing value chains, transforming industry boundaries and creating new competitive spaces."[31]

"Keeping on to redefine a career with one's interests I think is most important for personal and professional success, even if it means to move over to a new discipline and trade past achievements for personal development," explains Vierlinger. "Although appearing inconsistent, subsequent educational tracks in information technologies, economics, structural engineering and architecture now ultimately let me understand and work on different fronts of a project."

10 and 11 Robert Vierlinger with Melanie Kotz de Acha, Structural Analysis and Optimization, 2016.
Structural analysis and optimization of a complex shape by sizing and insertion of stitching beams with Karamba3d.

INTEROPERABILITY
Interoperability is about the way design professionals' tools communicate. "Interoperability refers to the ability to make different systems talk to one another,"[32] is the way the folks at CASE explained it. They continue: "This is more than just a problem of 'middleware' or 'file format' and should be viewed as a critical project process. At a technical level, 'interoperability' might refer to the process of streamlining information exchange between two or more model authoring platforms. At an organizational level, 'interoperability' can refer to the ability for different stakeholders to work together towards a common goal."[33]

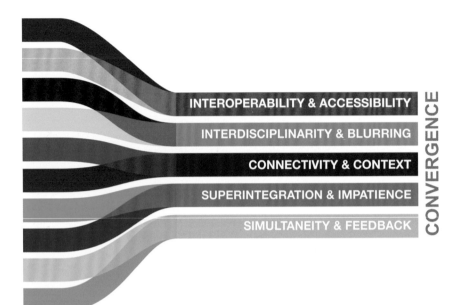

INTEROPERABILITY & ACCESSIBILITY

INTERDISCIPLINARITY & BLURRING

CONNECTIVITY & CONTEXT

SUPERINTEGRATION & IMPATIENCE

SIMULTANEITY & FEEDBACK

CONVERGENCE

12 Deutsch Insights, Convergence Bottleneck, 2017.
Drivers provide opportunities for further convergences. Are there limits to how far design technologies and work processes can converge?

The National Institute of Standards and Technology (NIST) estimates that the cost of poor interoperability for new and in-place U.S. construction amounted to $15.8 billion. A more recent survey conducted by McGraw-Hill estimates that, on average, poor interoperability can raise the total project cost by 3.1%.[34]

Rhynamo is an example of an interoperability tool that leverages file format conversion to achieve a desired workflow. But addressing one tool at a time won't contribute to industry convergence. So those at the former GoogleX moonshot project, Flux, took it upon themselves to create a method that scales to exchange data between multiple design tools. The result is Flux Interoperability Tools, which provide seamless data exchange between Excel, Grasshopper, Dynamo, and many more tools via the Web. Elsewhere, tools such as Dynamo can connect tools in the design pipeline, improving the flow of data, such as BIM 360 field data to structured COBie data.

SIMULTANEITY
In this era of connection, convergence is enabled by the Internet and access to the cloud. As the industry moves away from a product-based model toward software-as-a-service (SAAS), software seats have been supplanted by cloud-based subscriptions.[35] Autodesk, a forerunner in the field, experimented with cloud-based SAAS as far back as 2001, when it acquired the Buzzsaw file sharing and synchronization service.[36] Another example of convergence in this area is PlanGrid, which marries cloud-based file storage with software on the iPad. This was

soon followed by document management tools that could be leveraged in the field, as well as real-time material at the construction site, via the cloud. With its speed, storage, and computer power, the cloud increasingly provides access to, and serves as a home for, large, complex BIM files.[37] The cloud also encourages and enables collaboration—a prerequisite for convergence.

SUPERINTEGRATION

As discussed earlier in the chapter, where convergence is concerned, integration alone isn't enough. Tools and work processes have to be *superintegrated*. Early parametric tools such as BIM introduced the idea that a change in one place is a change everywhere. Change a door size or type in a plan in a BIM tool, and it changes automatically in elevation, and in the schedule. That was not the case with either labor-intensive hand drafting or CAD, a fact that often led to errors and omissions because every change wasn't manually identified and made.

Developing the ability, over a career, to manage an increasingly larger set of variables enables the ability to edit out systematic generation of useless alternatives. Phil Bernstein has described the difference between young designers and older designers as the ability to manage an increasingly larger set of variables: "When I was working for Cesar Pelli, that was one of the amazing things about him—he could keep so many things in his head and he could balance them and weigh one against the other, and he could edit out what he called the systematic generation of useless alternatives. He would prevent us from going down that avenue."[38] Being able to weed out alternatives before iteratively acting on or testing them saves time and resources—a critical skill set assuring the continuation of convergence.

Vierlinger described his investigation of digital design representation in terms of convergence. "A digital design tool defines the relation between user and algorithm," explains Vierlinger. "It is a matter of designing good user experience when trying to make complex algorithms approachable for designers. Not leaving your software environment, no coding, no excessive setup time are crucial factors for the application of advanced design methods. However, not just as an accessibility-interface, my [Multi-Objective Design Interface] thesis tries to perform as a means to communicate design, design problems, and design solutions. Through the negotiation of goals, many trade-off solutions are produced which reflect interests in a setting of conflict. This leaves the final decision to the human designer, and gives better insight to the nature of the task. It eases the identification of driving and driven factors, and hence finding an answer to the question of what to optimize at all. Disciplines are converging in the use of a tool that negotiates different optimized solutions as the interface between architects and engineers, clients and designers, the expert and the laymen. The solutions are the basis for interdisciplinary decision-making, they are the interface on which different interests come together and find consent."

CHALLENGES TO CONVERGENCE

What factors work against convergence? There are many, with the risk aversion and fragmentation rampant in the AECO industry leading the pack. Convergence flies in the face of fragmentation: Fragmentation suggests that you work small in silos, convergence implies that you work large. The silo effect will keep convergence at bay. Adapting to the new world of work requires learning to think simultaneously on several fronts, and from several points of view. This is the world of convergence.

The challenges to convergence don't end there. Despite Flux's efforts, the interoperability issues that keep tools and data from talking to one another continue throughout the building lifecycle. Others include boundaries brought about by specialization; forms that reward individual efforts over and above those of the team; showcasing discrete rather than interconnected project components; all of the above *plus* low investment in research and development (R&D). Architects and design professionals are battling with the convergences triggered by the changes brought about by computational tools, shifting work processes, and the introduction of the cloud, creating a digital/computational haves/have-nots divide in the AEC industry.

What's stopping the convergence framework from becoming a reality? Nothing—it is already here. What major barriers are there to more rapid advance of this convergence? Anything that focuses on the latest cool gadgets or tools at expense of interconnectivity.

What will it take to bring about more rapid convergence in the AECO industry? Standards. BuildingSmart, level of detail (LOD), interoperability, and Flux, among others, are working toward common standards that will help speed up convergence. However, it is not only technology that will speed things along. Also needed are trust, transparency, and the identification of common goals and living by them: these, plus working for the project rather than one's own personal gain (which, ostensibly, if you're working for the project, should take care of itself).

Where in the industry, you might be wondering, are we seeing divergence? Arguably, in areas where architecture is ceding turf to other entities: for example, with algorithmic generative design. Divergence is also apparent in architects' (for example, Bjarke Ingles) arguments that explain architecture in terms of an evolutionary relationship, inasmuch as evolution is depicted in diagrams that resemble tree branches. As we'll see in the chapters that follow, the convergence we are currently experiencing is anything but evolutionary. Ignore convergence at your own risk, for—in the one way it resembles evolution—it is a force of nature.

ENDNOTES

1 http://www.architectureanddesign.com.au/features/comment/in-profile-autodesk-s-philip-bernstein.

2 Phil Bernstein, "Future of Construction: Your Next Building Won't Be Built—It Will Be Manufactured," August 26, 2015, https://lineshapespace.com/future-of-construction/.

3 Sanjay Bhatt, "Callison Merges into Another Architecture Firm ... ," October 20, 2015, http://old.seattletimes.com/html/realestate/2027335327_callisonrtklxml.html?syndication=rss; "CallisonRTKL Launches New Brand Identity," October 20, 2015, http://www.callisonrtkl.com/news/callisonrtkl-launches-new-brand-identity/.

4 Terri Swiatek, "Pittsburgh Post-Gazette Touts CannonDesign/Astorino Merger as Success," August 15, 2015, http://www.cannondesign.com/news-insights/tag/corp/.

5 Kim Lyons, "Consolidation Changes Face of Pittsburgh Architecture as Industry Rebounds from Recession Lows," August 30, 2015, http://www.post-gazette.com/business/development/2015/08/30/Pittsburgh-architecture-firm-Astorino-consolidation-with-CannonDesign-brings-change-as-industry-rebounds/stories/201508300039.

6 Zach Mortice, "4 Ways a Robot or Drone 3D Printer Will Change Architecture and Construction," September 1, 2015, https://lineshapespace.com/drone-3d-printer/.

7 Ibid.

8 Ibid.

9 Jeff Kowalski, "CAD Is a Lie: Generative Design to the Rescue," December 16, 2015, http://www.themanufacturer.com/articles/cad-is-a-lie-generative-design-to-the-rescue/.

10 Lance Hosey, "When Buildings Design Themselves," December 21, 2015, http://www.huffingtonpost.com/lance-hosey/when-buildings-design-the_b_8851118.html.

11 Kate Greene, "A New and Improved Moore's Law," September 12, 2011, http://www.technologyreview.com/news/425398/a-new-and-improved-moores-law/.

12 http://www.autodesk.com/products/bim-360-plan/overview

13 Interoperability Planning & Implementation, Proving Ground website, https://provingground.io/services/projects/interoperability-planning/, 2016.

14 Michael Massing, "Reimagining Journalism: The Story of the One Percent," December 17, 2015, http://www.nybooks.com/articles/2015/12/17/reimagining-journalism-story-one-percent/

15 https://en.wikipedia.org/wiki/Digitizing.

16 Brian Ringley, interview with author, January 5, 2016.

17 Ibid.

18 Ibid.

19 Chris Razell, "Making the Complex That Little Bit Easier...," July 3, 2013, http://thecodebooklama.blogspot.com/2013/07/making-complex-that-little-bit-easier.html.

20 Farhad Manjoo, "iPhone 6s's Hands-Free Siri Is an Omen of the Future," September 22, 2015, http://www.nytimes.com/2015/09/24/technology/personaltech/iphone-6s-hands-free-siri-is-an-omen-of-the-future.html.

21 F. Hacklin, N. Adamsson, C. Marxt, and M. Norell, "Design for Convergence: Managing Technological Partnerships and Competencies Across and Within Industries," August 18, 2005, https://www.designsociety. org/publication/22903/design_for_convergence_ managing_technological_partnerships_and_ competencies_across_and_within_industries.

22 John Tobin, "OneDesign: Blurring the Lines Between Architecture, Engineering and Contracting," June 29, 2015, http://www.aecbytes.com/buildingthefuture/2015/ OneDesign.html.

23 Phil Bernstein, "Why Today's Architects Build Digital Cities Instead of Scale Models," October 2, 2014, http:// gizmodo.com/why-todays-architects-build-digital- simulations-instead-1638341197

24 Scott Simpson, "Moore's Law, Productivity, and Data- Driven Design," June 18, 2015, http://www.di.net/articles/ moores-law-productivity-and-data-driven-design/.

25 In Robert Scoble and Shel Israel, The Age of Context (Patrick Brewster Press, 2013), xiv.

26 Erin Green, "Project Aquila: Combining BIM and IoT," November 26, 2015, http://www.engineering.com/BIM/ ArticleID/11056/Project-Aquila-Combining-BIM-and-IoT. aspx.

27 Wanda Lau, "How the Internet of Places Can Validate (or Invalidate) Your Design," September 30, 2015, http://www. architectmagazine.com/technology/how-the-internet-of- places-can-validate-or-invalidate-your-design_o.

28 Brian Ringley, interview with author, January 5, 2016.

29 Tim Brown, "The Career Choice Nobody Tells You About," November 27, 2014, http://designthinking.ideo. com/?p=1412.

30 Ibid.

31 F. Hacklin et al., "Design for Convergence."

32 Nathan Miller, "Planning Your Project for Better Interoperability," May 18, 2015, http://www.case-inc.com/ node/508.html.

33 Ibid.

34 Ibid.

35 Alexander Eule, "Autodesk's Bet on the Cloud Will Generate Big Returns for Shareholders," September 26, 2015, http://www.barrons.com/articles/autodesks- bet-on-the-cloud-will-generate-big-returns-for- shareholders-1443248123.

36 Bernard Marr, "Big Data at Autodesk: Getting a 360-Degree View of Customers from the Cloud," August 10, 2015, http://www.forbes.com/sites/ bernardmarr/2015/08/10/big-data-at-autodesk-getting-a- 360°-view-of-customers-from-the-cloud/#76a963965092.

37 Hadley Jones, "Introducing the 3D (4D, 5D…) Cloud," http://www.cloudwedge.com/introducing-the-3d-4d-5d- cloud/.

38 Randy Deutsch, "How We Can Make Collaboration Work," February 4, 2014, http://www.di.net/articles/how-

we-can-make-collaboration-work/.

IMAGES
Figures 1, 2, 4–7, 12 © Deutsch Insights; figure 3 © Proving
Ground; figure 8–11 © Robert Vierlinger

1

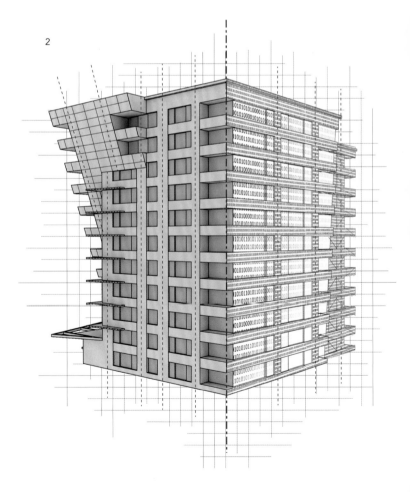

2

CHAPTER 2
DATA AND INTUITION

The world is being re-shaped by the convergence of social, mobile, cloud, big data, community and other powerful forces. The combination of these technologies unlocks an incredible opportunity to connect everything together in a new way and is dramatically transforming the way we live and work.—Marc Benioff[1]

1 Deutsch Insights, Data and Intuition Convergences, 2017. The book explores convergences in contemporary design practice that now occur at the meeting of two seemingly opposite forces.

2 Deutsch Insights, Convergence of Data and Intuition, 2017. Do data and intuition really represent extremes? Are there places where they start to approach each other?

What is the relationship between data and intuition? They appear to be on opposite ends of a spectrum: one rational, the other embracing emotion; one objective, the other subjective; one hard, the other soft; one quantitative, the other qualitative; one requiring thought, the other a more immediate response. But let's not let this devolve into a critique of machine vs. man. Data and intuition are related. But *how*?

Let's start by asking: Do the two really represent extremes? Are there places where they start to approach each other? Places where they remain different? Are both needed? Does one supersede the other? If so, always, or only when using certain tools, design methods, or in certain situations?[2] In this chapter, we'll look at both data and intuition, and see where the two converge, and what the implications are for architecture. As I explained in my last book, *Data-Driven Design and Construction: 25 Strategies for Capturing, Analyzing, and Applying Building Data*,[3] data informs intuition, where intuition provides the hunch, and data proves the rule. But data doesn't just inform intuition, data *improves* intuition. Imagine a model that turns green when you are designing within predetermined parameters, constraints, or rules. As soon as what you model goes out of compliance, it turns red. Then, based on that feedback, you modify the design until it turns green again. You go through this for a while and, as you navigate the model, you start to internalize and anticipate the rules. You are reacting to the data, and then suddenly you are reacting to your gut, your eye, your intuition, which have internalized the data. In this instance, data supports, backs up, and improves one's intuitions. There's a name for improving intuition: *learning*. Improving intuition is the human equivalent of machine learning. The feedback that data provides enables us to learn and grow on the job.

A LOOK BACK AT THE DATA

In discussions about data for my last book, I noticed there was another underlying conversation occurring that wrestled with the realities of data and intuition, shedding light on the convergence of these forces: one machine-based, the other human. Architects act—and make professional judgments—from a combination

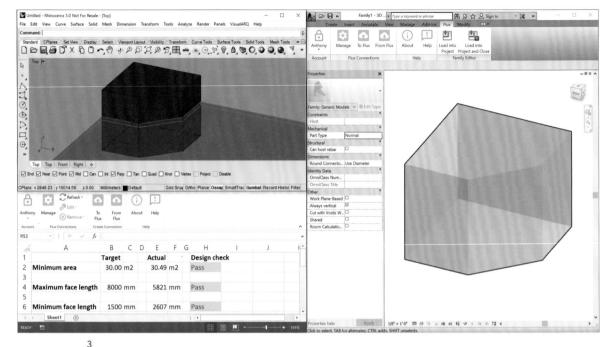

3

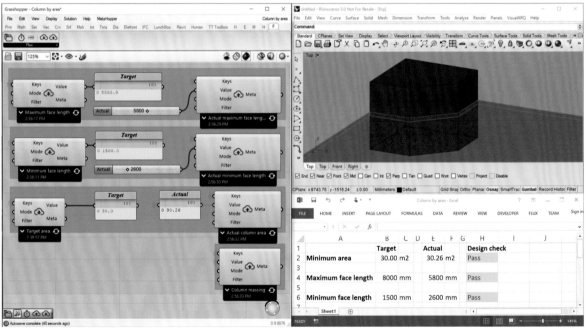

4

of experience, knowledge, and intuition. "What better way to reinforce intuition if you can prove it right? And when it is wrong, we can demonstrate that it is wrong," asked Jonathon Broughton.[4] As I wrote at the time, there's a place for hunches and intuition, but better buildings are backed up by better data.[5]

What exactly is it that data does for architects and their building projects that standard knowledge, experience, and intuition can't? It eliminates paths that don't lead anywhere, and reveals hunches and assumptions that were enabled by preconceived notions that turn out to be incorrect. The beauty of gathering and leveraging data in building projects is that it enables designers to save time and valuable resources by eliminating false positives.[6] What exactly does data do for Broughton in his projects that craft and knowledge, intuition, and experience, can't accomplish? "Data allows you to do that much more of it. Data allows you to be that much better. You can be more efficient. Wouldn't it be good if you could learn so much observing yourself doing something that the next time you do it you can do it better. Or quicker. Or cheaper. Or more effectively or sustainably," offered Broughton.[7]

When NBBJ's Ryan Mullenix and his project team use computational design to get the best views, does he always trust the tools? Does he feel the need to override them with intuition and common sense? Mullenix talked about trust factors. "We test our algorithms on a variety of cases. We even test them on ourselves sometimes in our office. The third part of this trust is related to intuition. I can say that intuition factors in a lot. We'll look at a daylighting analysis, for example, and your gut will tell you if the outcome is in line with what you should be seeing. And if it's not, it's actually a fun opportunity to explore deeper. Is my intuition off? Is the algorithm off?"[8] Mullenix described his experience working with Google on their Mountain View campus in California. "We proposed to them before even being hired that design computation could allow more time for creativity. I wrote a blog post that speaks to both my belief and our firm's belief on how design computation provides more room for creativity because quick iterations and rapid prototyping determine ideals faster. When you find better outcomes faster, you provide more time to spend in the creative phases with your client."[9]

Anthony Buckley-Thorp, Application Engineer at Flux Factory, explains the convergence in terms of accessibility and ease of use. "Some people have been doing—and will continue to do— some excellent things. But the overhead that they have to carry, to achieve their goals, seems unfair. Somebody like Flux could make their life much easier. The plug-ins that we have—we're not really in the business of building plug-ins because anybody can build them. What we feel we can do that is truly unique is the whole Internet infrastructure. The ability to not just send the data between two different softwares on your local machine, but across the web encrypted, backed-up, authenticated, and secure. That's where 90% of Flux's engineering effort is currently embodied. Through such things as SDK and other plug-ins to build apps that

3 and 4 FLUX, Column sizing: Arup Shanghai, Raffles City Chongqing, China 2014. Residential super high-rise corner mega column and floor plate. Rather than prescribe fixed column dimensions, the structural engineer provided targets for three critical variables, permitting the architect freedom to comply with the structural requirements via a multitude of potential geometric configurations.

5 LMN Architects in association with Marmon Mok, Tobin Center for the Performing Arts, San Antonio, TX, 2014.
Combining one of San Antonio's most beloved architectural icons with advanced technology to create one of the most flexible multipurpose performance halls in the United States.

6

7   OVERVIEW

Early concept sketches exploring form, opening, and shadow.

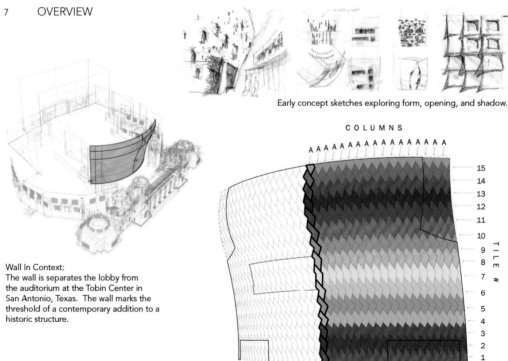

Wall In Context:
The wall is separates the lobby from
the auditorium at the Tobin Center in
San Antonio, Texas. The wall marks the
threshold of a contemporary addition to a
historic structure.

COLUMNS

A A A A A A A A A A A A A A A A A

15
14
13
12
11
10
9
8
7   T I L E #
6
5
4
3
2
1

Tiling Concept:
The surface of the wall is created with repeating columns made up of 15 unique tiles.
The tiled column is repeated along an arc to form the geometry of the wall.

connect design tools, it's going to make it easier for people such as Thornton Tomasetti or Proving Ground to build their own plug-ins. Or to build them in such a way that as soon as you build one link you've built all the links. That's not a new idea, but nobody has been able to achieve it at critical mass." Buckley-Thorp continues, "The other fundamental difference is Flux's mindset. You can't copyright it and we wouldn't want to copyright it. It's this idea about thinking about data, and not files. For some reason our industry is so much in the mindset of files, when I'm going to exchange data with someone I'm going to send them a file. It's just so ingrained we need to unveil the revolution in the way we think about our data."[10]

QUANTITATIVE VS. QUALITATIVE DATA
In an article on smart cities and the New York City development Hudson Yards, Dr. Steven Koonin, Director of CUSP, indicated that the combination of quantitative with qualitative information will lead to a convergence of areas of study and research, and potentially even professions. "One result will be to change traditional disciplines. Civil engineering," said Koonin, "has traditionally centered on physical systems rather than human behavior. In the future there may be careers in 'human-centered civil engineering' or 'civic engineering.' Architects and interior designers study how people interact with buildings and rooms, but without much quantitative information. … 'Quantitative design,' he said, 'may be a career of the future. Disciplines will merge,' Dr. Koonin predicted, 'as a result of the data.'"[11]

Sam Miller of LMN/LMNts spoke about the role of design technologies in his office, but could have been describing the role data plays. "One of the important roles that LMNts [LMN's tech studio] has evolved into is not just enabling design technologies within the office, but customizing design technologies to work with our design process," said Miller. "So that the tool is adapted to what we are trying to achieve and the way we are trying to achieve it. And not the other way around."[12] One can take this logic and apply it to data and intuition, where one doesn't allow the data to dictate outcomes but instead applies data in a way that adapts to the natural way one designs—ostensibly by making intuitive design decisions. "The term *data-driven* tends to imply that the outcome is largely driven by the data. We're striving to make the best informed decisions we can, but also knowing that there is only so much in design that you can capture with data," Miller continued. "There's also a quality, an aesthetic, and other contextual issues that need to be woven into the solution in a way that data alone isn't going to achieve," he explained.[13]

One of the most counterintuitive take-aways from my conversations with data experts in the AEC industry was that the more data-driven their practice, the more they talked about what they do in terms of intuition. I said to Mads Jensen of Sefaira (now Trimble) that data, technology, and software are fairly rational tools, then asked: *Why an emphasis on intuition?* "Human intuition is so unbelievably powerful, and it shapes every moment of our

6 LMN Architects in association with Marmon Mok, Tobin Center for the Performing Arts, San Antonio, TX, 2014.
Each of the 15 tiles is sculpted with subtle ripples conceptually generated from the water patterns in the San Antonio River that runs next to the site.

7 LMN Architects in association with Marmon Mok, Tobin Center for the Performing Arts, San Antonio, TX, 2014.
15 tile variations, arrayed vertically, lock together to create the geometric expression of a sensual mosaic pattern.

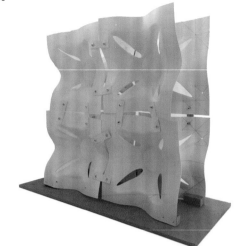

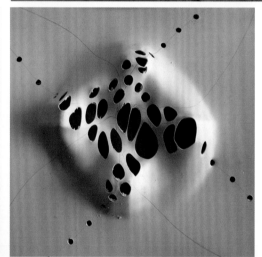

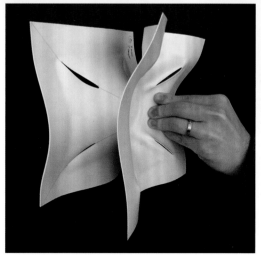

lives and every part of our history. We have been greatly inspired by Kahneman's and Twersky's incredibly powerful research on human psychology [popularized in Kahneman's *Thinking Fast and Slow*] and it seems clear to us that our intuition is always with us—sometimes for good and sometimes for bad, but always there. Building physics is a complicated discipline. Sometimes it gives counterintuitive answers (such as reducing the size of your windows might make your building consume more energy), sometimes just answers which your intuition could have figured out on its own." Jensen continued, "The intuitive qualities of architects are what we find in the very best of the arts—those ephemeral qualities that computers just can't replace. We simply see [the] interaction between man and machine as a great way to leverage the things humans are great at and designating the things we are less great at to computers."[14]

However, this line of thinking is still somewhat linear, in that it does not acknowledge the convergence between data and intuition, but instead assigns one role to machines and the other to humans. It doesn't make the best of both—as when a human collaborates with a laptop computer to compete in chess.

Data and intuition: the two aren't mutually exclusive after all. Just as predictive analytics doesn't have a crystal ball, but instead relies heavily on past behavior, so too does intuition. Intuition, in other words, is an aggregation of the past: experience, facts, beliefs, and yes, data. All of these reflect the past and may no longer be true, just as past performance does not necessarily predict future results. What does this data/intuition convergence mean for architecture? What are the implications for practice?

There is, of course, a danger in siding with either data or intuition over the other. As Brian Ringley, Design Technology Platform Specialist at Woods Bagot, indicated concerning his students, "It is as if once the data is there, common sense just falls to the wayside. That is a huge danger of data—there is trust in data that removes our critical thinking."[15] The same can be said of abandoning the certainty of data in favor of intuition. This in turn raises the question of whether there is an ideal order by which one approaches either data or intuition. Do you start with a hunch and back it up with data? Or do you get the data on something and run it past your instincts for a gut check? As Jonathon Broughton noted, "Sherlock Holmes was highly intuitive, but only after he had collected sufficient data to eliminate the false positives."[16] The implication is that without data, intuition alone is not sufficient to back up our hunches.

ARCHITECTURE STARTS WITH INTUITION
It makes sense that humans would have an affinity for both data and intuition. "When it comes to the ability of a human to quickly evaluate a scenario, and come to a decision, when compared with the latest advancements in AI, there's no comparison. Humans win every single time," suggests Proving Ground's Nathan Miller.[17] "It comes down to pattern recognition. I don't see the technology

8 Brian Ringley, Pratt GAUD, with students Nada Asadullah, Changbum Park, Cansu Demiral, Maria Echeverry, and Ricardo Diaz, New York, NY, 2016.
Pratt GAUD students robotically fabricated shell prototypes from panel connection mock-up (left) to ¼-scale assembly (center, right).

9 Brian Ringley, Pratt GAUD, with students Maria Nikolovski, Christopher Testa, Milad Showkatbakhsh, Sandra Berdick, Nada Asadullah, Changbum Park, Cansu Demiral, Maria Echeverry, Ricardo Diaz, Fayad Shadhim, Emma Weiss, Alex Behnke, and Takuya Toyama, New York, NY, 20152016.
Pratt GAUD students' HIPS (high-impact polystyrene) plastic forming studies for the production of a robotically manufactured double-skin shell.

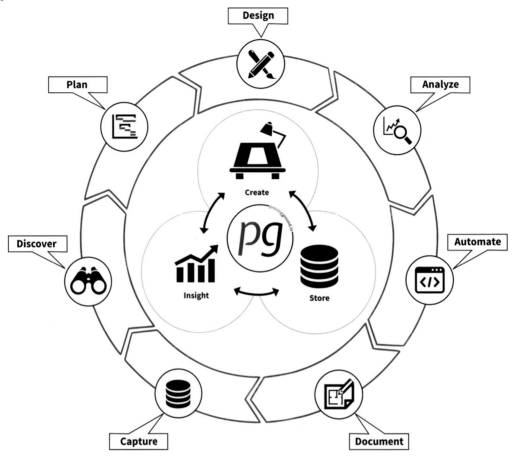

10 Proving Ground, Data
Cycles and Feedback Loops,
2016.
A sketch for a data cycle that
can drive a creative process.

11 LMN Architects,
Optimization Loop, 2015.
Convergence iteration
diagram with architect leading
the decision-making process.

or data replacing intuition. We're so far away from that. Human intuition is far too evolved and sophisticated."[18]

THE LIMITS OF DATA IN ARCHITECTURE

LMN Partner Sam Miller recently spoke about convergences in architecture in terms of the amount of information that is available to architects, and how much is necessary to make decisions. "The topic of convergences in architecture is great, because there is a lot of talk about it but nobody quite knows, not just what it means, but what it means especially for the profession. As an architect, there are some existential questions that come along with that question that have been in the background for quite a while. With design technology, with changes in delivery methodologies (including IPD among others); with performance space design and building procurement: there is a fundamental question about who's driving this thing and what's the architect's role in all of this. So it's an intriguing question in a lot of ways." Miller continues, "My take obviously is coming at it with the architect's hat on and what these things mean for me, and our practice. The diagram that we drew and the diagram you put together are different takes on a similar thing, which is that we have all these different inputs and all this information and processes—with the hope that we are aligning the information and the processes in such a way that the outcome is better than it would otherwise be. In parallel with that, it raises the question of who is doing that aligning?"[19]

Miller takes the topic back to data and the ways architects make decisions. "Similar to the question around data-driven design versus data-informed design, there is all this new additional information and new opportunities, but it doesn't change the end goal of wanting to do great work, however you measure 'great.' What I have envisioned with that spiral and the little arrow at the center of the spiral—this may have been the optimist in me—I have always thought of that arrow as being the architect. Because the architect is in a central role and position they have an opportunity; the contractor develops or inserts himself into this. Architects are in a unique role in that we have the skills that are needed."

Miller continues: "Another way to look at it is, is there an asymptote? Is there a limit to how much we can handle? That's a great question. I don't know. It's not a question of 'is there a limit to how much convergence' or 'how much data and variables we can handle?' Perhaps the question is 'how much is worth considering?' We can consider all of that information, but how valuable is it to do that? One example I can think of is building information systems, or a BMS [building management system] system for a building, a control system. I wish I had the statistic so *don't* quote me on this one, but something like every week a typical high-rise BMS system generates the equivalent of all the works of Shakespeare. It's just this huge amount of data that's being generated. And to what end? What's the value there? That's an example of where there is more data than value. We don't need all that information to design a building that's going to perform

AMBIGUITY   CLARITY

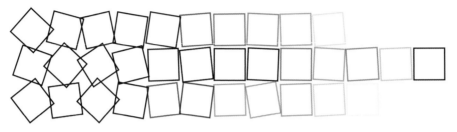

UNCERTAINTY   CERTAINTY

12 Deutsch Insights,
Ambiguity to clarity diagram
after Georg Nees's Gravel,
2017.
Architectural decision-making
via convergence moves from
ambiguity and uncertainty to
clarity and certainty.

13

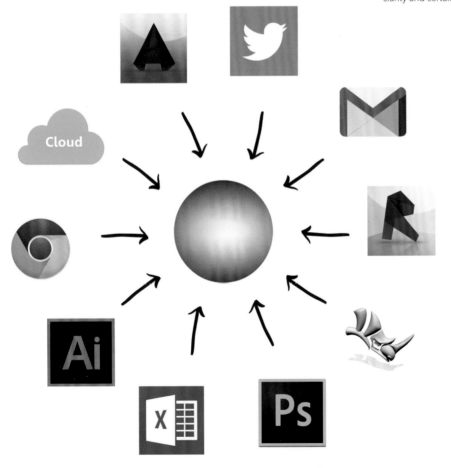

well. So in my mind maybe it's not that we can't handle that data, but at some point we have to filter. That's true even today: we are generating more information than we really need, or that we effectively utilize, so we do have to filter. That's the role of the architect to some degree because we are in a position to balance. We're getting input from a mechanical engineer, the contractor, structural, and we have to make decisions that are balancing these different systems. Every system can't be designed in a vacuum. It all has to work together in the end. We have to be the ones to assimilate all this information into a coherent whole. There's a filtering that happens as part of that, and we have to be able to say 'Okay, we adhere with that. But that's not as important as this piece of information over here, so therefore we're going to make this decision.' It's the filtering of the information and there is a certain limit to how much you can take on and still pull together to a coherent whole. It's just the value of the information, and the value of the change that might be associated with a particular piece of information and how that compares to everything else that's going on. And it's not good if you're dialing one system to a particular level of accuracy and you're missing a whole other piece on the other side."[20]

We of course have the human capability to apply data in our critical thinking by means of rational thought. One instance of this is Phil Bernstein's description of Cesar Pelli's handling of alternatives: "[T]hat was one of the amazing things about [Cesar Pelli]—he could keep so many things in his head and he could balance them and weigh one against the other, and he could edit out what he called the systematic generation of useless alternatives. He would prevent us from going down that avenue."[21] More recently, Phil said that when he worked in Cesar Pelli's office, Pelli didn't allow the computer to be used for the systematic generation of useless alternatives.[22]

THE CONVERGENCE OF EVERYTHING
How does a design technologist see convergence applied to the AEC industry? "What comes to mind for me is accessibility to other industries' workflow and data," says Ringley. "It is also accessibility to a larger amount of the AEC industry workflow. It can be anything from I now have access, as a designer, to material information through a tool like KieranTimberlake's Tally in the realm of material science, to something where I now have access to Karamba Grasshopper workflow where my design is being directly driven by structural knowledge, which is typically outside of my field, which is directly controlling a robot, which is also not necessarily central to my field. This kind of control—openness and connectivity to the traditional design model—is largely due to big data, interoperability, more accessible algorithms through user-friendly software, and computational power through contemporary hardware."[23]

Rhynamo, an open-source plug-in authored by Proving Ground's Nathan Miller, which exposes new visual nodes for reading and writing Rhino 3dm files inside of Dynamo, represents another

13 Deutsch Insights, Apps to Platforms, 2017.
The focus today is less on the individual software tools than on the project data and platform the tools are designed to run within.

14 COMPLEX

SIMPLE

TIME INTENSIVE

INSTANTANEOUS

15

FORM-FINDING

STRUCTURAL ANALYSIS

PANELING

TOOLING

ROBOTIC MANUFACTURING

14 Deutsch Insights, Less Complexity, 2017.
Convergence moves from the individual, complex, and time-intensive toward the integrated, simple, and instantaneous.

15 Brian Ringley, Pratt GAUD, New York, NY, 2016.
A single Grasshopper definition with subroutines for form-finding (Kangaroo), structural analysis (Karamba), panelization (Kangaroo and SmartForm), tooling, and robotic manufacturing (HAL).

By converging multiple disciplinary aspects of a holistic design process, such as ancillary analyses and downstream fabrication, design changes can be accommodated much deeper into the project lifespan.

convergence tool. "Rhynamo has allowed a kind of connectivity that has been difficult for some of us to achieve before it existed," continues Ringley. "Then Flux came out and is a few degrees better to that end. Flux is more open source in the sense that can transfer more data from thing to thing. But it is much less open in terms of it's still like a corporate product that someday we're going to have to pay for." Ringley contends that the same applies, to a large extent, to Grasshopper. "It wasn't open. It was just made to be really easy to use. It made coding itself accessible. It made development accessible. I can write a Grasshopper definition or Python scripts to achieve the same thing where I used to have to compile in Visual Studio," says Ringley. "It seems like an oxymoron, but it seems like open source has an accessibility issue. Not everyone knows how to code. Not everyone knows what to do with that stuff. It's like big data. Yes, there are huge datasets out there. Do you have the algorithms to connect that to a model and do something useful with it? What we are working towards is that everyone has an access point to the model."[24]

WHAT CONVERGENCE WORKS AGAINST

Brian Ringley points out that convergence dictates what platforms or modes are to be used when designing and collaborating, which has implications for the transfer of data and the sharing of intuition and insights. "I'm not about to throw my computer away, but what's another way of working? That's a little bit more multimodal? Convergence works against that. Convergence wants everyone to be in the same framework—the same environment—to have that kind of fluidity," explains Ringley. "If I have to read a book and then write down data from that book, then hand-enter that data into the system, I'm not going to do that. I'm going to Google that database and find it. The problem with Googling the database is that I'm just retrieving numbers. If I actually go through a document, maybe it explains those numbers. Explains those numbers in a nerd way—there's a whole world of metadata surrounding every database that could be in the form of a book. I'm referring here to first principle or conceptual understanding of datasets. When everything becomes just numbers, you're going to lose the power of getting any insight out of it. You're also not going to be able to temper it with common sense. You can't be the *human override* for these data processes if you don't have the critical understanding or the common sense."

Ringley continues: "I read an interesting article recently on parsable vs. unparsable datasets, a coder telling the reader that they're losing appreciation for the paragraph, a centuries-old way to format information. But you can't parse a paragraph. You can parse an XMTL file. Any time a culture values only one mode of thinking or communication, that's a very dangerous moment for us," says Ringley. "There is something about making something work that I liken to when I was repairing fabrication machines such as CNC routers. I remember feeling trepidation or fear in taking the risk on production. I was nervous about taking a machine apart—to figure out what was wrong with it—in the event something broke. Over the years I realized as I watched other

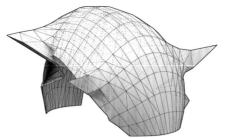
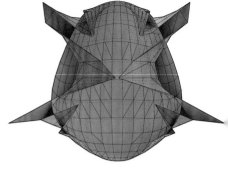

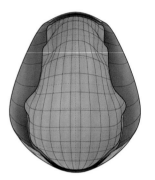

16

16 Brian Ringley, Pratt GAUD, New York, NY, 2016.
From left to right, top to bottom: Initial form-found NURBS shell, exaggerated visualization of shell deflection under gravity load, underside view of deflection visualization, resulting variable offset of double-skin NURBS shell, underside view of double-skin shell. The deflection visualization indicates where the resulting double-skin shell might benefit from increased thickness for stiffening purposes and can be remapped to be used directly for the shell offset operation as a data-driven operation.

17 Deutsch Insights, Convergence Architect, 2017.
Architects today are expected to wear many hats. While that has always been the case, what differs today is that architects are increasingly expected to wear these hats all at the same time.

17

| Architect | Hacker | Data Scientist | Algorithm Builder |

VS

Architect/Hacker/
Data Scientist/
Algorithm Builder

people who were successful in that area, they had this fearlessness, not even caring about knowing. I thought you had to know everything you were about to do before doing it. That could be very stifling. Versus the embracing of the fact that I'll learn as I go. Part of what has enabled that is more accessible data. If I make a mistake, I can Google it and figure it out."

Ringley weighed the pros and cons of the convergence we are currently witnessing. "Convergence is nice because the more you keep things fluid, the more that ad hoc strategy works. Is this enabling bad behavior? At the same time, if you do have the convergence—if everything converges and everything starts to feed into the model—there are good sides to this because I can pull HR data: I know how much people bill, how much experience they have in a certain area, I know if they are available or not, and almost automate team creation," explains Ringley. "Convergence also seems like it can potentially be good because if you do have a more holistic management strategy, then I'm not checking off a box that I've completed a particular task. The software knows I've done the task because the software can see the model and saw me do it. I talk about this a lot with the people I work with about the systems we are creating here. I'm working on a tool in Rhino that enables you to submit screen captures of what you are working on continuously to the cloud. As you feed data into the project. And there will be all of this metadata about that. Some people who are less in the know say that they don't have time to type in all of that metadata. You don't need to do that. The computer knows who you are. The computer knows what the file's called and where it's stored, therefore it knows the project. It can count the tools you're using."

Ringley shared his holistic view of the convergence of technologies. "This is an academic exercise. Let's do it—let's push it—let's talk about how it may not make the most sense but let's push the idea. What comes from that? Once we had the holistic model in Grasshopper, we had much greater ability to do multi-objective optimization. Now I can simultaneously look at manufacturing limitations and structural concerns. And daylighting concerns simultaneously for the purposes of outputting robotic motion, for the purposes of ostensibly constructing a building. So then pushing the multi-objective stuff in Galapagos and Octopus is the current focus, even if the focus is technically on robots and automation. I emphasize the word *automation*. Now that all of the data has converged, how do we start to train all of our models?"[25]

The idea of using intuition—instead of data—in making decisions in architecture is predicated on relying on a single individual. This reliance on individuals becomes problematic at a time when firms are relying on integrated teams to solve intractable problems commonly experienced on large-scale, complex building projects. Whose intuition exactly are we going to base our decisions on? Nathan Miller recently addressed a diagram I presented to him of a hacker/algorithm builder/data scientist/architect sitting side by side vs. these roles all in one person. "I'm resistant to the notion of

CROSS DISCIPLINE

SPECIALIZATION

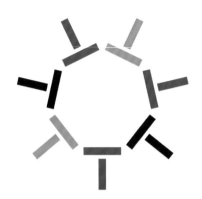

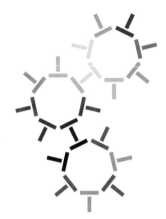

trying to put too much on a single individual," said Miller. "When it comes to all the things someone needs to know, architects need to know too much already. There's a ton of stuff you need to know as an architect when in practice you rely on other people. You rely on other people's body of knowledge. There might be something to say about the generalist mentality. You do need to know the component parts. I'm not one who believes you need to be an expert in all of them. Look at this in terms of scrum and the cross-functional team. You know enough about the subject matter that if one of the pieces on the team falls off, or gets sick, or goes away, the rest of the team can fill in the gap. The people on the team are there for a reason. They're specialists. They have deeper knowledge in certain areas of the project than other people. The diagram is right in one sense: you have a data scientist on an architecture team. Ideally, they also have enough of an awareness about all of the other moving parts that are going on around them. They know where the team is. They can support other team members as needed. And be pulled into other conversations. They aren't the guy in the corner that is isolated. They have an awareness. You have a situational awareness about where you are sitting. That person with situational awareness may be strong in one area but they are able to have a meaningful conversation."[26]

Miller continues: "Language is important across the board when it comes to being able to communicate what is happening. If I'm an architect, the language of the day is data. So I need to be able to talk about data—and work with it—in a manner where I'm not necessarily a data scientist but I have that in my vocabulary. If you're a hacker on the team, an effective hacker is able to hack systems, get into systems, find solutions and workarounds, they know where the holes are in the process. They know where the workarounds are. You can only have that in our industry if you understand the process of building, even though you may be coming at the problem from a very different angle. Today, data is a foundational element of building and how we practice. I look at the hacker as less of a role and more of a way of learning. The act

18 Deutsch Insights, T-Shaped individuals diagram, 2017. Managing technological partnerships and competencies across and within industries requires a redefinition of what it means to be a firm, and a rethinking of firm boundaries.

of hacking as problem solving, as a way of learning a new skill set or concept, or finding new solutions. As being more effective than a couple days of Revit training."

Miller contends that he does see convergences in the industry driven in part by data. "What we see in the industry—and we actually see it now, with the pace that things are evolving—on the technology front and the data front, we can and do see convergences," says Miller. "For example, convergence of ideas: the converging of data and technology. One of the things people are coming around to now is interoperability. We know this is an issue. We have all of these technologies and tools. How are we going to get them to talk to each other?" GoogleX project spin-off Flux represents one way our industry's tools will begin to talk to each other. "We're seeing start-ups like Flux engaging in interoperability from a product standpoint," says Miller. "The idea of creating a data glue that connects various parts together. It's one of those ideas that are now hitting the mainstream. These subjects like interoperability that existed on the fringe have now become important issues. When something hits the mainstream— it's a form of convergence."

Miller offers an example of how data is sometimes misused. "This is one of the issues I have with the current state of BIM," explains Miller. "The promise of BIM is still yet to be realized in a mainstream way. More often than not, BIM is used as CAD 2.0. A faster way of cranking out the same deliverables that they're always made. That's why there's all this interest in standards—they want their BIM to look just like CAD. Then they'll get into the model and get through any workarounds they can in order to get the drawing to look just right. The way they're used to seeing it … overriding dimensions, etc. The drawing, the document, is the be-all and end-all. I can't point to a firm where this hasn't been the case to some degree. What baffles me is you have the potential for a really powerful database that *can* be the be-all and end-all. It can be this thing you can hang your hat on. But instead, they're hanging their hat on potentially manipulated 2D abstractions of that data—views into the data rather than the data itself." It's as though intuition wins out over the data.

Does it make sense to go the route of the Master Algorithm—and is it a form of convergence? "For this to happen, available data sources would have to become shored-up to the point where it made sense to take advantage of that," says Miller. "It is still the Wild West when it comes to having consistent ways to structure data in our industry from design to operations. You need to gather normalized data before you can use a data-driven design process at scale with building design. Take health care, for example. It is arguably one of the more data-rich opportunities for delivering a data-driven design process. Yet, it's a similar problem when it comes to various providers. Data is different from project to project. Sometimes there's postoccupancy data. Sometimes there isn't. Sometimes there are sensors collecting the information. Sometimes it's observational. You have to adapt the process to the

19

20

situation you find yourself in. You can't have an all-encompassing algorithm to figure it out. It is always going to have to be very nuanced. There's this specificity that needs to occur. Some of the information can be generalized: this is going to be relevant, this is going to be relevant. I'm going to build my toolkit around this. Also, there's the expense."[27]

DATA AND INTUITION IN DESIGN TOOLS

Morpholio co-creator, Proxy Design Studio co-director, and GSAPP Cloud Lab co-director Toru Hasegawa spoke about the role data plays in his research. "When we are developing some of these drawing tools, we're collecting data in order to understand and find the environment in which we ideate," explains Hasegawa.[28] "The benefit of this: search space is fast and big. It's about identifying the needle in the haystack. So far humans have acquired a brain through Malcolm Gladwell's 10,000-hour rule to make the filter mechanism in our brain. When we see something we don't search in a directory and assess what it is. Our brains have evolved to instantaneously respond. To evaluate through experience. Memory is much more reliable to the extent that you accumulate experience. If an architect has been looking at floor plans for 35 or 40 years, how she sees it is ten times different from how an emerging professional sees it. But at the get-go, without the experience, we're all the same. This is where it touches big data: good solutions actually exist that are generalizable in the vast dataset. Some people will argue that there is no innovation in that. I don't see how it would operate all that differently for a nonaugmented human to define that problem. The input you're seeking can be augmented to that. So the benefit is that you would find the solution much faster."

19-22 Toru Hasegawa and Mark Collins, Columbia GSAPP's Cloud Lab with Van Alen Institute, DUMBO, 2014.
A visualization of mental phenomena set within a neighborhood of New York City. A group of volunteer citizen scientists contributed their brain waves in a collective visualization of a day in the life of a neighborhood's mental states. The map visualization overlays many people's subjective experience to discover patterns and common responses to environmental stimuli such as parks, infrastructure, and the block structure.

21
22

While looking at the Morpholio user interface, I pointed out to Hasegawa that on the right-hand side in Morpholio a user can go through different sources, and questioned whether this merging on the screen is a form of convergence. "On the mood board, now when you select a product or move it around your mood board, you are choosing a product with certain values," explains Hasegawa. "Here's a product with similar values. Or here's a color palette that it might match. Stuff that is suggested by what they are intending is what we are trying to envision. If you selected two chairs, you're probably looking for a table. If you decided to buy a hundred chairs, you're probably designing a large conference room, chapel, or small concert hall. They are pieces of data that will heuristically tell you something. The more you can do that in the process, you will have better suggestions on the design side."

"The Revit ribbon works similarly," Hasegawa explains. "There are so many things we can possibly show, why would we show X,Y and Z? That's problem #1: There are cajillions of options. Google decides what to rank higher and what to rank lower. It is similar to this design problem. To an extent the software is designing with you. It's a very blurry line. I don't think it's a crisp line. Machine learning some of these processes caters to just one person. As you accumulate more data in your machine-learning algorithm, it starts to pick up your interests. As a designer, you almost want to see that occur. A good example is Pandora. When it first came out it was interesting and considered cool by a lot of people. You would just scroll up or down and it would try to cater to you. You realize after a month that it plays the same songs over and over. It becomes so boring. That is why designers are always trying to destabilize themselves. Is it a paradox that a software can do that?"[29]

In this chapter we looked at both data and intuition, to see where the two converge, and what the implications are for architecture. We looked at ways in which data and intuition can be thought of on a continuum, as opposed to representing polar extremes. If intuition is an ability to understand something immediately, without the need for conscious reasoning, then the merging of data and intuition points to the opportunity for making more assured decisions in less time. While experts such as cognitive psychologist Gary Klein suggest that we trust our instincts over analysis,[30] no matter how good our intuition is, it inevitably fails us for certain things. But also, no matter how good data is, it also fails us for certain things. Even data has its limits.[31] Neither one nor the other alone is adequate. We need both to make assured decisions, and the convergence of the two—data and intuition—is how this will come about. The convergence of data and intuition opens the door to the overlap between analytics and the model, as discussed in the next chapter.

ENDNOTES

1 Shel Israel, "Mark Benioff to Write Age of Context Foreword," Mar. 18, 2013, http://www.forbes.com/sites/shelisrael/2013/03/18/marc-benioff-to-write-age-of-context-foreword/

2 "The 'new cohesion,' the current, global convergence of creative forces that I have been calling Parametricism … ." Patrik Schumacher, "Convergence vs. Fragmentation as Condition for Architecture's Societal Impact," *Fulcrum*, no. 19 (June 2011).

3 John Wiley & Sons, 2015.

4 Randy Deutsch, *Data-Driven Design and Construction: 25 Strategies for Capturing, Analyzing, and Applying Building Data* (Hoboken, NJ: John Wiley & Sons, 2015), 9.

5 Ibid., 12.

6 Ibid.

7 Ibid., 103.

8 Ibid, 147.

9 Ibid.

10 Anthony Buckley-Thorp, interview with author, May 16, 2016.

11 Steve Lohr, "Huge New York Development Project Becomes a Data Science Lab," April 15, 2014, http://bits.blogs.nytimes.com/2014/04/14/huge-new-york-development-project-becomes-a-data-science-lab/?_r=0

12 Deutsch, *Data-Driven Design*, 158.

13 Ibid.

14 Ibid.

15 Ibid., 20.

16 Ibid., 5.

17 Nathan Miller, interview with author, February 23, 2016.

18 Ibid.

19 Sam Miller, interview with author, April 12, 2016.

20 Ibid.

21 Randy Deutsch, "How We Can Make Collaboration

Work," February 4, 2014, http://www.di.net/articles/how-we-can-make-collaboration-work/

22 Overheard at AIA National Convention 2016, Architect Live, Philadelphia, PA, May 20, 2016.

23 Brian Ringley, interview with author, December 20, 2015.

24 Ibid.

25 Ibid.

26 Nathan Miller, interview with author, February 23, 2016.

27 Ibid.

28 Toru Hasegawa, interview with author, April 19, 2016.

29 Ibid.

30 Gary Klein, *The Power of Intuition: How to Use Your Gut Feelings to Make Better Decisions at Work* (New York: Crown Business, 2004).

31 Peter Chen, "Big Data: Analytics versus Intuition," November 27, 2015, *Algebraixdata*, www.algebraixdata.com/how-data-algebra-improves-business-analytics-2/

IMAGES

Figures 1, 2, 12–14, 17, 18 © Deutsch Insights; figures 3 and 4 © Flux Factory Inc.; figures 5–7, 11 © LMN Architects; figures 8, 9, 15, 16 © Brian Ringley, Pratt GAUD; figure 10 © Proving Ground; figures 19–22 © Toru Hasegawa/GSAPP Cloud Lab with the Van Alen Institute

1

2

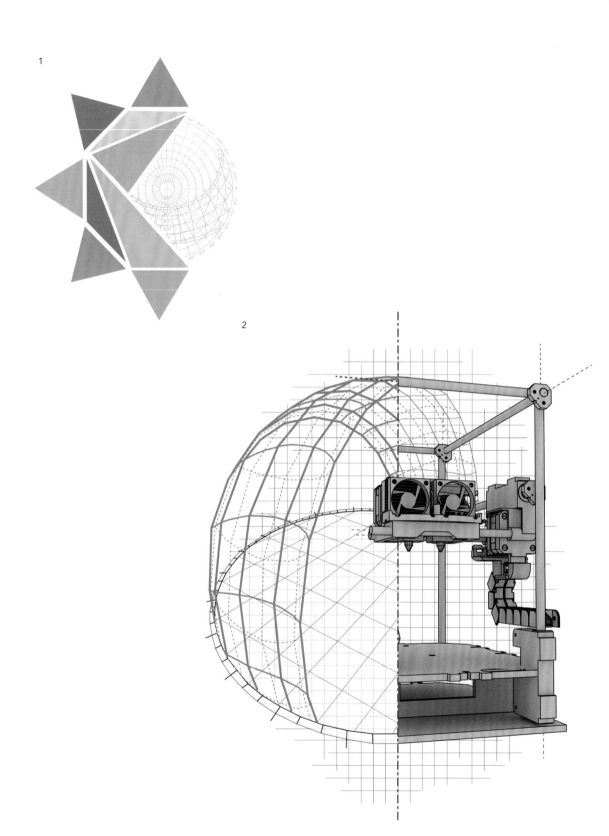

CHAPTER 3
ANALYTICS AND MODELS

The way you want to make a city today is one that creates convergence. It's probably the most important thing architecture can do.—Bruce Kuwabara[1]

What does it mean that there is a noticeable convergence between analytics and models? That digital building models have the capacity to be more than 3D virtual representations of buildings? That virtual models increasingly incorporate a feedback loop—through simulation, analysis, and optimization—that not only informs designers but can also influence design outcomes? In this chapter, we'll look at some of the ways in which analytics and models are converging and what that means for design and construction.

One example of convergence between analytics and modeling is in the design phase: Based on the design criteria, a model can be set up to turn green when the designer is working within the constraints and to turn red when she exceeds them. Here, it is important to note that the data and analytics don't require separate data visualization. The model itself serves as the data viz in real time. In doing so, the data—and subsequent analytics—not only inform the design and designer, but over time *improve* the designer's ability to design within parameters, design criteria, and predetermined constraints.

INTEGRATED ANALYTICS
Yun Kyu Yi, Assistant Professor at University of Pennsylvania School of Design, acknowledges that there are trade-offs when using one modeling method over another. For example, is there a noticeable time savings or a reduction in quality of the results in terms of accuracy for the Kriging method vs. another type of analysis such as the Radiance method? "Radiance is a physics-based modeling tool, whereas Kriging is a statistical prediction model," explains Yun Kyu Yi. "The greatest benefit of utilizing the Kriging method is in reducing time in comparison to Radiance. While different modeling methods can be used to reduce time compared to Radiance, utilizing the Kriging method allows one to generate an estimated surface contour from scattered data points with reasonable accuracy, something that is very difficult with other methods."[2] But what are the actual trade-offs of using one modeling method over another? Is the Kriging method not as precise as the Radiance method? Are there times when we can live with less accuracy (for example, when there's reduced computational time)?

1 Deutsch Insights, Analytics and Model Convergences, 2017.
Convergences in contemporary design practice continue to occur at the meeting of two seemingly opposite forces.

2 Deutsch Insights, Convergence of Analytics and Model, 2017.
Do digital building models have the capacity to be more than 3D virtual representations of buildings?

3

Energy Simulation	Decision Making (BCVTB)	NURBS (grasshopper)	Kirigami Shading Control

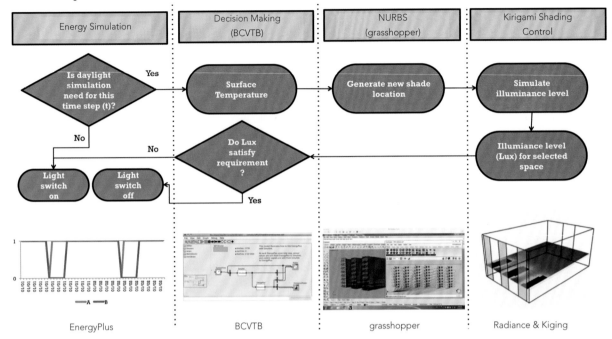

EnergyPlus — BCVTB — grasshopper — Radiance & Kiging

Flowchart contents:

- Is daylight simulation need for this time step (t)? — Yes → Surface Temperature → Generate new shade location → Simulate illuminance level
- No → Light switch on / Light switch off
- Illumiance level (Lux) for selected space → Do Lux satisfy requirement? — No → (Light switch) / Yes

4

Individual A	Individual B	Individual C	Individual D	Individual E
6.94	4.82	6.40	3.38	7.12
5.42	5.51	6.65	8.02	6.04
7.15	6.99	8.06	5.29	8.52
5.31	5.31	5.31	6.04	5.31
3.48	3.48	3.48	3.48	3.45

3 Yun Kyu Yi, Energy Simulation
Diagram, 2016.
With time, our tools—both hardware
and software—are becoming easier to
navigate and use. With accessibility to
otherwise complex and proprietary tools
comes convergence.

"Modeling methods for various behaviors can vary depending on the goal. If the goal of modeling is analyzing exact behavior of phenomena, using a comprehensive model is a great choice; however, the goal of modeling is to understand general behavior of phenomena in various conditions," explains Yun Kyu Yi. "Simplified modeling will be adequate to answer such questions. Expensive high-end tools and technology are not always the best solution. Sometimes using inexpensive, simple tools can do a good-enough job for certain tasks. In the schematic design stage with various options available for improving performance, it is best to use a tool that is fast but also shows a reasonable outcome, instead of a tool that provides an accurate prediction but is time consuming." So, should we equate "easier to learn" tools with less accuracy? If so, why? Is less accuracy better at times than a "perfect" or optimal solution? If so, when? "If you are learning a new domain, there is no easy way to learn it. Instead, one should say 'easy to use' or 'simple to learn use of tool,'" Yun Kyu Yi comments. "Most tools claim that without deep knowledge of a tool's domain, their tools are easy to use. This is where we have a common misunderstanding. If you don't know what your tool is for, you have a very high chance of misusing the tool. Tools can become easier to use by reducing human interference. If tools can automatically populate boundary conditions for the user, this will make it easier for the user to use tools, but the user has to understand what these variables of boundary conditions are for in their calculations. Tools are developed for a certain intent or purpose, and if a user knows the intent, no tool is less accurate or better. It is a user's knowledge that impacts a tool's accuracy more than a given tool's capacity."

4 Yun Kyu Yi, Genetic
Algorithms Breed Best
Performer That Generates Still
Better Offspring, 2016.
We are at the edge of a new
era where computation is no
longer a tool to support or aid
the design process, but rather
becomes itself a method for
design.

Yun Kyu Yi describes dynamic integration between building energy simulation (BES) and computational fluid dynamics (CFD) simulation for outdoor conditions. "Energy simulation tools are developed to capture a whole year of energy usage of a building," he says. "For that reason, there are too many variables (boundary conditions) to consider, requiring a significant amount of computational power and time to compute. This is why energy simulation tools are developed with a multitude of assumptions based on experimental experience. For instance, convection flow near an exterior wall is very difficult to calculate because wind speed and direction change dramatically and other factors such as the roughness of surface, slope of surface, etc. [come into play.] For that reason, energy simulation tools develop a simplified model to calculate convection heat flow around surfaces. This simplified model is easy to calculate, but it is based on very general cases. If a building has very different material than a conventional material, or the building shape is very different from a conventional shape, this model will have difficulty finding an accurate convective heat flow. For that reason, I propose a method to link CFD to BES that is able to provide a reasonable convective heat flow value [faster] than existing methods in energy simulation tools."

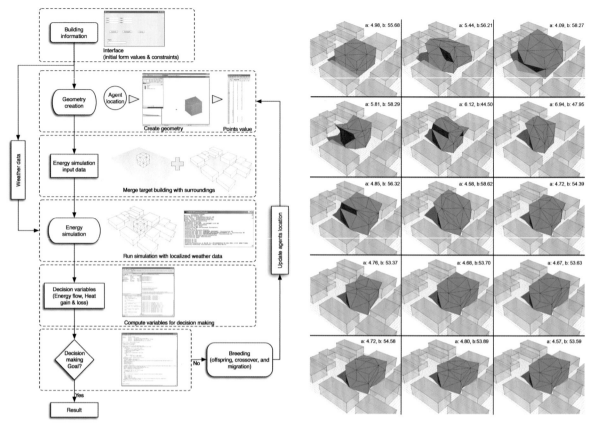

5 Yun Kyu Yi, Genetic Algorithm Data-Informed Geometry Creation, 2016. With genetic algorithms (GA), we can control complex geometry with fewer variables, thus enabling us to use GA more efficiently.

What are the ways in which we are redesigning design? Are we doing so via an integration of tools, the convergence of work processes, or in terms of simulation? "The design process has changed and will continue to change because of the knowledge and technology that each generation has at their disposal," says Yun Kyu Yi. "We are at the edge of [a] new era where computation is no longer a tool to support or aid the design process, but rather where computation becomes itself a method for design. Integrating with different domains provides opportunities that weren't possible before, but simply merging different domains under one roof shouldn't be considered integration. Among many other major elements to consider for integration, among the priorities would be (1) integration for finding better solutions, (2) integration for simple solution, and (3) integration for effortless use. Most tools these days are aimed to be effortless but they neglect better and/or simplified solutions. It is important to consider all three to truly be considered integration."

One such potential of the redesign of design is the analysis vs. synthesis cycle. Yun Kyu Yi describes this process, explaining its benefits over other design methods and processes. "Design is based on a thoughtful process of reasoning. Some current design processes are based on infinite form searching to find unexpected shapes or form, selecting a morphological shape without proper reasoning," he notes. "A proposed method of synthesis is to use simulation tools to help support the design process. This method uses heuristic searches to find answers set by the designer. Proposed methods attempt to design form based on reasoning, not by random selection."

Yun Kyu Yi explains the process of using genetic algorithms (GAs) to find the best (i.e., most optimal) solution. "GA is an evolution algorithm breeding a best performer that will generate better offspring. This method has been developed a while ago but, until recently, was difficult to use in architecture. One major reason is that buildings have very complex geometry and [we] want to have a great deal of flexibility on the choice of shape or form." Yun Kyu Yi proposed an idea for utilizing Non-Uniform Rational B-Splines [NURBS] to control geometry with fewer variables—which means we can use GA more efficiently. "Integrating simulation tools with GA, I was able to discover the performance for a very complex goal that I was not able to find when using GA alone," he said. "For instance, adverse wind conditions or indoor light levels require advanced tools to calculate. With integration between NURBS, simulation tools, and GA, I was able to find an optimal solution more efficiently."

"I would like to add one domain in the equation, which is time," suggests Yun Kyu Yi. "Evolution is rather slow and revolution is rather fast. In certain periods, radical change is necessary in order to cope with the needs and demands. I agree we are in the age of revolution, but I would like to add a note that the fast track is not always good. As we compressed the time for design, we lost certain important factors such as perception or scale of space in architecture. Computational space (virtual space) do[es] not have physical dimensions and we should aware of this and think about

6 Proving Ground, Trello Apps for AEC Software, 2016.
New project management tools create an opportunity to leverage agile processes within BIM and design tools.

6

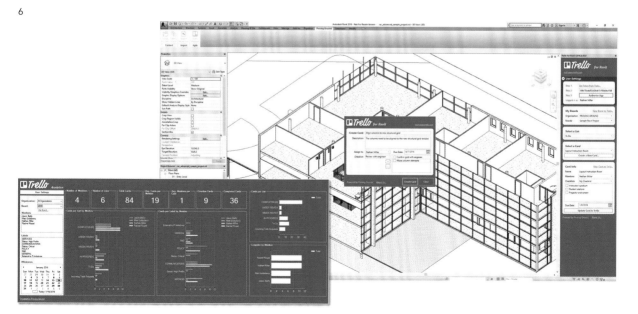

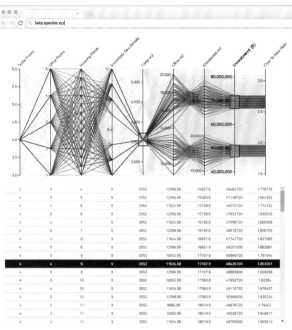

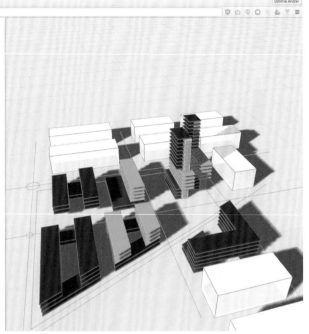

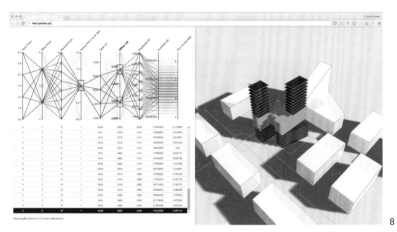

8

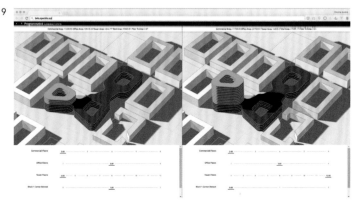

9

how to compensate for what we lost by compressing the time."[3]

MODELING AND SIMULATION

When we say *model*, what comes to mind? Physical models, whether of a plane or a building? Mathematical models? Computational models? There is a new theory in modeling called *similarity*, which is offered as an account of the relationship between models and the world.[4] Building performance simulation (BPS) tools help building designers make better decisions by delivering the performance consequences of design choices to the designer before those choices are made. However, there are limitations to these tools, due to inaccessibility to average users and time constraints. "BPS tools often require deep technical knowledge and [are] too time-consuming to use to effectively support the design exploration in the early design stages. To solve this challenge," researchers propose "sentient building performance simulation systems, which combine one or more high-precision BPS tools to provide near-instantaneous performance feedback directly in the design tool. Sentient BPS systems are essentially combining: 1) design tools, 2) parametric tools, 3) BPS tools, 4) dynamic databases, 5) interpolation techniques, and 6) prediction techniques as a fast and valid simulation system for the early design stage."[5]

The acts of combining and instantaneous feedback, as we've seen, are hallmarks of convergence. Software tools now come packed with built-in simulation capabilities enabling easy-to-use analysis throughout the various design stages. And yet, despite the tool's visibility at professional venues, outside the trade show circuit, the number of firms that routinely model their projects is surprisingly low. A recent AIA firm survey "found that 12 percent of architecture firms used energy modeling software for 2013 projects, with 61 percent of firms reporting no immediate plans to purchase software … . The primary reasons include cost and its frequent accomplice, time."[6]

Models simulate reality—at real scale, in real time—helping us to anticipate the consequences for any course of action, even human behavior. "Models that integrate computational logic into design permit us to discover, predict or orchestrate the nuanced behaviour of architecture," according to the Design Modelling Symposium website. "Our current modelling practices, those which represent what a thing looks like and how a thing may behave, are dominated by procedural logics of computation, which often artificially delimit phenomena, scale and time, not only reducing the quality of feedback but also its rapid implementation during the design process."[7] The aforementioned site's mash-up of diverse inputs and models as a shared interface for multiple disciplines—architects, engineers, planners, and fabricators as well as material scientists, ecologists, and physicists—is an unmistakable simulacrum for convergence in architecture.

Today, when we discuss modeling, we are often referring to BIM. "BIM is a tool, but it can also be a roadmap for required change," says Markku Allison.[8] "If you push it to its limits in every

7- 9 Dimitire Stefanescu, Beta. Speckle, 2016.
Speckle makes parametric models universally accessible when you display and explore parametric models in your browser.

bata.speckle: online

parametric design software ◀

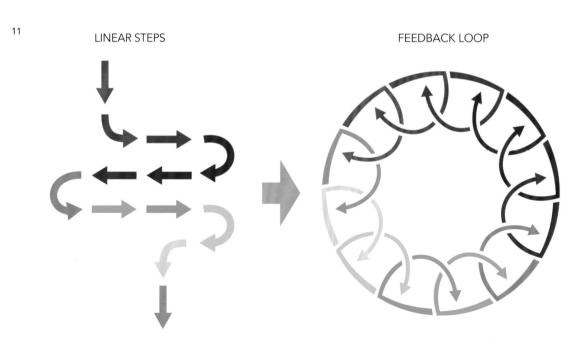

Design Problem

Design Parameters

Performance Measures

Parametric Model

rinse & repreat

LINEAR STEPS

FEEDBACK LOOP

10 Dimitire Stefanescu, Beta. Speckle design iteration diagram, 2016.
Parametric models can enable design transparency and form the basis of collaborative decision-making.

11 Deutsch Insights, Feedback Loop, 2017.
Traditional linear thinking no longer works in this converged-upon world that finds us moving beyond the linearity metaphor and thinking in terms of simultaneity, superintegration, and convergence.

area of its practice, you're going to bump up against business and cultural boundaries, and you're going to want to remove them. It'd be great if I could share this model with a mechanical contractor—I don't usually have a relationship with him so I can't. Effectiveness—eventually owners will understand the benefits that will accrue through the implementation of these technologies. Technology delivers lots of benefits within our individual silos. But those benefits are multiplied when they are supplied to a collaborative environment. As the technologies become more robust they will require cultural change. That doesn't seem unlikely to me at all. It seems like something that can easily happen. Ten years ago I would have said [it will take] 510 years, but today [it will take] another 510 years. We are starting to understand that problems of business and culture today are complex problems. We are starting to see it in every business sector—collaborative models employed to greater benefit. You've heard the software engineering role of programming. One guy is driving, one guy is watching. That's spending twice the amount of money on that, all the benefits on the backside prove it out. I think that, as an example, is the direction of where we're going. The technology is pushing us in that direction and the construction industry is pushing us towards more transparent collaborative behaviors. That's going to be par for the course."[9]

ENERGY MODELING

By organically defining constraints along the various parameter/performance axes, one can dynamically explore solutions that match one's queries. Beta.Speckle is an example of an open-source modeling tool that simultaneously explores both design solutions and building performance, from a one-directional graph to a bidirectional solution and performance-space matrix from a model exported from Grasshopper.[10] Tools such as this enable designers to keep track of design trade-offs. The latest version of Autodesk's BIM tool, Revit, provides energy modeling in just a few clicks—the equivalent of a Staples "Easy Button" for energy analysis. Although preparing a model for energy analysis may seem like a minor feature, it is vital to encourage architects to conduct performance analyses "early in their projects rather than waiting until the late stages of design. The only thing you need to start an analysis is a project location," according to Autodesk, which opted to hide more advanced features behind a button to reduce the intimidation factor.[11]

We tend to think of impacts on the environment as separate topics, rather than the more likely scenario of the synergy between topics. For example, Arup Thoughts recently explored how economics, energy, and the built environment all impact each other. Convergence certainly points to a commingling of forces when explaining large, intractable problems such as global warming and climate change. Arup University has been working on an economic modeling tool called 7see, using an evidence-based approach to make projections about the nature of economic activity in the near future, helping to explain how economic activity creates carbon emissions, and identifying potential routes for change, in an effort to explain how economics, energy, and the built environment all impact each other.[12]

Building performance is increasing in priority, and the performance modeling or energy modeling tools to predict it are becoming more accessible.[13] This accessibility ought to reduce the time required to incorporate energy modeling into the architect's workflow, increasing the impact of the convergence. "What often was the case perhaps ten years ago was the energy modeling that was typically done was done for validation purposes only, either for energy code or for LEED," says LMN's Sam Miller.[14] "It wasn't done in an exploratory way. It was done for confirmation of the design strategy. We kept moving through our design process and then they would validate the results to comply with the energy code. And that has changed radically in the last 10 years, where nearly all of our projects are undergoing energy modeling as a tool to evaluate design ideas early in the process. We make sure we're writing that into our contracts with our modelers. Some of it we do in-house, but typically the buildings are complex enough that we want to work with third parties who have a broader scope in that regard. We want to bring them in early to the process, and the Holy Grail, frankly, is a seamless workflow where as we're updating our model that information is feeding back to us. There is a lot of effort in that regard, but nothing I've seen that achieves the ultimate goal of instantaneous feedback. The feedback loop is getting shorter, for sure. And not just energy modeling, but simulation in general. The feedback loop on things like daylighting is very, very short because we are linking our models to daylight analysis so we're getting quite close there. The energy model piece is a little more challenging, there is just more complexity to it, to have confidence in how it's working. But it's far, far better than 10 years ago."[15]

COMPLIANCE MODELING
Another interface between analytics and modeling is code compliance modeling, and recent advances to automate that process. Code compliance in model checking is not new.[16] BIM itself has enabled code compliance checking and "has been responsible for even considering that code-checking could be automated in the first place."[17] Despite progress made in recent years, Lachmi Khemlani contends that automated code compliance in BIM may not happen any time soon, suggesting that the industry "wait to work on commercializing it until BIM has matured and is universally adopted, perhaps even mandated."[18] Rafael Sacks suggests that for code compliance to occur in BIM, one needs to shift the onus from the BIM modeler (human) to the application. "If one could shift the onus of generating explicit information from the BIM modelers to the receiving applications, in this case the code-checking applications, then it becomes possible to envisage code-checking systems that can receive generic BIM models and 'semantically enrich' them as a pre-processing stage before checking them."[19]
"The major barrier to automating code compliance was and

12 Deutsch Insights, Venn diagram, 2017.
Diagram representing the convergence of data, computation, and project management.

13 Deutsch Insights, Venn diagram, 2017.
Diagram representing the convergence of BIM, GIS, and geodesign.

remains the content of the models. In order to check whether a corridor meets some minimum width requirement, for example, the space itself must be defined, the space function must be identified as a corridor, and the check needs to be performed along the full length of the corridor, through turns and doors," explains Sacks. "The geometry is not enough—if the semantic information of the design subject and intent is not explicitly made available, the code check cannot be performed." Sacks's recent research in this area looks like the future is promising for code compliance in BIM.[20]

Specification is another opportunity area for BIM. e-SPECS, for example, integrates construction drawings and specifications, originally with a simple interface to AutoCAD a decade ago and more recently with a version for Revit not long after its acquisition by Autodesk.[21] More recently, there has been some success writing specs in DynamoBIM.[22]

Cost analysis is yet another area that is gaining traction in BIM. Architects are typically discouraged from cost estimating. First, architects are not typically trusted by some owners with budget oversight. Do they consider first costs vs. lifecycle costs? How should they go about contextualizing cost? For example, by bringing world events and natural events into consideration? Think of the impact Hurricane Katrina or Super Storm Sandy had on the cost of plywood at the time. If architects estimate costs, they will do so primarily by providing a preliminary design cost estimate rather than a detailed cost estimate. There are good reasons for this. Architects don't deal with materials day to day the way that contractors do. Architects aren't familiar with labor costs and equipment costs. Architects typically either work with contractors on integrated teams to get accurate costs and project pricing at the various stages, or work with consulting cost estimators.

In recent years, reports have been made available to the industry that purport to help project teams leverage BIM for cost estimating. Despite the availability of these guides, design professionals have relied on professional judgment and peer network knowledge to make cost estimating decisions.[23] Navisworks Quantification enables project teams to complete late-stage tasks in the earlier stages, by using floors from early mass models to provide rough estimates of construction cost.[24] Nevertheless, BIM-based cost estimating is still a work in progress. In a white paper that examines cost-estimating practice and procedure in the UK and the impact of the use of BIM, the authors note that "for Quantity Surveying (QS) profession, BIM presents huge challenges and opportunities, particularly in the area of cost estimating and quantity take-off. BIM offers the capability to automatically generate quantity take-offs and measurement directly from a digital model of a building, a process that traditionally is very time consuming for quantity surveyors. However, there is little evidence that BIM is systematically introduced in quantity surveying profession in UK largely due to majority of the BIM-based cost estimating or take-off tools

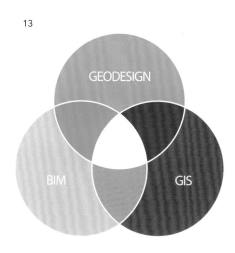

12

13

14 SOM, Guiyang World Trade Center Tower,
Guiyang, China, 2016.
Crown of Guiyang World Trade Center Tower.

15 SOM, Guiyang World Trade Center Tower,
Guiyang, China, daylight autonomy, 2016.
Daylight autonomy for all-glass façade vs.
proposed façade in plan and section.

developed outside UK and adopted the different practice and
rules in quantification."[25]

GEODESIGN, GIS, AND BIM

Geodesign is a set of techniques and enabling technologies
for planning built environments—including civil infrastructure,
and even natural environments—in an integrated process,
including project conceptualization, analysis, design specification,
stakeholder participation and collaboration, design creation,
simulation, and evaluation (among other stages).[26] There is a
diversity and complexity of domain knowledge across building
information modeling (BIM) and geographic information system
(GIS) systems, resulting in their not being capable of completely
sharing the semantic information that is unique in each system.
Various technologies and work processes must be in place to
assure interoperability between existing BIM and GIS tools.[27]
In an article entitled "Geodesign Combines Strengths of BIM
and GIS in New Convergence Platforms," the "related links"
give further indication of the technologies and processes that
are converging: Big Data, point clouds, and GIS delivering on
promises with building information modeling and geographic
information systems. According to the Davidson article, BIM
generally combines performance, scheduling, acoustics, and
other parameters with physical geometry, while GIS analyzes
spatial relationships within the natural and built environments;

15

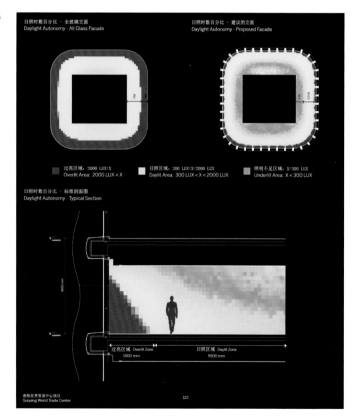

16 SOM, Guiyang World Trade
Center Tower in context,
Guiyang, China, 2016.
Guiyang World Trade Center
Tower seen in relation to other
structures.

17 SOM, Guiyang World
Trade Center Tower facade,
Guiyang, China, 2016.
Façade of the Guiyang World
Trade Center Tower.

however, users often find it difficult to exchange information between the two environments.

Besides the challenges posed by utilization of GIS in construction and design, most often the functions of the BIM and GIS convergence software are discussed.[28] One application of geodesign, GIS, and BIM technologies at the ambitious scale of an entire city-state or country is Virtual Singapore, due to be released in 2018. Among its many applications, Virtual Singapore can calculate the perimeter, area, and volume of a building, and can create a database with information on buildings and civil infrastructure. "Virtual Singapore is a 'digital twin' of the real one, said George Loh, director of the National Research Foundation's programs directorate, which is leading the project."[29]

When mandatory submission of BIM models for new buildings was phased in by Singapore, "it required three levels of detail. These can be plugged into the Virtual Singapore software, but they require tweaking. The huge amounts of data involved in the design and construction of buildings would overwhelm the processing power of the computers accessing the database. The trick is to extract only the data needed for the task at hand."[30]

Addressing the future of geospatial/BIM convergence in 2014, a day-long collaboration session was organized by ISO/TC 59 (International Organization for Standardization), buildingSMART International (bSi), and the Open Geospatial Consortium (OGC), considered at the time a major milestone for the development of standards as a foundation for the convergence of building and civil engineering design and geospatial technology.[31] This pilot program, which integrates BIM and GIS to improve urban management, points out that BIM and GIS intersect at all four main stages of a facility lifecycle: Stage 1, Planning and conceptual design; Stage 2, Detailed design and construction; Stage 3, Operate and manage; and Stage 4, Renovate and repurpose.[32] Urban Canvas, Autodesk's software-based simulator for planning and analyzing urban development and master plans, was created to help planning professionals more effectively create and communicate urban plans with easy-to-use design and analytical tools, thereby helping users to visualize spatial data in 3D, collaboratively edit urban data in the cloud, and study alternative scenarios.[33] For indoor mapping and indoor positioning, one can consider the recent convergence of GIS and BIM. One such convergence is between the full line of Leica iCON robots and the Autodesk BIM 360 Layout app used by BIM and virtual design and construction (VDC) professionals.[34]

DOES TECHNOLOGY FACILITATE CONVERGENCE?

"Technology can certainly prompt and facilitate convergence," says Robert Yori, senior digital design manager at Skidmore, Owings & Merrill LLP.[35] "The world has gotten smaller. Our ability to recognize and jointly develop solutions is greatly improved through technology, by minimizing the time between ideation, analysis, and team communication. The collaborative

18 LMN Architects, photo by Doug Scott, Brooks Sports Headquarters Building, Seattle, WA, 2014.

An office building is paving the way for a new generation of highly sustainable market-rate buildings in the Pacific Northwest region. Developed by Skanska Development, the project targets energy and water use reductions of 75% from baseline. The project is certified LEED Platinum.

19 LMN Architects, Brooks Sports Headquarters Building Seattle, WA, 2014.
Iterative daylight analysis of various fenestration strategies to determine overall level of effectiveness.

FENESTRATION STUDIOS - LMN TECH STUDIO

19

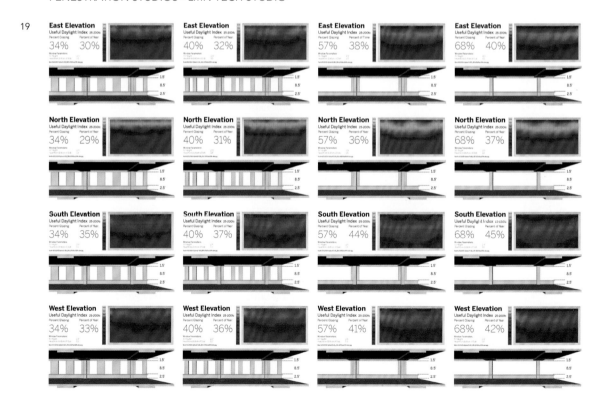

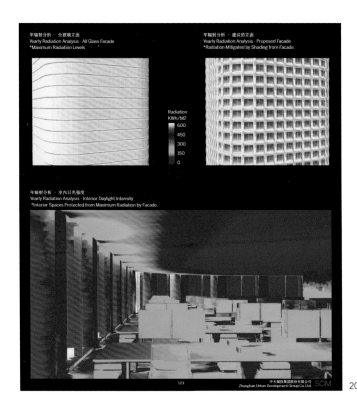

年辐射分析 - 全玻璃立面
Yearly Radiation Analysis - All Glass Facade
*Maximum Radiation Levels

年辐射分析 - 建议的立面
Yearly Radiation Analysis - Proposed Facade
*Radiation Mitigated by Shading from Facade.

Radiation
KWh/M2
600
450
300
150
0

年辐射分析 - 室内日光强度
Yearly Radiation Analysis - Interior Daylight Intensity
*Interior Spaces Protected from Maximum Radiation by Facade.

123
中天城投集团股份有限公司
Zhongtian Urban Development Group Co. Ltd.
SOM

20

20 SOM, Guiyang World Trade Center Tower radiation glare, 2016.
Annual radiation analysis indicating maximum radiation levels for all-glass façade vs. proposed façade. Annual radiation analysis for interior daylight intensity.

21 SOM, Guiyang World Trade Center Tower structural system, 2016.
Structural system of the GWTC Tower.

21

塔楼A结构系统描述
Tower A Structural System Description

外抗弯框架筒
External Moment Frame Tube

+

内核心筒
Inner Core Tube

+

组合重力框架体系
Composite Gravity Framing System

=

双筒中筒系统
Dual Tube-In-Tube System

锥型塔楼减少风荷载及反应
Building taper reduce wind loading and response

收缩核心筒以增加酒店层租赁跨度
Core setback provides larger lease spans through the hotel zone

南北向立面图
North-South Elevation

东西向立面图
East-West Elevation

137
中天城投集团股份有限公司
Zhongtian Urban Development Group Co. Ltd.
SOM

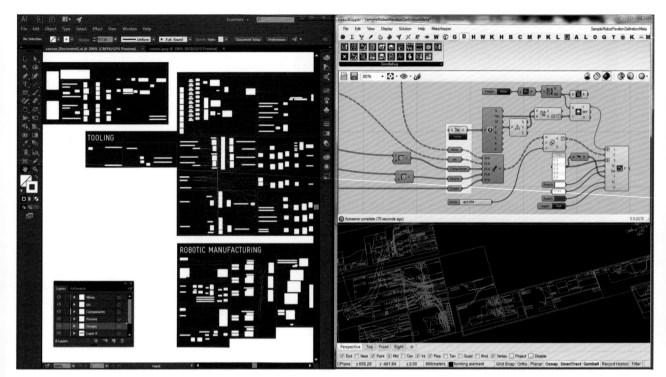

22

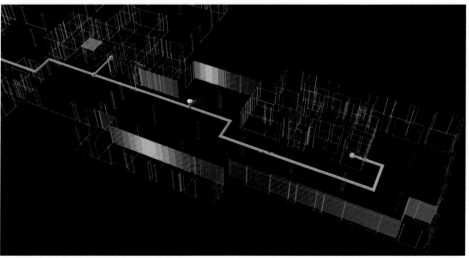

23

22 Brian Ringley, Pratt GAUD, New York, NY, 2016.
Andrew Heumann's Metahopper and Doodlebug libraries being used for automated Grasshopper self-documentation. The graphic representation and documentation of a Grasshopper definition intending to encapsulate a holistic design process can be contained within that very same definition.

23 Proving Ground, Walking Path and Sightline Analysis, 2016.
Creative applications of computational tools can allow designers to measure space in ways that inform human experience.

process is key. The cloud, Internet, the availability of information, they're all catalysts—but I don't know that they are elements of convergence themselves."

Yori continues: "A perfect example of accessibility in the AEC world: Years ago one of our studios used Digital Project as the primary design and BIM tool for a large project we were working on at the time. We were quite impressed with it, and bought a number of seats and explored using it in other studios. While we still use it for specialty analysis and problem solving, it didn't become one of our core tools. Reducing the time between synthesis and analysis is a tremendous benefit. One of the things that we need to be careful about, is that analysis isn't simply a button that gets pushed, with a report or a graph as the result. The friendliness of the software should not replace the assumptions that need to be made. That's why subject matter experts are still essential to the process. The simpler an analysis tool, the fewer the buttons, the more assumptions that are being made for you. It's not necessarily a bad thing, but you need to be aware of it."

Reducing the time between synthesis and analysis requires increased speed. "Speed will always be one of the benefits," says Toru Hasegawa. "At the pace we're working at, we'll have this super-accelerated ability to find more accurate, deeper assessment of what you are trying to do. We're seeing the version 1.0 of how we truly interact with machines. We're still in the first season. The future that we'll see—that Facebook and Google are already doing—there are so many computers spinning with one click. They are spinning servers to analyze your data on a single click. That's why some people who really understand this are paranoid about it: they [Facebook and Google] can understand you way better than you can understand yourself. This will become the reality—if it is not already."[36]

"It's the filtering of the information, and there is a certain limit to how much you can take on and still pull together to a coherent whole," says Sam Miller.[37] "It's just the value of the information, and the value of the change that might be associated with a particular piece of information and how that compares to everything else that's going on. And it's not good if you're dialing one system to a particular level of accuracy and you're missing a whole other piece on the other side. So, for example, in an energy model you've got your systems, your envelope, and you've got your plug loads, and one thing that we're learning as we're designing buildings that are more efficient is the plug loads and the process loads start to become a much bigger part of the equation. And you can add another inch of insulation on the envelope but if you're not paying attention to what is happening elsewhere, you're chasing your tail, you're getting too far into the weeds on that particular system. That convergence piece has to do with balancing the criteria across all disciplines and making sure that you're not missing the big moves in one area and not getting too fine-toothed comb on another area. That's related to the question of 'is there a limit?' Because there is always this

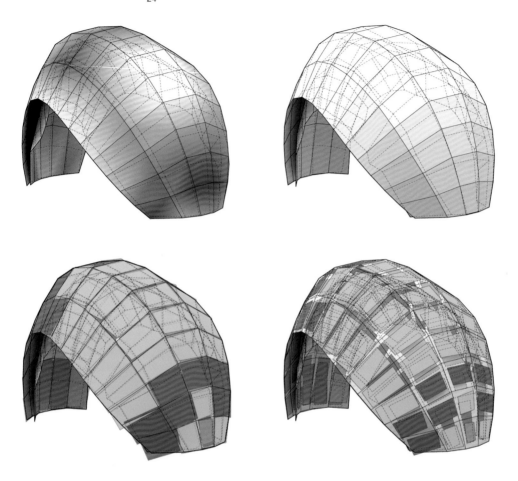

balancing that needs to happen across, and so in that sense that's suggesting there is."[38]

"I don't know that technology enables convergence," notes Yori.[39] "Architects and engineers are jointly coming up with solutions for large or complex projects that require an intense level of expertise at the early stages. Think supertall design. There's very little distinction between structure, architecture, and sustainability at that scale. That's convergence in my mind. Not the architect throwing something over the fence to the engineers, and the engineers complaining that it's not going to work, and then throwing it back to the architect. Convergence is sitting around a table and jointly, collaboratively, working out those issues, in service of the holistic solution—whether that happened last week or 40 years ago, and regardless of what technology was used." He continues, "That said, technology can certainly prompt and facilitate convergence. The world has gotten smaller. Our ability to recognize and jointly develop solutions is greatly improved through technology, by minimizing the time between ideation, analysis, and

24 Brian Ringley, Pratt GAUD, New York, NY, 2016.
From left to right, top to bottom: Color indication of panel corner deviation from planarity, planarized panels (Kangaroo), K-means clustered panel shapes (SmartForm), and optimized K-means results (Galapagos). The automated discretization of the shell forms into panels must be handled in a manner that anticipates the downstream manufacturing techniques being utilized.

team communication. The collaborative process is key. The cloud, Internet, the availability of information, they're all catalysts—but I don't know that they are elements of convergence themselves."

DATA, ACCESSIBILITY, AND CONVERGENCE

For convergence to occur, there must be an increase of accessibility to the model. "What we are working towards is that everyone has an access point to the model," explains Brian Ringley.[40] "Ultimately, the way to do that is through the web. There are a number of projects underway for both Dynamo and Grasshopper that, for the select few, is still very easy to use. But then you add an ease-of-use wrapper where you are only exposing what people need locally through an interior interface—which is the web." Ringley continues: "At this point most people in our field are web-literate, as are most people. Especially mobile web— some people are skipping desktop computers. We can create these type of interfaces such as specify the models. What model? Ask a question and tell me what deliverables you want, and make that happen. We can get to a point where it is that seamless. The danger is that there is this diminishing return. The more and more we democratize access to the model, the less people have control over those mechanisms."

"That's just making a tool work. It's not actually solving a problem or answering a question," continues Ringley. "The question may be, can I harvest enough solar radiation on my site for this to be a self-sufficient building? The question isn't, can I get solar radiation onto my model? It's important, but it's missing a larger point. In the spirit of KieranTimberlake's Billie Faircloth, we should be asking intelligent questions of our model. That is what should be driving the production of that model."

THE POINT WHERE ALL OF THE INTELLIGENCE CONVERGES

"Convergence is nice because the more you keep things fluid, the more that ad hoc strategy works. Is this enabling bad behavior?" asks Ringley. "At the same time, if you do have the convergence— if everything converges and everything starts to feed into the model—there are good sides to this because I can pull HR data: I know how much people bill, how much experience they have in a certain area, I know if they are available or not, and almost automate team creation. I can pull information about prior bid information, prior project success, and client profiles. All of that stuff can be centralized on the web—with the actual models that are under development. Convergence enables bad behavior of the ad hoc mentality. We don't have to think too hard about this, because mistakes are easier to fix and we can make changes later in the game." Ringley further states, "Convergence also seems like it can potentially be good because if you do have a more holistic management strategy, then I'm not checking off a box that I've completed a particular task. The software knows I've done the task because the software can see the model and saw me do it."

"Revit was made in response to people who were frustrated with what had happened to AutoCAD," adds Ringley. "Look at some

25

26

of the BIM technology that existed in the UK in the 1980s. Then all of a sudden we all went to AutoCAD and everything was 2D. People such as Matt Jezyk wanted something better—wanted the industry to be better. Charles River Software became Revit. My frustration arises from the fact that Revit was made for a very specific thing, which was automated revisions to 2D drawings. Now in an era of coming model-based delivery, it's just not working for that end. Revit's dead. Revit is a collection of elements that combine a particular kind of geometry class with metadata specific to building object types, or building components such as a window. A lot of that metadata and geometry—everything that goes into that element package is predicated upon a specific means of scheduling, and a specific means of 2D representation. If all of your data element types are completely predicated upon 2D representation, I cannot use those in a contemporary model-based workflow. If I'm orbiting a 3D view of a Revit model, and I want to place rooms, because room elements are a very easy way to query things like square footage, renumbering a room, there's so much that that is useful for. So I go to place that object. That object cannot be placed in a 3D view, because it is so tied to being about a 2D documentation process. There are these huge interface issues. Dynamo enhances the ability to tap into Revit, and enhances our ability to do model-based delivery. But for a system predicated upon 2D, Revit achieved the thing it was supposed to do. But by the time it did, there was a new need, revolution and paradigm shift," says Ringley, then adds: "But we are 100% committed to using it because it is the least dead of all available options. It took over the market by virtue of everyone having it. Our lives will be easier if we just keep using it. And that's true. So we're fully committed to it. But in order for it not to make our lives miserable, we need active development on the Band-Aid, which is Dynamo. Dynamo's utility is getting us more and more access to the Revit API so we can do the things we need to do. Because Revit can't or won't do them."

"What we'll see now is a greater focus on web dashboards and web interfaces, because a lot of stuff is predicated on people being in the model," explains Ringley. "But you don't necessarily need to be in the model to use the model. So finding these easier portals or access points for everyone in the team seems to be the next big thing. The convergence has really been about model-to-model. It's how I connect my structural model to my design model to my documentation model to my fabrication model. Now that all of those things have converged, the next step in convergence is how I connect the model to the web. Because maybe the web is where a number of my other databases already exist. Such as HR, intranets, knowledge management systems, for a more holistic connection. And theoretically, everything could just be in one system that happens through the web."

Ringley continues: "One thing I say to my students is, I have been teaching for seven years now, and we're at the point where each of these new connections is making my life easier. Now, I'm at the opposite point where you shouldn't put all of this stuff

25 LMN Architects, WSCCA\
Washington Convention
Center Addition, Seattle, WA,
2020.
Designing with digital and
physical modeling tools.

26 LMN Architects, WSCCA\
Washington Convention
Center Addition, Seattle, WA,
2020.
Large-scale physical models
are an integral part of the
design process at LMN.

into one model. I try to get my students to think about it a little more critically. OK, we have gotten to a point where we can put everything in the model. What we have is a design model, a structural model, we have optimization routines, we have tool-pathing, we have robotics. There's so much stuff—planarization, rationalization—all of that stuff is in a single model. I'm sure I'm overwhelming them with the complexity at this point. Is it really that smart to put everything in one environment?"

"Now we're at a point where all of the intelligence can converge. The next obvious question is: Do I even want that? Now that I've gotten what I wanted, I realized it's excessive. So maybe I can back away and ask what makes sense?" Ringley queries.

"All of this leads toward machine learning. Google just open-sourced all of their machine learning algorithms," says Ringley. "So we're probably going to see that creep its way into the AEC industry. We can now truly teach our models, through machine learning and AI. That is ultimately what is now possible. So if we could just say, in theory, we have converged the model. There are always going to be little nitpicky connections that need to be made. In theory, I can now have an entire model in a single space. Have access to all of the data simultaneously—at will—and any user can. Now that that is true, we can now start to think about AI in our future. I'm going to start to give consciousness to these machines now. The laser cutter is only aware of the question you ask the model. You ask the model what are the 2D components of this model, or what are the edge lines of this model, whatever the case may be. The robot is holistically aware of my model. It knows how to construct the entire thing. Because it can see the entire model. You can pick apart that argument, but there is a fundamental difference there. When you are converging, you're making different models aware of one another. Within the context of the larger integrated model, federated model, or converged model. Everyone has access to Ladybug and Honeybee, but no one knows anything about energy analysis. Everyone has access to Karamba and Millipede, which have done a great job of dumbing-down structural analysis for designers, but no one knows anything about those principles."

"Education can't be all things to all people in architecture because it's too much," explains Sam Miller.[41] "You can't, in a three year M-Arch program, you can't teach everything that we need to know. A big question for academia is of all of this, what parts are best addressed by the architecture academy? That's a really important question because is our time well spent teaching professional practice to students, or are we better spent teaching them things that they might not be learning as much once they get back into the office, for example? And then the other one is to embrace the diversity. One of the most eye-opening things for me in becoming an architect was when I was in a three-year M-Arch program and, coming from my civil engineering background, I thought I knew something about buildings and putting a building together but I was seated with all these people with unrelated backgrounds.

There was an artist, econ major, a philosophy student, and there were all these different people who came at everything in a very different way, with a very different mindset. It was amazingly rich, and it was such an eye-opener for me because I had a very pragmatic approach on how to put a building together. They had a very different paradigm on how they were viewing architecture and what it meant to build a building. We fed off each other, and that soup, if you will, of backgrounds created this rich environment where there wasn't a right answer, there was just a lot of different ways to think about a particular problem. We all learned a lot from each other and appreciated how deep architecture goes into all of these different areas. It's humbling, too, because you recognize that you're never going to know it all. There is just way too much to know. But it also points out that you need a team. You need other people to provide those insights that you, yourself can't have. The message is not any one person is ever going to know it all, so we need to be better team members, better collaborators. What are the skill sets that students really need to come out of school with and what are they going to learn on the job more effectively? The hours spent in school are better spent focusing on particular areas that are harder to teach in the workplace."

"Architecture and design has always been an iterative process," adds Miller. "Today, there are more variables, and it's more robust. We are still using lots of trades today. Modeling is part of our process and a powerful tool, to create a lot of great physical models. We need both: the physical and virtual. We still need these analog tools with the digital tools and it's the combination of the two that's really powerful. We're still using Moleskines, still using trace. Architecture has always been iterative. It's just more so now." Especially when it comes to the convergence of parametrics and computation, the subject of our next chapter.

ENDNOTES

1 Jonathan Migneault, "Think Big, Urges Architect," September 18, 2014, https://www.sudbury.com/local-news/think-big-urges-architect-251840.
2 Yun Kyu Yi, interview with author, April 21, 2016.
3 Ibid.
4 Michael Weisberg, Simulation and Similarity: Using Models to Understand the World (New York: Oxford University Press, 2013).
5 K. Negendahl, T. Perkov, and A. Heller. "Approaching Sentient Building Performance Simulation Systems," in Proceedings of eCAADe 2014 (Vol. 2), ed. E. M. Thompson, 49.
6 Wanda Lau, "The Case of the Missing Energy Model," Architect Magazine, May 31, 2016, http://www.architectmagazine.com/technology/the-case-of-the-missing-energy-model_o.
7 "Modelling Behaviour," October 2, 2015, Design Modelling Symposium Copenhagen 2015 (Copenhagen Denmark, September 30October2), https://www.design-

modelling-symposium.de.

8 Markku Allison, interview with author, May 11, 2016.

9 Ibid.

10 http://beta.speckle.xyz.

11 Sean David Burke, "Five Standout Features from Autodesk Revit 2017," Architect Magazine, April 21, 2016, http://www.architectmagazine.com/technology/products/five-standout-features-from-the-newly-released-autodesk-revit-2017_o.

12 Simon Roberts, "Arup Thoughts," April, 7, 2016, http://thoughts.arup.com/post/details/536/modelling-the-economy-7see-and-low-carbon-scenarios.

13 Lau, "The Case of the Missing Energy Model."

14 Sam Miller, interview with author, April 12, 2016.

15 Ibid.

16 Lachmi Khemlani, "Automating Code Compliance in AEC," AECbytes, October 22, 2015, https://aecbytes.wordpress.com/2015/10/23/automating-code-compliance-in-aec/.

17 Ibid.

18 Ibid.

19 Rafael Sacks, commenting in Khemlani, "Automating Code Compliance in AEC."

20 Ibid.

21 e-SPECS for Revit: Integrating Building Information Models and Construction Specifications, 2014, http://e-specs.com/downloads/Sales/e-SPECS%20for%20Revit%20BIM%20Integrated%20Specifications%20Paper.pdf.

22 "Writing Specs in DynamoBIM," December 4, 2015, http://therevitsaver.blogspot.com/2015/12/dynamo-specification-file.html.

23 David Mitchell, "BIM for Cost Managers—RICS UK Guidance Note 1st Edition," released January 28, 2016, https://sourceable.net/bim-cost-managers-rics-uk-guidance-note-1st-edition-released/#.

24 Lee Mullin, "Using Navisworks Quantification for Early Stage Estimates," February 19, 2016, http://beyonddesign.typepad.com/posts/2016/02/using-navisworks-quantification-for-early-stage-estimates.html.

25 Song Wu, Gerard Wood, Kanchana Ginige, and Siaw Wee Jong, "A Technical Review of BIM Based Cost Estimating in UK Quantity Surveying Practice: Standards and Tools," Journal of Information Technology in Construction (ITcon) 19 (2014): 534563, http://www.itcon.org/2014/31.

26 https://en.wikipedia.org/wiki/Geodesign.

27 E. Karan, J. Irizarry, and J. Haymaker, "BIM and GIS Integration and Interoperability Based on Semantic Web Technology," Journal of Computers and Civil Engineering (2015), http://ascelibrary.org/doi/abs/10.1061/(ASCE)CP.1943-5487.0000519.

28 Kelly Davidson, "Geodesign Combines Strengths of BIM and GIS in New Convergence Platforms," February 11, 2014, http://www.enr.com/articles/8485-geodesign-

combines-strengths-of-bim-and-gis-in-new-convergence-platforms?v=preview.

29 Ryota Ieiri, "A Singaporean Building Information Modeling Project Could Revolutionize Urban Planning," Nikkei Asian Review, June 9, 2016, http://asia.nikkei.com/magazine/20160609-TAKE-TWO/Tech-Science/A-Singaporean-building-information-modeling-project-could-revolutionize-urban-planninga.

30 Ibid.

31 Geoff Zeiss, "Multi-Disciplinary Interoperability Standards for the Convergence of BIM, 3D and Geospatial," November 3, 2014, http://geospatial.blogs.com/geospatial/2014/11/progress-in-developing-multi-disciplinary-interoperability-standards-for-the-convergence-of-bim-3d-a.html.

32 Ron Exler and Bart De Lathouwer, "Building for the Future: Pilot Program Integrates BIM & GIS to Improve Urban Management," http://www.directionsmag.com/entry/pilot-program-integrates-bim-gis-to-improve-urban-management/457829.

33 Adam Beck, "The Collision of Tech and Master Planning," May 14, 2015, http://ced.berkeley.edu/events-media/news/the-collision-of-tech-and-master-planning.

34 "Leica Geosystems and Autodesk Advance BIM-to-Field Layout with Next-Generation Robotic Total Station Connectivity," December 1, 2015, http://www.amerisurv.com/content/view/14542/.

35 Robert Yori, interview with author, April 19, 2016.

36 Ibid.

37 Sam Miller, interview with author, April 12, 2016.

38 Ibid.

39 Robert Yori, interview with author, April 19, 2016.

40 Brian Ringley, interview with author, January 5, 2016.

41 Sam Miller, interview with author, April 12, 2016.

IMAGES

1

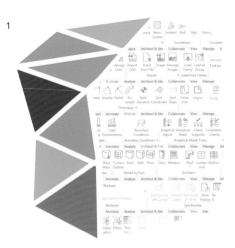

1 Deutsch Insights,
Parametrics and Computation
Convergences, 2017.
The book explores
convergences in contemporary
design practice that now
occur at the meeting of two
seemingly opposite forces.

2 Deutsch Insights,
Convergence of Parametrics
and Computation, 2017.
BIM lends itself to converging
with other technologies,
tools, and work processes,
but notably so in the case of
integrated project delivery
(IPD), among other delivery
methods and workflows.

3 Deutsch Insights, Venn
diagram, 2017.
Diagram representing the
convergence of BIM and
computation.

2

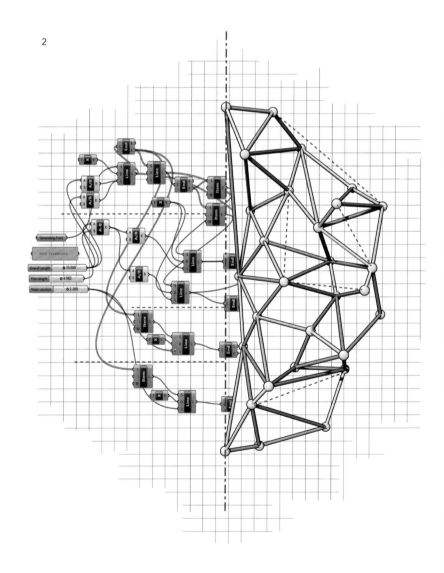

CHAPTER 4
PARAMETRICS AND
COMPUTATION

*What we're beginning to see is a kind of convergence of intelligence
in the design process—that cultural, physical, representational,
sociological issues are becoming far more entwined in the way we
can piece things together. Just as all kinds of information converges
on our screens, I think it is beginning to in the things we design.*
—Sam Jacob[1]

Building information modeling (BIM) software enables the creation
of three-dimensional parametric models that include both geometry
and nongeometric design and construction information. A change
made to one element in BIM software, for example, is reflected
consistently across the model to keep other components, views,
and annotations consistent. In other words, with parametric BIM,
a change in one place is a change everywhere. This ability assures
increased coordination and decreases the likelihood of design or
documentation errors, while easing collaboration between teams,
because it ensures that when changes in the model are made,
all information—whether door type, floor area, or schedule—is
updated both automatically and dynamically. Because BIM is
rule-based, other parameters in BIM could include positional data,
dimensions, manufacturer's data, and algorithms describing form.

BIM TOOLS
In one estimation, currently 25 different software vendors offer
some or all of the functionality needed to deliver BIM.[2] There are
also a variety of parametric tools available to design professionals
that are not limited to BIM. Some parametric software can,
for example, provide a comprehensive modeling, animation,
simulation, and rendering solution. Because this book primarily
discusses the convergence of parametric and computational tools,
the focus in this chapter is limited to BIM. Due to its dynamic
nature, BIM lends itself to converging with other technologies and
tools, but also, in the case of integrated project delivery (IPD),
among other delivery methods and workflows, to converging with
other work processes. Because BIM increasingly has applications
throughout the building lifecycle, from earliest planning and
design through construction, facility management, and building
operations, as tools go it has the opportunity to converge at many
points across the design/build/operate spectrum.

Computational tools today—like their BIM counterparts—are
legion. For the sake of discussing their convergence, in this
chapter they are referred to here as *graphical programming*

3

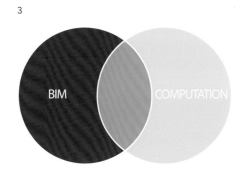

BIM   COMPUTATION

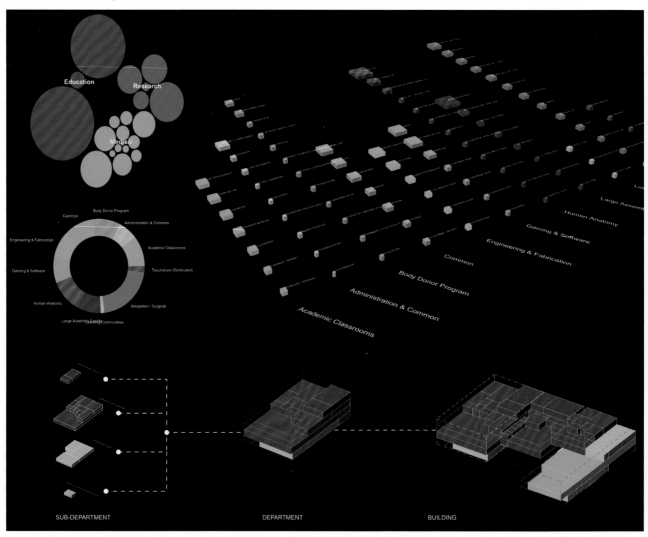

SUB-DEPARTMENT   DEPARTMENT   BUILDING

4 Proving Ground, Program Blocking and Stacking Algorithm with Dashboard, 2016.
Computational tools give planners and designers the ability to gain insight into program complexity and relationships.

environments for design. One such tool, Dynamo, extends BIM with the data and logic environment of a graphical algorithm editor. Today, parametric and computational tools are merging, with Dynamo coming preloaded in Revit, and Rhino and Grasshopper now interoperable with and accessible from ArchiCAD.[3] The combining of a parametric tool such as BIM with a computational tool such as Dynamo is natural, even when the motivation or impulse for doing so is not entirely clear—so natural, in fact, that pointing out their convergence may seem obvious to some who are immersed in those tools. However, this was not always the case. The two technologies are combined for all of the practical reasons discussed so far: to perform functions faster and therefore more efficiently, and perhaps at decreased expense; to ensure that results are coordinated and rationalized, and thus of improved quality—even when the motivation is not always made clear as to *why* the two technologies have been combined. Hence the convergence of parametrics and computation, such as pairing a BIM platform like Revit with a visual programming platform like Dynamo. The fact that, starting with the 2017 release of Revit, Dynamo came preloaded in the software assures not only that the convergence is well underway, but also that before long few will remember a time when they were even considered separate tools. As Philip Bernstein, FAIA, has suggested, in the near future "there will be a stronger connection between what's designed, built, and how it operates."[4] That connection is a factor in the convergence we are seeing in the profession and industry today. In part, the merging of parametric and computational tools enables this to come about.

Nathan Miller of Proving Ground provides a scenario involving a queuing system where the parametric and computation tools (a discrete event simulator that ties into Grasshopper) work together to bring about improved results via an iterative feedback loop. "I've got a shop. At rush hour I have this influx of customers and I need to know how many servers I need to have on staff. Parametrically you can run the simulation, increase the number of servers, and you actually see this fall-off where adding more servers doesn't make any sense. There might be a giant leap from going from one to two servers. Another modest leap from going from two to three servers. Three to four servers doesn't increase performance based on the anticipated influx of customers. We can model it parametrically, run it through design scenarios. Think about typing that into a building system where you are getting instant feedback. I'm going to parametrically increase the number of patient rooms. I'm going to add a couple more bays of checkpoints on this tolling station. You're all of a sudden tying design to this operational performance. You always see the charts of the linear thinking of design to construction to operations. Why can't operations go right back into design? And therefore, what are the tools and systems that we need to integrate? We have the operational data, and know how the building has to function. Why don't we fold that right back into design where the tools now not only allow you to think about the design problem, but think about the operational problem."[5]

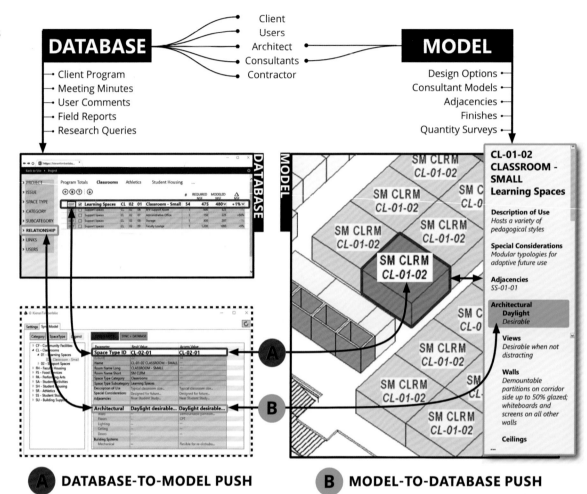

A DATABASE-TO-MODEL PUSH

B MODEL-TO-DATABASE PUSH

5 KieranTimberlake, BIM Workflow for Integrated and Informative Programming, 2016.
The architects developed a relational database and linked it to the BIM model, creating a generative building programming workflow that gains intelligence over time.

For convergence to take place, data and geometry must be integrated across multiple platforms. "A lack of true software interoperability within the modeling and simulation ecosystem continues to limit the capability of BIM to fully leverage its rich information potential," explains Matthew Krissel, Partner, KieranTimberlake.[6] "While engaging in multivariate design work, teams need to be able to bring diverse datasets together and make information conversant, accessible, and relevant while maintaining fidelity and efficiency across platforms. When developing a building program, a design team systematically captures and tracks data from numerous stakeholders. Work often begins with a spreadsheet created by the client or the design team, and the data typically remains separate from the building model. The designer has to move back and forth between disaggregated data and software platforms; an inefficient workflow that risks data loss or misinterpretation. As the project evolves, the spreadsheet(s) are often managed by select individuals on the team, making the information even more remote to designers. Yet the data culled in the programming phase from user groups and the design team provides some of the most useful qualitative and quantitative information."

Krissel continues: "During the programming phase of a multi-use educational building, we needed a database that could evolve with the project and continue to provide value downstream. Because no third-party software could meet our aspirations for an efficient and generative building programming workflow, we designed a relational database that combines qualitative with quantitative information and is linked to the BIM model. The resulting database gains intelligence over time, allowing the design team to build, organize, and query in more ways than they could with a spreadsheet. The data flows back and forth from the database to the model, ensuring that the design process and the people modeling the geometry are persistently working with live data. Key to the success of this workflow is giving the whole team access to the data within the modeled environment as well as the database environment by removing hindrances like Revit access, cost, and training in interacting with it throughout the platform. We solved this by hosting the programming data in the cloud with a free app in SharePoint to create an interactive yet simplified version of the database that democratizes the information flow in a web browser. With the web app, we created a simple workflow to capture information across a number of mutually defined parameters. This allowed us to collect and access defined values, notes, and experiential narrative conveyed by the users in real time. It made data such as adjacencies, size, and finishes, acoustic requirements, lighting design criteria, and user narratives regarding intrinsic qualities, atmosphere and cultural purpose spatially explicit and associated with the geometry of the project. We can also push modeled data back to the programming database to identify moments when the design does not match certain project requirements. This feedback loop, coupled with the confluence of data and design narrative present in the modeling environment, creates a more holistic design space and encourages

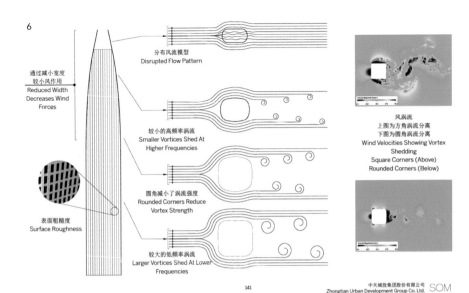

6

通过减小宽度
较小风作用
Reduced Width
Decreases Wind
Forces

表面粗糙度
Surface Roughness

分布风流模型
Disrupted Flow Pattern

较小的高频率涡流
Smaller Vortices Shed At
Higher Frequencies

圆角减小了涡流强度
Rounded Corners Reduce
Vortex Strength

较大的低频率涡流
Larger Vortices Shed At Lower
Frequencies

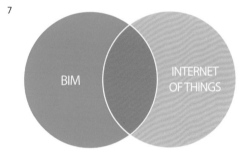

风涡流
上图为方角涡流分离
下图为圆角涡流分离
Wind Velocities Showing Vortex
Shedding
Square Corners (Above)
Rounded Corners (Below)

中天城投集团股份有限公司
Zhongtian Urban Development Group Co. Ltd. SOM

greater discourse. It is important to find ways to fluidly transfer information across software platforms to eliminate the redundancy and information loss that occur when operating within a multi-tool design environment like BIM. With this workflow, we set out to establish a dynamic, relational framework where we could ensure that project knowledge is pervasive, evolving, and effectively informing the design. We have since taken this workflow beyond the programming phase to support iterative energy modeling workflows with consultants."

CHALLENGES TO THE CONVERGENCE

A great deal of time and attention in the discussion of BIM implementation in the industry has been on standards—a focus that may be ill-advised or misguided. For a complete convergence to occur between BIM and computational tools, and their attendant work processes, the promise of BIM has to be realized in a thorough, comprehensive, and widely accepted way. It requires the understanding of BIM as not only a document-generation tool but also, and more importantly, as a sharable database containing a project's information. Seeing BIM as the next generation of CAD keeps both practitioners and academics—the industry, profession, and education—from benefiting from the convergence.

One of the factors distinguishing between CAD and BIM is that BIM is not only a technology, but also a process—a collaborative process. It is this collaboration that gives BIM the opportunity to merge with other tools from the beginning design stages, through construction, and increasingly during operations. The BIM technology and process have led to innovative workflows that enable convergence to occur throughout the project lifecycle. Workflows that were decidedly linear have become iterative, and, as they make their way toward a solution, convergent. "Back in the day, MEP consultants would receive drawings from

7

BIM INTERNET OF THINGS

6 SOM, Guiyang World Trade Center Tower, Guiyang, China, 2016.
Reducing the tower width reduces wind forces.

7 Deutsch Insights, Venn diagram, 2017.
Diagram representing the convergence of BIM and the Internet of Things.

8 SOM, Guiyang World Trade Center Tower, Guiyang, China, 2016.
3D model of the Guiyang World Trade Center Tower's structural system.

an architect, work to map the air flow requirements for each of the spaces and functions, and work out an HVAC system that met the project's requirements," explains Robert Yori, Senior Digital Design Manager at Skidmore, Owings & Merrill.[7] "They accomplished those very discrete tasks sequentially, which added up to a completed design. It makes perfect sense. But in this era of convergence it's not as cut and dried. One can't execute in the same manner—solely through discrete tasks. There needs to be a more broad awareness of one's role in the process, or how one's role adds to the process and how it impacts others. We don't have the luxury of being able to cast some of that aside the way that we have in years past. We need to have an awareness of those impacts. And I think it all comes together, not just with BIM and construction: Sustainability principles and cradle-to-cradle thinking involve a great deal of convergence as well."[8]

While in recent years we've seen BIM converge with the Internet of Things (IoT), with gaming engines, and virtual reality, to name just three emergent technologies, some researchers anticipate that there are limits to what can converge with BIM, both in terms of current technologies and also *when* it occurs in the design/construction process. "In the BIM world, there is nothing to guess or even search, because it is just a management construct," says Toru Hasegawa, GSAPP Cloud Lab Co-director. "I don't see much in the way of machine learning or artificial intelligence [AI] when it comes to BIM. It will only play in the realm of ideation. That is what it's for—to identify new solutions or possibilities."[9]

COMPUTATIONAL TOOLS

What does a user hope to achieve by the use of computational tools? Automation, increased speed, ease of access? Dynamo, for example, is a visual programming tool that lets designers create logic and adds behavior to a BIM to explore parametric designs and automate tasks. It binds with Revit to create very powerful workflows without needing to understand a programming language. Design professionals use Dynamo (also known as DynamoBIM) to complete work that otherwise might take days in a matter of hours. This saves their clients money, but it also makes them heroes to their managers and employers, many of whom don't understand the tools but appreciate the outcomes nonetheless. The user interface (UI) on some BIM tools, such as Revit, can be perceived by some users as, at best, tedious to work with. The merging of Dynamo with Revit provides greater accessibility and ease of use.[10] In addition to current technologies such as BIM, there are new digital tools being introduced nearly every day. These BIM add-ons and plug-ins represent robust technologies in their own right, but, because they are often designed as modifiers of existing software, there is a convergence component to them as well. Instead of waiting for manufacturers to release the latest versions of their industry software, both emerging and established professionals are taking matters into their own hands. They're introducing workarounds where existing tools don't enable them to accomplish required tasks. But *why* they do this isn't always clear.

8

有限元模型-三维视角
FE Model - 3D View

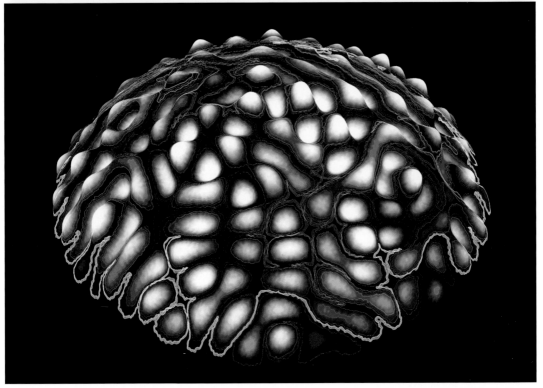

Earlier in the book we identified millennial impatience as a factor or driver behind custom tool creation and, importantly, free distribution via social networks. Why author a new tool like Octopus for an existing tool such as Grasshopper? Generally, what triggers the need for you to create a new tool? Is it one thing, or are there multiple triggers? As an academic-practitioner, Robert Vierlinger, Design Research, University of Applied Arts Vienna & BollingerGrohmann, considers tool creation as a category of applied research. "The limits to the practically possible are a key driver to research, to create something which is justified by a real-world, full-scale application," explains Vierlinger. "Needs and problems from practice provide research questions and ultimate testing grounds for the hypothesis and methods developed. What is created? For which problems? On what level has it been, what will be the future? Our research group creates tools which are tested and used at Bollinger+Grohmann Engineers, but further [by] many people around the world. This ensures relevance and provides context. A sometimes criticized split of focus between academia and building industry can be easily outweighed by the matter of relevance."[11]

There are unmistakable signs that BIM and computational tools have been converging. We need look no further than the fact that Grasshopper has integrated with Rhino, and more recently, Dynamo within Revit, as Autodesk Dynamo's scripting capability and visual programming platform now comes built into Revit without any additional installation needed. That's convergence. Proving Ground founder Nathan Miller, in a Designalyze podcast, mentioned Project BIM Manager, Practice Technologies at Walt Disney Imagineering, Michael McCune's IFC schema chart developing Anvil for Dynamo-to-Solibri interoperability via Dynamo.[12] "The reason Michael was able to do that project was because a group had put together the start of an open source tool that could read that schema," explained Miller.[13] "It's projects upon projects upon projects now converging around things that can sit on a designer's desktop. Interoperability is one topic. Computation is another. The idea of computational design has been around for a while. I originally used generative components for a while before Grasshopper came out. There were, of course, parametric modelers around well before that. We had GC providing one of the first more intuitive user interfaces for designers. It served as a steppingstone. It was available at NBBJ to use but there wasn't a push in the firm to go computational with the design process. Or to push that as a mode of practice. It wasn't a top-down thing. Within a couple of years, Grasshopper comes out, there's a little more energy from a bottom-up standpoint with myself and a couple other folks pushing the boundaries with it, and there were some significant returns on investment (ROI) that were measurable. Having a computationally-driven project such as NBBJ's Hangzhou Stadium running with a high multiplier didn't hurt when trying to sell the story of using computational tools on our projects. With very small teams, we suddenly had a tangible case study of a small team doing more with less, delivering a design with a very high level of

9 and 10 Robert Vierlinger, Buckling Shapes, 2016.
Geometric studies using the buckling mode analysis of Karamba3d on a spherical cap.

11

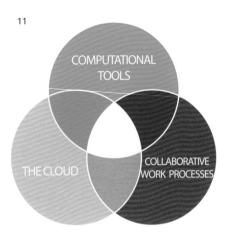

11 Deutsch Insights, Venn diagram, 2017.
Diagram representing the convergence of the cloud, computational tools, and collaborative work processes.

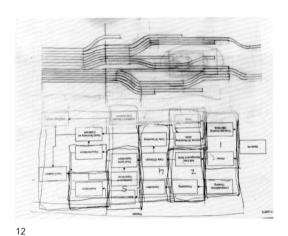

12

13

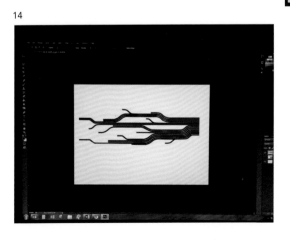

14

12 -14 Jamie Farrell, Sankey diagram studies, 2015.
Early progress studies for what would eventually become the computational thinking/3D modeling Sankey diagram. See image 16 in this chapter.

complexity in a short amount of time. With a very provocative aesthetic to it. It became a very good story that started to drive the conversation and point the way toward organizational shifts around computational tools. OK, we're going to build a team around this. Put a strategy together. How do we cultivate this so that it's not one project but every project? How does this idea work at scale? That starts to signal a form of convergence."

Miller continued: "Take a concept—whether technological or data concept—give it traction, a structure so it can operate at scale, with the ability to promote organizational change. Beyond that, domain specific change, then industry change. Taking something and putting it scale. Something that is repeatable. User-friendly. When I am trying to measure a level of maturity around a computational design implementation, one of the questions I ask is: How do you deploy? How do you take this algorithm you've made and put it in the hands of many people? If you haven't done that, that's usually the next step. It's a question a lot of software engineers ask: How do I deploy this piece of software? Ease of use can help with the diffusion of software. All Grasshopper is, is a visual language. It's coding. You can either be coding with text or coding with scripts. Coding with visual nodes is far more intuitive for designers. Tools such as Grasshopper will democratize the ability to give access to an algorithm and lower that barrier to entry. When you look at something such as Human UI by Andrew Heumann, it introduces an aspect to the conversation that many people doing algorithm making and tool making in a computational sense don't always think about. And that's: How do I give it an interface? How do I design how someone is going to use this thing?"[14]

ON THE EVOLUTION OF A PARAMETRIC/COMPUTATIONAL CONVERGENCE
Jamie Farrell, Research Assistant at Massachusetts Institute of Technology (MIT), explained the evolution of his parametric/computation convergence Sankey diagram. "The diagram was the result of a marketing effort," says Farrell.[15] "[The Boston Architectural College BAC] said, 'We need to get more Revit training. We need to get building data, parametric logic on top of Revit, not just Rhino.' It was a tough sell. 'Revit doesn't do that. It's for modeling 3D buildings, not necessarily data or computer science.' That launched a conversation on what the learning objectives of the course are and structure of it. That's where this diagram came out—something to put on the table to communicate that idea. The director of digital media at BAC loved the idea of this course as a laboratory and giving us as much room as we want. He said, 'This syllabus is great, but I'd like to see what this looks like digitally.' It started as a hand drawing. It was me articulating how these ideas connect and where they cross over and how that starts to play out in time."

"The superuser concept came to be because on the terminal or command prompt, if you type (SUDO super user: do), it is a way to override any restricting constraints. One of my goals was making this more computer science class with design thinking and

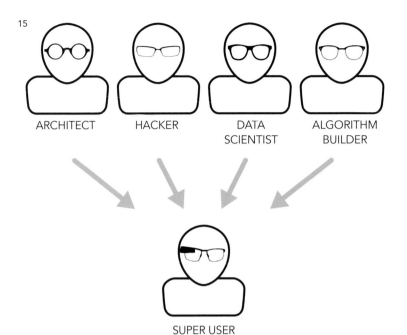

ARCHITECT   HACKER   DATA SCIENTIST   ALGORITHM BUILDER

SUPER USER

15 Deutsch Insights, Super Users diagram, 2017.
Diagram representing the convergence of the architect/hacker/data scientist/algorithm builder in a master superuser.

16 Jamie Farrell, Sankey diagram, 2015.
Sankey diagram depicting the convergence between computational tools and BIM.

16

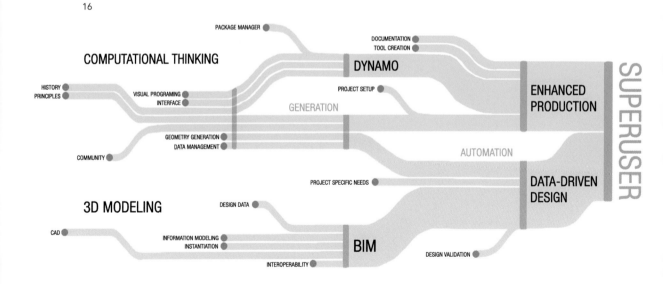

drawing. We'll think about data structures and then we'll sketch in the same night. How can I go to these other disciplines, learn something, and take it back to architecture to the collective built environment, but not get too distracted in what I'm learning in these other disciplines?"

Farrell continues, "It's a Sankey, a diagram that comes from the 1980s or earlier. There are definitely moves in circuitry and the organic. It was one of those things if it wasn't done by hand it would not have come out like this. I originally did it by hand and used another layer of sketch paper on top to smooth out the lines. Then I took that, scanned it, brought it to Photoshop, and painted each curve on top of my underlying hand sketch. Normally I would do this in Illustrator, but [I didn't] because I didn't want to worry about the line paths were correct and line weights and liked it the way it was. There was one iteration that had a circular arrow at the beginning that indicated we were bouncing back and forth with computational thinking and 3D modeling. It wasn't reading nicely, and it implies it by being parallel like a timeline. Just because there isn't a physical convergence with the lines, having them stack on top of each other is somewhat temporal. There is a level of a timeline to this, but the convergence isn't really until the skills are so natural on either end that they're able to then utilize each other to support advanced production superuser. In some cases it was also a bit of reluctance to commit to how these modules tie together."

Architects' espoused reasons for delving into combinatory technologies are varied, and often deeply personal. "My own world has tended to gravitate to increments, with small group conversations and neighborhood-level organization," explains practicing visual artist, architect, and professor Philip Beesley.[16] "My parents were deeply affected by the Second World War and responded with an activism rooted in local ethics and in immersion in nature. I have tended to respond with urban scales and with strong interest in artificial technologies. Seen as multiple cycles, perhaps this makes a personal narrative of overlapping, stuttering movements, in which wholes are progressively sought. One can think of more systematically engineered living systems and other examples of movements that have a tremendous optimism about unification. Conversely, there are some fertile examples that resist whole-systems thinking and insist on decoupled, granular divisions. A good example might be our recent focus on emergence in computational design. This might resonate with a social model of agency rooted in individual action. In a hopeful sense it results in highly resilient, complex, extremely interesting assemblies. I savor the kind of churn that happens from the intersection of those different scales."

Philip Beesley also explains the role team integration plays in his work. "A model like integrated project delivery … would instruct us to ensure that all parties have conversations from the earliest possible point in launching a design project in order to foster integration," says Beesley. "I appreciate the spirit of that, but the

17

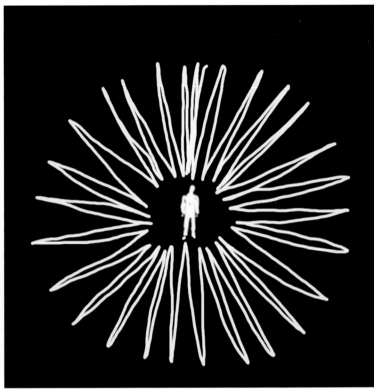

18

19

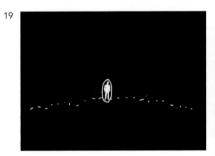

20

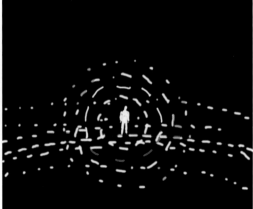

19 - 21 Philip Beesley LASG/PBAI, Architectural
responses to the environment, historical and
contemporary, 2016.
In contrast to historical conceptions of the
world as an eternal fundament, contemporary
conceptions are dominated by turbulence and
uncertainty. In response, some conceptions
of architecture might seek to archive tightly
bounded, highly secure boundaries.

circumstance of my own work and relationships means that the model is far more one of a hiccupping, punctuated mongrel of multiple convergences combined with a great deal of work that is decoupled as well. So it's far from a model of utter harmonic communication. Plato would really disapprove of the way we work. It does not have a purity to it. My work goes through a multitude of cycles of development. There are five streams happening in my projects right now. That is lightweight resilient scaffolding and mechanisms requiring distributed computation and algorithmic development as well as electronics and synthetic biology, psychology and neurology working with synthetic responses. How can we put these things together and how might we verify things and how might we turn this into design models? How can we make some of the design methods useful for young children?"[17]

Not everyone must know how to use Revit or Grasshopper for real convergence in our industry to occur. "This addresses one of the reasons I came to Flux," says Anthony Buckley-Thorp.[18] "The amount of things that I need to achieve that kind of integration that we achieved on the Safdie Architects project, they had to be at a certain level, I had to be at a certain level, the willingness to share data in a new way—the stars had to align. If we are going to change the whole industry, we will be waiting forever for that to happen. One of the things about Flux is that we really go to where people are today. Take BIM as an example. We're on the BIM train, so you've got to hop on the BIM train. From the other person's perspective, it's scary. They don't know if it's going to work out."

SIMULATION AND AUTOMATION

Along with analysis and automation, one function of computational tools is providing simulation for design teams. Simulation can be thought of as a form of construction: the construction of a model, usually a mathematical model, to reproduce the effects or behavior of a phenomenon, system, or process.[19] Design simulation helps design teams explore highly complex projects, but how do they compare with real physical conditions, and how reliable are their results? How do simulations work, under what conditions are they reliable, and what is the nature of the results they produce?[20] Dynamo is used in conjunction with Revit to automate what would otherwise be redundant or time-consuming processes, freeing up design professionals to put their time and attention into tasks that require their core competencies. Dynamo in Revit, for example, can automate evacuation plans to address demands of building codes.[21]

Other add-on and plug-in tools, such as Lunchbox, a set of computational design plug-in tools for Dynamo and Grasshopper, include component nodes for managing data and geometry for activities such as generative form making, paneling, rationalization, and interoperability. Lunchbox's creator, Nathan Miller of Proving Ground, says the LunchBox tool is, and always will be, free to use for educational and commercial purposes.[22] As we've seen, this level of accessibility both enables and encourages continuing convergence in the industry. The convergence of BIM, computational, and take-off and estimating software tools is making possible automatically generated, fully automated

17 and 18 Philip Beesley/LASG/PBAI, Form-language Paradigms, 2016.
Classical paradigms for design tend to be based on conceptions of optimum use of resources, resulting in minimum-surface pure bounded constructions. Conceived as building designs, these schematic forms result in minimized reactions with the surroundings.

21

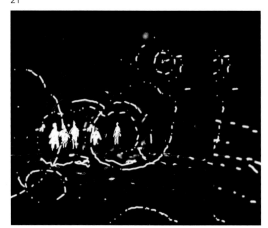

URBAN DENSITY PLANNING DASHBOARD

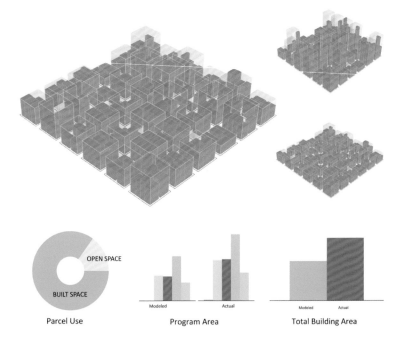

Urban Density Planning
powered by Proving Ground

1) Rhino Layers and Geometry: ✔ Retrieve Rhino Layers refresh

CITY BLOCK PLAN BOUNDARY

Select Rhino Layer to retrieve City Block Property Line Boundary geometry:

Setback ▾

BUILDING FOOTPRINT

Select Rhino Layer to retrieve Building Footprint geometry:

BLDG ▾

Verify the Rhino Model Units is set to Feet: Launch Rhino Document Properties

☐ Retrieve Rhino Geometry refresh

2) Write to Excel:

EXCEL FILE [WRITE]

C:\Users\You\Masterplan\Masterplan_DEMO.xlsx   Select File

Worksheet Name for Buildings Area by Building

Building Name Prefix BLDG-

Worksheet Name for Blocks Allowable Height by Block

Block Name Prefix BLOCK-

WRITE overwrite

3) Input Desired Areas in Excel Document:

OPEN

4) Retrieve Desired Areas from Excel Document:

EXCEL FILE [READ]

C:\Users\You\Masterplan\Masterplan_DEMO.xlsx   Select File

READ

OPEN SPACE

BUILT SPACE

Parcel Use

Modeled   Actual

Program Area

Modeled   Actual

Total Building Area

22

23

take-off and estimating from the BIM's architectural plans and specifications.[23] Why automate synthesis and design? Because automation means the project will be designed and completed faster. The exploration of solution spaces in simulation means that the project will be better, while optimization assures that it will be completed more cost-effectively.[24]

THE ALGORITHM OF EVERYTHING

Does it make sense for designers to go the route of the Master Algorithm? "For this to happen, available data sources would have to become shored up to the point where it made sense to take advantage of that," explains Nathan Miller.[25] "It is still the Wild West when it comes to having consistent ways to structure data in our industry from design to operations. You need to gather normalized data before you can use a data-driven design process at scale with building design. Take health care, for example. It is arguably one of the more data-rich opportunities for delivering a data-driven design process. Yet, it's a similar problem when it comes to various providers. Data is different from project to project. Sometimes there's postoccupancy data. Sometimes there isn't. Sometimes there are sensors collecting the information. Sometimes it's observational. You have to adapt the process to the situation you find yourself in. You can't have an all-encompassing algorithm to figure it out. It is always going to have to be very nuanced. There's this specificity that needs to occur. Some of the information can be generalized: this is going to be relevant, this is going to be relevant. I'm going to build my toolkit around this. Also, there's the expense."[26]

22 Proving Ground, Parametric Masterplan Interface, 2016.
The ability to customize interfaces allows planners and designers to scale their tools and make them usable by a wider audience.

"In Stephen Wolfram's *A New Kind of Science*, he discusses how fixed rules are said to always converge," explains Toru Hasegawa.[27] "If there are a finite set of rules, they are thought to converge to a point. Wolfram finds out, based on his research, that this isn't true. There are certain rules, for example, that never converge. In other words, you could create chaos with various rules that never displayed a repetitive pattern. You could say that chaos is a certain pattern. But it doesn't illustrate that property that was said to be a general rule/a general rule of thumb: If you have a finite set of rules, they will always converge. In line with this I-Robot problem, just because the set is finite, doesn't mean that everything is predictable. This is higher metaphysics stuff here. The point being that just because you have said everything is programmed, you can't guarantee the outcome. The genetic algorithm is one of many ways to evolve a solution. I teach a course at Columbia University on evolutionary design. We specifically use Grasshopper's Galapagos that uses genetic algorithms to look at the search spaces for certain design problems. The problem with generative (setting the rule-sets to find a solution) and genetic algorithms is that they have been heavier on the form-finding side. Very few go beyond the fillet-ification of architecture. It's only used up to the point to find the form. Once it's built, it doesn't exist. It doesn't matter how you got there. You could have sketched it, for that matter. This is closer to my research. How do you program the environment? How do you program the environment in real time? You're living in your

23 Toru Hasegawa and Mark Collins, Columbia GSAPP's Cloud Lab with Van Alen Institute, DUMBO, 2014.
Van Alen Institute joined Columbia GSAPP's Cloud Lab in DUMBO, Brooklyn, to gather 50 EEG datasets recording brains' response to outdoor urban environments.

living room, or going to your classroom: how can the architecture be more responsive to the environment? We have made some progress in this direction: windows opening when someone enters. What is the level of response and how can it get better? Or is this something that humans just don't appreciate? We've seen it with Francois Roche's robots changing of the environment all the time. One example I've seen is where the environment was shifting toward some solution. This is one side that generative design has been limited to that solution alone. The genetic algorithm is a sophisticated yet finicky tool. It will find some crazy solution. But it would not be applicable. It is really good at finding weird shapes, not so much great solutions. Do you give it more control or less control? You debate what's the point of even trying to automate that process if you start to constrain it more and more? It's like instead of making a software-guided solution that you have imagined, it now finds a solution that you couldn't imagine. That's the chicken-and-egg problem of some of these problem sets genetic and generative algorithms are encountering. The results are highly detailed and asymmetrical because they don't have any constraints. It's what nature does best, too. It goes for the best solution, gradually shifts things around. The question arises: do people even want Baroque anymore? That's a whole different discussion."[28]

While most of the buzz on generative design has been in product design, it begs the question as to whether there are applications for the generation of building-scaled projects. The question then arises as to whether large portions of the design process could become automated, requiring only minimal human intervention (the acquisition and uploading of building information, including the building program, building code, local ordinances, project budget, etc.) and human override (in the selection of the most optimal output that meets all criteria plus common sense as well as *design sense*). It is a question between explicit algorithms and generative design. What if an engineer could encode smart information into an architect's design space, asks Anthony Buckley-Thorp of Flux?[29] "I recall the first time I saw Antonio Gaudi's hanging chain model in the crypt of the beautiful Sagrada Familia in Barcelona. The idea of designing by adjusting weights on a hanging chain model and then building the upright mirror image of it was truly inspired. In a time when architects could be masters of all disciplines, designs attained a level of integration and beauty that is rarely achieved today. What are the hanging chain models of today's design studios? Surely technology should have enabled everyone to attain the greatness of these ancient master architects, but I don't think anyone would argue that mediocre practice is still too often encountered. BIM models are today aiding and improving the construction of the Sagrada Familia, but they are fundamentally different from the hanging chain model used to find its shape and form. When Gaudi adjusted the weights on his hanging model, he got immediate feedback and built an intuition for the forces flowing through the structure. With all the technology afforded to design professionals today, it was Gaudi who enjoyed the greatest freedom to explore his ideas and express his creativity to the fullest extent."[30]

GoogleX spin-off Flux has explored generative design of buildings at the urban scale. "Because Flux came from GoogleX, the whole idea was moonshots," explained Anthony Buckley-Thorp.[31] "Everybody realized after our introduction of Metro, OK, that was great. That was a lot of manpower by software engineers working on this long project. But you could only really configure a building now in California. Our industry is so local. It's all about the people, all about the client requirements. It's really a cottage industry in a way. It's about local knowledge. And so Flux has gone through being this all-encompassing building configurator to recognizing that what we need to do is just get the tools to individuals, so they can customize their own personal configurator. All these people, when we're speaking to structural engineers, mechanical engineers, architects, they can express in words how they can take this open-source dataset and this 3D model and combine them in such a way that there will be a really interesting insight or innovative design. But they just don't have the means to put their ideas into practice."

Buckley-Thorp continues: "When I was based at Arup in Shanghai, I worked on a big project with Moshe Safdie Architects in western China. I was designing a skyscraper with huge, 5 meter by 5 meter, corner columns. From my consideration, what I really cared about, was the cross-sectional area of the column. The architects cared more about whether the column was square or triangular. That impacted how they laid out the apartment units. I couldn't just write an area on the AutoCAD drawing or in the Revit model and give it to them. You can't do that. You have to draw something physical. On a trip to their office, I noticed one of the younger architects using Grasshopper. I was just like, oh, I can just give you a Grasshopper script with a number slider. And then that cross-sectional area that I need for my column, I can just balance some other parameters, and I can give you an infinite number of column shapes, making sure that they conform to the minimum required area. So I sent him a Grasshopper script, and in doing so, gave him a boundary of solutions. Without giving him a specific solution. So, even though I was in Shanghai and they were in Boston, I communicated the entire design range of what was possible. It occurred to me, this is how it should be in the future."

Generative design has been used in BIM, for example, by incorporating a generative design add-on for creating mechanical, electrical, and plumbing (MEP) systems in Revit.[32] New software uses real-time clash detection and sophisticated algorithms to draw out the best route for an MEP system, potentially reducing the time spent on a project by eliminating human error. One can anticipate that before long there will be other generative design plug ins and add-ons for building systems. In the same category of generative design are genetic algorithms, search heuristics that mimic the process of natural selection in evolution. Genetic algorithms are great tools for problem solving, and have been used in engineering for a long time. "For instance, if the algorithm can shift the positions of a bridge's pillars along its length, it can propose the safest and cheapest ones," explains

24

Robert Vierlinger.[33] "Or, it changes the positions of diagonals of a structural truss from chaotic configurations into stiffer ones. Step by step it will come up with more informed versions of the initial chaos, but probably the solutions will still look random in the beginning. Eventually, after the algorithm has run for long enough, a placement has evolved which resembles patterns of repetition, symmetry, or variation that a human designer also would have drawn. If the algorithm is given no hints to those patterns, this can take a lot of time. Another example for this is the production of drawings: Imagine one should come up with patterns for a façade by randomly altering the greyscale values of each pixel: the degrees of freedom are so many that it would take a long time to find good solutions. Again, without any hint on patterns, any idea of what an edge or a gradient is, it will take a long time for good solutions to come up."

ALGORITHMS AND MACHINE LEARNING

Many machine learning methods use artificial neural networks, very often to first learn from training examples and then predict results for new inputs. "They work by superimposing basic mathematical functions, and a side effect of that concept is that any random network of those functions will always, despite all randomness, produce patterns which are readable by the human eye when turned into geometry," says Vierlinger.[34] "Evolution designed us to recognize patterns, from simple pre-processing steps happening in our retina to high-level abstractions happening in our brain. An interesting step for me now lies in the negotiation of computational chaos and rational regularity, systems and forms that exhibit a high degree of logic but are not regular by definition.

24 Robert Vierlinger with Walraff Architects and Bollinger+Grohmann Engineers, 3D print studies, 2015.
3D print of studies for the competition entry of an Info-Pavilion or "Info-Box" for the Vienna Main Station. On the basis of structural information from Karamba3d, Octopus's search algorithms drive the stitching of the platform to the partially occupied ground. Structural, spatial, formal, and economic goals are negotiated in a single search process, creating solutions that are differentiated in form and performance measures.

Open systems which are able to reflect any unforeseen state and stabilize to converge on a particularly meaningful solution. When a human engineer designs a truss, the diagonals probably are arranged in a very regular repetitive way, neglecting the minor influences of irregular boundary conditions. When a genetic algorithm designs the truss, it can react on the smallest influences to find a good solution for a particular situation. Still, it would take a long time to find efficient patterns which are obvious to the human designer. But if the genetic algorithm optimizes an artificial neural network, it comes up with creative and novel solutions within just seconds."

How does machine intelligence (MI) contribute toward convergence? Vierlinger has presented on MI and AI. "Science and design are meeting in many fields of architecture, and each can be highly complex," explains Vierlinger. "Octopus is designed to be an interface to complexity, to untangle interrelations and provide a platform for high-level negotiation of conflicting goals. An expert approaches a problem in the best possible way of her choice; afterwards the results are presented in a unified and structured [form]. The solutions can be examined, understood, and chosen by others. It is a way to interface disciplines without turning them into black boxes, putting emphasis on mutual understanding, insight, and inherent choice of results without leaving the familiar environments and fields of expertise. Machine learning methods can contribute in a similar way by transporting outcomes of an expert approach to a lay user in a slim and simple way: The results are not some single solutions which were found, but instead the entire knowledge gained is given to the user, without the clutter of the actual calculations. It is not a search for solutions but a search for the mechanisms producing good solutions. Time-

25 Robert Vierlinger, Octopus optimization of a structural truss, 2016.

The machine learning algorithm discovers concepts of repetition, variation, alignment, and symmetry within seconds.

25

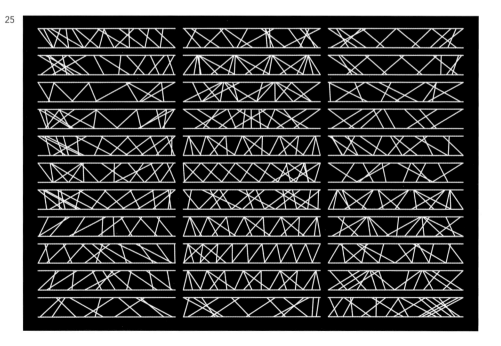

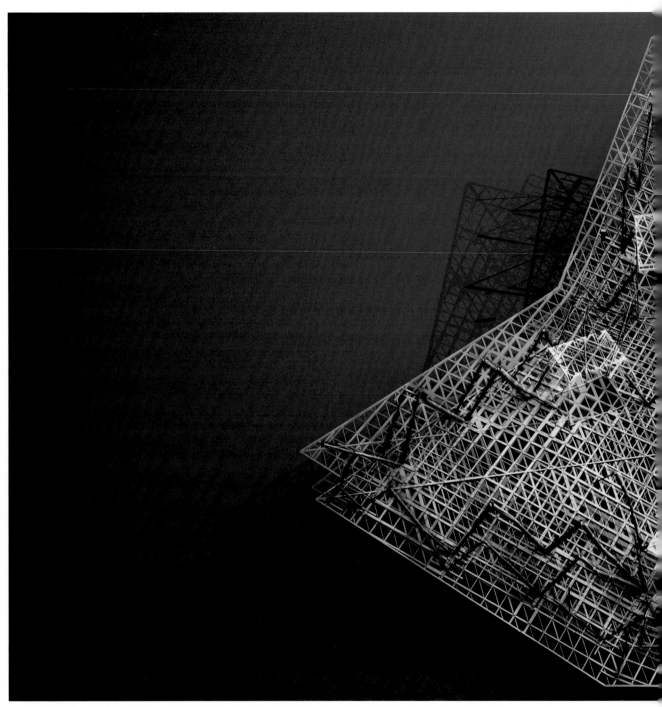

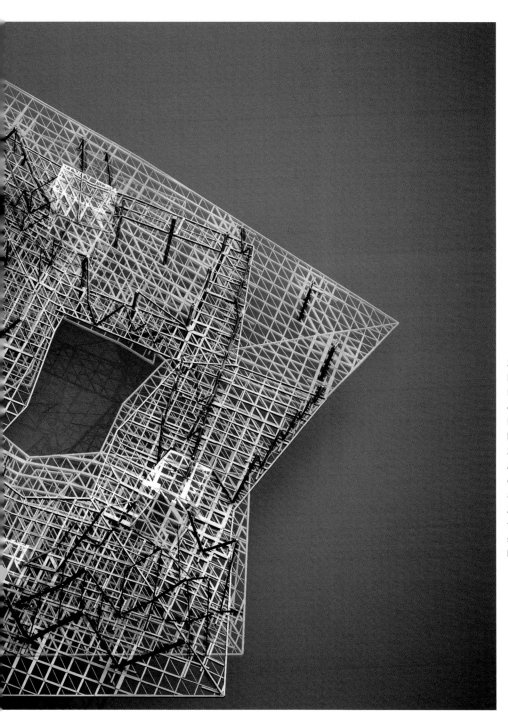

26 Robert Vierlinger with Bollinger+Grohmann Engineers and Snohetta, in collaboration with Melanie Kotz de Acha, Structural Drawing Agent Behavior, 2016.
A drawing tool generates different truss structures within an architectural envelope. Artificial neural networks ease the parameterization of the structural drawing agents' behaviors.

intensive classic search algorithms evolve towards ones which act 'by experience,' with a most significant effect in their immediacy of application and their usability by nonexperts. It means the expert elaborates and teaches a machine how to produce good solutions to a problem domain, which takes time and know-how. After learning is done, the machine then can be deployed and quickly applied to different settings within the problem domain, without the need of expert knowledge or tools. A set of those pre-trained machines, each specialized with knowledge on a specific task, could help (for instance) the architect to perform preliminary engineering design tasks instantly and without having to have expert knowledge or special software skills. The level of collaboration shifts, where one party actually gives ready-to-use knowledge to another instead of working out single solutions. Machine learning provides ways to encapsulate knowledge gained by experts of one field for the use by experts of another field."

What does the term *convergence* mean when applied to the AEC industry? The combinatory opportunities for parametric and computational tools goes a long way to explain what is meant when design professionals say that a convergence is underway in their industry. This is taken even further by the convergence between the virtual and physical, which is explored in Chapter 5.

ENDNOTES

1 James Taylor-Foster, "Sam Jacob on the 'Post-Digital Phase,'" November 26, 2014, http://www.archdaily.com/572314/sam-jacob-on-the-post-digital-phase\.

2 Andy Hamer, "BIM Technology Overload!," February 24, 2016, https://www.linkedin.com/pulse/bim-technology-overload-andy-hamer?trk=hb_ntf_MEGAPHONE_ARTICLE_POST.

3 Lachmi Khemlani, "ArchiCAD 20," July 7, 2016, http://www.aecbytes.com/review/2016/ArchiCAD20.html.

4 Philip Bernstein, "There Will Be a Stronger Connection Between What's Designed, Built, and How It Operates," October 21, 2015, http://www.architectureanddesign.com.au/features/comment/in-profile-autodesk-s-philip-bernstein.

5 Nathan Miller, interview with author, February 23, 2016.

6 Story relayed to author by Matthew Krissel, KieranTimberlake, "Integrating Data and Geometry Across Platforms", July 14, 2016.

7 Robert Yori, interview with author, April 19, 2016.

8 Ibid.

9 Toru Hasegawa, interview with author, April 19, 2016.

10 Truevis user comment, "Create Calculated Values in Schedules?" January 30, 2016, http://dynamobim.org/forums/topic/make-calculated-values-in-schedules/.

11 Robert Vierlinger, interview with author, April 21, 2016.

12 Nathan Miller, "Episode 9," July 6, 2015, http://designalyze.com/blog/podcast/episode-009-nathan-miller.

13 Nathan Miller, interview with author, February 23, 2016.
14 Ibid.
15 Jamie Farrell, interview with author, June 6, 2016.
16 Philip Beesley, interview with author, June 8, 2016.
17 Ibid.
18 Anthony Buckley-Thorp, interview with author, May 16, 2016.
19 Kristina Shea, "Computational Design-to-Fabrication: The Role of Simulation," ED+C, May 15, 2014.
20 Isabelle Peschard, "Science in the Age of Computer Simulation," March 31, 2011, http://ndpr.nd.edu/news/24666-science-in-the-age-of-computer-simulation/.
21 "Evacuation Path Analysis with Dynamo," April 22, 2016, https://revitbeyondbim.wordpress.com/2016/04/22/evacuation-path-analysis-with-dynamo/
22 Nathan Miller, interview with author, February 23, 2016.
23 Richard Voreis, "Trends in Automation—Building Information Modeling, Part II," February 23, 2016, http://dollarsandsense.usglassmag.com/trends-in-automation-building-information-modeling-2/.
24 Shea, "Computational Design-to-Fabrication."
25 Nathan Miller, interview with author, February 23, 2016.
26 Ibid.
27 Toru Hasegawa, interview with author, April 19, 2016.
28 Ibid.
29 Anthony Buckley-Thorp, interview with author, May 16, 2016.
30 Ibid., based on Buckley-Thorp's "Design Augmentation, Not Automation," November 30, 2015, https://www.linkedin.com/pulse/design-augmentation-automation-anthony-buckley-thorp-1?trk=prof-post.
31 Buckley-Thorp, "Design Augmentation."
32 Erin Green, "How to Use Generative Design in BIM," May 4, 2016, http://www.engineering.com/BIM/ArticleID/12010/How-to-Use-Generative-Design-in-BIM.aspx
33 Robert Vierlinger, interview with author, April 21, 2016.
34 Ibid.

IMAGES

Figures 1–3, 7, 11, 15 © Deutsch Insights; figure 4 © Proving Ground; figure 5 © KieranTimberlake; figure 8, 6 © ATCHAIN; figures 9, 10 © Robert Vierlinger; figures 12–14, 16 © Jamie Farrell; figures 17–21 © PBAI; figure 22 © Proving Ground; figure 23 © Toru Hasegawa/GSAPP Cloud Lab with the Van Alen Institute; figure 24–26 © Robert Vierlinger

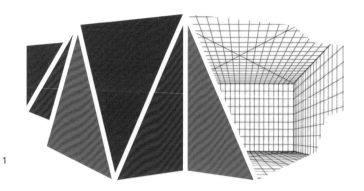

1

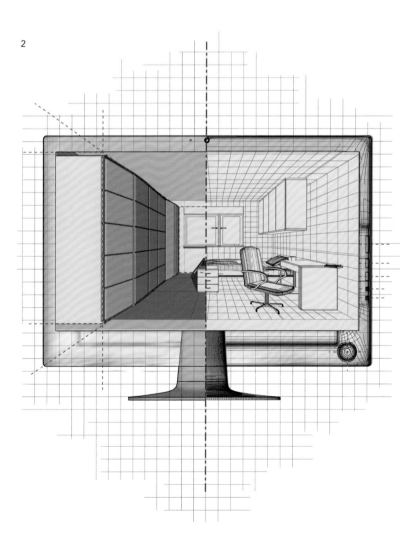

2

1 Deutsch Insights, Virtual and
Physical Convergences, 2017.
The book explores
convergences in contemporary
design practice that now
occur at the meeting of two
seemingly opposite forces.

2 Deutsch Insights,
Convergence of Virtual and
Physical, 2017.
Virtual reality, augmented
reality, and mixed reality are
entering the construction
space, each with implications
for how buildings are
designed.

CHAPTER 5
VIRTUAL AND PHYSICAL

I jokingly call this convergence of games into reality the "Gamepocalypse": the moment when every moment of life is actually a game.—Jesse Schell[1]

As we design for the built environment, we introduce the virtual—in the form of ideas, sketches, rough models—into existing conditions: the building site, local features, and surrounding context. The design could be described as a reconciliation between the digital and the real, in that the still-emerging building design adjusts to the physical realities of soil conditions, the presence or absence of vegetation and landscape, adjacent buildings, and so on; at the same time, the physical reality of the existing site adjusts to the presence of the newly introduced building. In the best situations, the two meet about halfway, each—the virtual and physical—making concessions or adjustments for the other. In its own form of convergence, unlike virtual reality, augmented reality can be said to fill the space of virtual objects layered on top of the real world.

To arrive at the newly conceived building in its realized (built, completed) state, architects today make use of the virtual, be it for laser scanning of the existing conditions, digitizing existing site surveys, using sensors to mine data from external forces or presences at the site, using GIS to map utilities and infrastructure, and analyzing that data for energy, daylighting, crowd control, and other means of performance—or just to see what it is like to experience a virtual reality (VR) environment.

ADVANCES IN VIRTUAL REALITY

An increasingly impactful tool used by design professionals and others in design, construction, and real estate, among other markets and industries today, has begun to converge the actual and the digital into a third reality: the virtual. Virtual reality—born of gaming, game mechanics, and game engines—is on the verge of disrupting architectural practice and the way design professionals engage with both project teammates and clients. The latest VR tools enable design professionals to move from operating a mouse and keyboard to working immersively in a virtual environment. The advent of CAD use by the design professions took approximately 20 years, whereas the adoption of BIM took approximately half that time. The uptake of virtual reality by design firms has, in comparison, been swift: in 2014 Facebook acquired Oculus for $2.2 billion, and in so doing legitimized the VR industry overnight.[2]

Although we're a few years from indistinguishable-from-reality, fully immersive simulations, this chapter is premised on the idea that virtual reality will change the way architects design, review their designs, and communicate with others. We don't yet know

3

3 Deutsch Insights, Venn diagram, 2017.
Diagram representing the convergence of gaming, spatial analysis, and virtual reality.

4

5

6

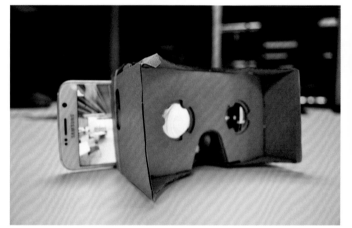

7

8

4 Yulio Technologies, Yulio
plugin for SketchUp, Toronto,
2016.
Yulio's plug-in for SketchUp
integrates directly with the
SketchUp interface, allowing
users to render and upload
to Yulio.

5 Yulio Technologies, Yulio
viewer app for Android,
Toronto, 2016.
The Yulio Viewer app is
available for iOS, Android, and
through to Oculus Store on
Samsung's Gear VR.

6 Yulio Technologies, Yulio
viewer app for iOS, Toronto,
2016.
Yulio makes virtual
reality available on users'
smartphones through the free
Yulio Viewer app.

7 Yulio Technologies, Yulio
viewer app with Google
Cardboard, Toronto, 2016.
Yulio is a fully immersive
experience, giving viewers the
impression of being physically
inside a design. This helps
with decision-making and

whether we will design and present designs using virtual models, or whether VR will ultimately become one more tool in an ever-expanding toolkit. Instead, the purpose of this chapter is to look at how virtual reality and reality are merging, and the potential implications for the design professions. We'll look at how virtual reality is converging with other tools, such as gaming engines, that when coupled with architecture transform the way designs are interacted with and experienced.

To understand the convergence of the actual and virtual, you need look no further than the drivers of convergence mentioned in Chapter 1. Part of what will enable this convergence is accessibility. Virtual environments are often much more intuitive to work and navigate around in than many of professional 3D tools available to the industry. As Oculus CEO Brendan Iribe predicts, "We definitely aim long-term to get a billion people in VR; these two areas and categories will converge and deliver an incredibly comfortable VR experience in a set of sunglasses."[3] Headsets are becoming lighter weight and less invasive, more like goggles or soon even the sunglasses we place over our eyes today without giving them so much as a second thought. The less invasive, the more immersive and accessible the technology will become. Part of what will enable the convergence of the virtual and physical is simultaneity with little or no latency. Virtual reality devices aim to provide a real-time experience without the nuisance or aggravation of a time delay as you look from side to side, turn your head, or walk through space.

Part of what will enable the convergence of the virtual and physical are the following: the blurring between pixels and the actual physical objects and spaces people experience when wearing headsets; the ability to make decisions by engaging with the design in the midst of the larger project context; the receipt of valuable feedback that the immersive VR experience provides; and the interoperability of being able to move in, around, and through the building model using modeling software—bringing a BIM model into a virtual reality space while translating a BIM model into a virtual reality experience. As a further point of convergence, BIM software enables design teams to create the 3D environments necessary for VR applications. "Digitisation is spearheading a transformation of the built environment and creating a space where digital and physical built assets interact," explains David Philp, Global BIM Consultancy Director, AECOM. "At the heart of this shift is the use of Building Information Modelling."[4]

VR AND REALITY CAPTURE
In 2016, Autodesk thought leaders considered the fact that "reality can be captured, augmented, and made virtual through big data to create a digital mirror of the physical world in near real time" among the top trends for the AEC industry.[5] Experiencing virtual reality requires a convergence of tools, combining a gaming engine with a headset, or stereo panoramic renderings viewed on a smartphone.[6] The Google Project Tango app and smart device represent the convergence of 3D scanning and indoor navigation with a gaming engine to scan and instantly model spaces in 3D, and also to track

predicting design errors prior to construction.

8 Yulio Technologies, Yulio Viewer app with Homido MINI, Toronto, 2016. Yulio is designed for mobile viewing, and is compatible with accessible, pocket-friendly mobile headsets such as Google Cardboard and Homido MINI.

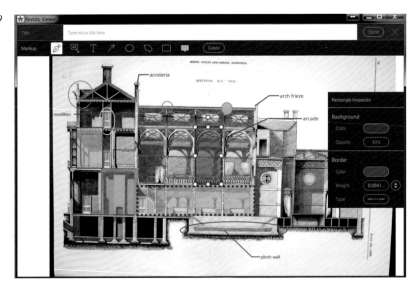

9 Dan Stine Interior Design, law office, Duluth, Minnesota, 2015.
Annotating 2D drawings with customizable markup tools in Revizto Viewer.

10 Dan Stine Interior Design, law office, Duluth, Minnesota, 2015.
Marking up on 3D in Revizto Viewer provides an extensive list of markup tools to help convey ideas and directives in a clear, comprehensive way when marking up on 3D.

11 Dan Stine Interior Design, law office, Duluth, Minnesota, 2015.
Issue Tracker keeps track of everything that's going on in the project. The user can note all project-related issues, assign and follow up on tasks, be notified about all project updates, and generally manage all teamwork and project activities in one place that everyone has access to.

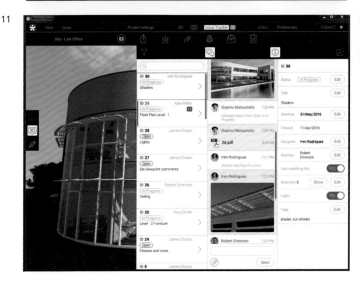

motion, potentially replacing expensive laser scanners in the future. With Project Tango, laser scanning comes to handheld smart devices.[7] In fact, researchers from ETH Zurich have been able to 3D-map an entire building exterior with a tablet (in just 10 minutes).[8] Importantly, reality capture is converging into a single device.

As the name implies, *reality capture* uses tools and applications to capture and document reality in 3D. Photogrammetry is a form of reality capture, as are 3D mapping, laser scanning point clouds, and visual sensing. ReMake—formerly known in beta as Memento—is an Autodesk tool that converts photos and 3D scans into high-quality, ready-to-use 3D models. Photogrammetry tools are convergence tools in that they allow smartphone users to capture objects from the real world and render them into digital 3D models. "What's most impressive about ReMake is that it can take two-dimensional photos, separate the primary object in that photo from its background and create a high-quality 3D model from a group of photos taken around an object."[9] According to Autodesk, ReMake/Memento "is an end-to-end solution for converting any captured reality input (photos or scans) into high definition 3D meshes that can be cleaned up and used for a variety of purposes including 3D printing."[10]

Photogrammetry can be used in construction, where the 3D model resulting from photographs taken at multiple locations and angles at the construction site can be stitched together and brought into various BIM applications.[11] The convergence of photographs with BIM can also help initiate effective site logistics workflows.[12] Besides handheld smart devices, unmanned aerial vehicles (UAVs) or drones can assist with reality capture and 3D mapping of construction sites.[13] Rather than capturing information as a point cloud, there are reality-capture drone-based applications today that generate site data into a "reality mesh" that "is built similarly to geometric engineering models so as to align itself with real-world context through photographs. It produces a form of photogrammetry that can generate 3D representations from photos taken with a digital camera, whether it's highly specialized or a regular smartphone, without the need to stitch a batch of photographs together."[14] From a convergence standpoint, reality-capture drones that transcribe 2D photographs into 3D BIM models collect, manage, and reconcile large quantities of data and information, saving time for design and construction professionals at the construction site.[15]

Beyond drones, handheld scanners can perform both building data capture and reality capture from a human scale and perspective. One such device, the Trimble DPI-8 scanner, can be used for immediate field verification of data. According to at least one architect who tested the device, the scanner is lightweight, intuitive to use (and therefore accessible), and includes a camera. In fact, the scanner is described in convergent terms as "just basic components that [are] connected together."[16] The scanning feedback is also simultaneous, not only informing your process, but ultimately improving it: "The information that is displayed on the screen

12 Dan Stine Interior Design, law office, Duluth, Minnesota, 2015.
Shows iIssue tracking for projects without 3D models. PDFs and 2D sheets can be imported into Revizto Viewer, and Issue Tracker is used to mark up any part of the document.

13 Dan Stine Interior Design, law office, Duluth, Minnesota, 2015.
Revizto Issue Tracker keeps track of everything that's going on in the project.

14 Dan Stine Interior Design, law office, Duluth, Minnesota, 2015.
Revizto Issue Tracker keeps track of everything that's going on in the project.

12

13

14

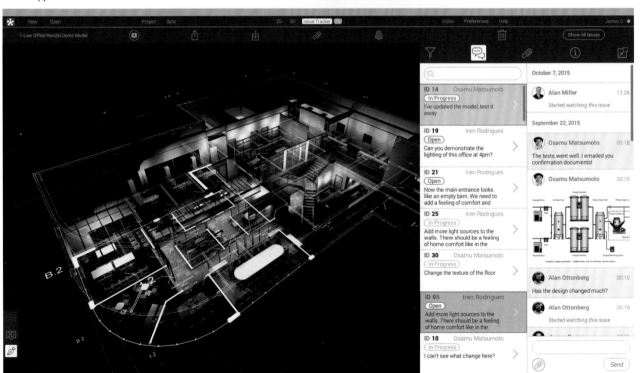

during the scan is constantly giving you feedback how you should proceed scanning, and what area you have scanned so far."[17]

REALITY COMPUTING

Another convergence takes place in a concept called *reality computing,* "a high-level concept that integrates the digital and physical worlds, bringing together many products and technologies to digitally capture existing conditions (laser scanning, photogrammetry, depth cameras, UAVs), manipulate and analyze that information in design software, and then realize the result back in our physical world with 3D printing and digital fabrication or visually thorough augmented reality or projection technologies."[18] Reality computing relies on advances in 3D scanning, ubiquitous sensors, rapid prototyping, and cheap, massively parallel (cloud) computing.[19] Converting flat 2D photographs into 3D models is still one step removed from a convergence between the virtual and physical. This is where augmented reality (AR) comes into play, representing an opportunity to bring the actual and virtual together.

USES FOR VR IN ARCHITECTURE

While many industries, including medicine and the military, are looking to leverage virtual reality, the focus here is on architecture, engineering, and construction (AEC). As VR technology is still emerging, there are several parallel fronts for combining VR with and using it in AEC. One includes the leveraging of gaming and video games in AEC, and more specifically, gaming in BIM. Before looking at the convergence of gaming and BIM, though, it helps to gain an understanding of the qualities of and uses for VR in architecture beyond the ability to take your client on a building tour. That said, the architect's clients can gain an immediate and visceral understanding of a design when they experience it in virtual reality, and that leads to improved—faster, less costly, more assured—decision-making on the part of the owner.[20] In one specific instance, during a demonstration that took place at SXSW Interactive 2016, "despite [the fact] that the design had already been finalized and that changes would incur extra costs, the designs were updated based on the client's realizations while wearing the VR headset."[21] From a faster/better/cheaper standpoint, the technology cannot always make convincing claims for return on investment (ROI). "Currently, using virtual reality in AEC can be time-consuming and expensive, but a few companies … are working to change that."[22] This current situation doesn't stop architecture firms such as NBBJ from exploring the possibilities of leveraging VR as a productivity tool, or even creating custom VR platforms "designed to make it easier to collaborate and make decisions about projects."[23]

For there to be a convergence between the virtual and the physical, pixels must provide the equivalent of the perception of depth and space (and by that I am not referring to *voxels*), as well as a sense of scale—especially when dealing with objects the size of buildings. Equally importantly, virtual reality must provide users with a *feel* for the place they are inhabiting, observing, or otherwise passing through.[24] Not limited to the vicissitudes of virtual reality, this feel for a space or place is something architects strive to give their clients no matter what technology, tool, time period, or dimension they are working in. For most building designers, it is a small step from modeling—whether with physical or virtual models—to designing in VR. "Architects are already designing in 3D, so it's a natural transition to VR-based presentations."[25]

Because VR represents opportunities for direct experience with a space or place, by removing steps, stages, or even phases in design-to-decision workflows that require the integration of client feedback into workable designs, a convergence is occurring that approximates the rapid prototyping of 3D printing or even the iterative approach of design itself, where the designer zeroes in on a design direction—taking the clients down the proverbial path—in less time, and with a great deal more certainty for their having *experienced* the design themselves, not just basing it on the designer's word.

VR AND AR IN ARCHITECTURE, ENGINEERING, AND CONSTRUCTION
Going back as much as 40 years, virtual reality is not new. Its application to architecture and construction goes back more than a decade. For example, a special issue of the online *Journal of Information Technology in Construction* was published on the theme, "Virtual Reality Technology in Architecture and Construction," in 2003.[26] Construction companies with 150-year histories today make use of virtual reality (primarily for visualization). "At its office in Roseville, Calif., McCarthy has been using VR technology for several years. In 2012, McCarthy built its own Building Information Modeling (BIM) Cave, which uses projection technology and 3D glasses to allow multiple users to see what a hospital room or office space will look like."[27] Despite having been around for a long time, and beyond those functions already alluded to, VR is still an emerging technology that is in an exploratory stage as to its ultimate impacts in AEC.

Autodesk University, held in Las Vegas, Nevada, near the end of 2015, showcased the virtues of virtual reality for a worldwide audience, addressing its implications for the way architects will work. Autodesk refers to its vision for the future of work as the *augmented age*.[28] "The [Autodesk] Fusion 360-HoloLens collaboration reaffirms the movement toward a more technologically advanced construction industry. Wearables like HoloLens are becoming more popular in all aspects of construction, from safety to design, and making it possible to better integrate building information modeling (BIM) systems into everyday workflows."[29] Autodesk suggests that this convergence of tools will save time, reduce errors, and minimize document overload and mismanagement waste.

In the construction space, the DAQRI Smart Helmet, marketed as "The World's First Wearable Human Machine Interface," integrates the VR/AR headset into the construction worker's hardhat gear.

Equipped with more than a dozen sensors, the helmet enables workers to overlay construction and augment data/information on top of construction site surfaces. Research is being undertaken on how to use BIM with the helmet, with the ultimate goal of gaining efficiencies across multiple sites.[30] For VR and AR to catch on at the construction site, let alone in the architecture firm, the technology cannot be perceived as requiring additional effort. Intuitive tools that are built on top of existing tools and devices—or software and apps that essentially teach you how to use it as you are using it—are preferred over stand-alone tools that require additional training and hardware. Until this convergence of tools and work processes can be achieved, architects will likely stick with rendering in the cloud, Google Cardboard, and a smartphone.

Some feel that augmented reality will have an even greater impact on the AEC industry than VR, in that AR breaks down the physical/virtual barriers even further. If visualized along a continuum, with reality on one end and the virtual on the other extreme, augmented reality would be situated somewhere along the middle. AR overlays the real world with digital assets.[31] Virtual reality creates a new reality, whereas augmented reality enhances reality.[32] "The whole point of that ugly word, augmented, is that AR takes your view of the real world and adds digital information and/or data on top of it."[33] AR enables users to "see both synthetic light as well as natural light bouncing off objects in the real world."[34] While, as we've seen, VR uses computer technology to create a simulated, three-dimensional world that a user can manipulate and explore while feeling as if she were in that world, AR can be thought of as an enhanced version of reality that is created by the use of technology such as sensors and algorithms to overlay digital information on an image of something being viewed on a device. "In contrast to the fully immersive experience of virtual reality, augmented reality 'augments; physical reality with additional relevant content instead of replacing it altogether."[35] Project Tango, mentioned earlier, can be used "for augmented reality by projecting digital on the phone's display objects over the real-world surroundings."[36] Project Tango's sensors and camera generate augmented- and virtual-reality visualizations into various headgear or goggles. Google Project Tango promises to produce augmented-reality BIM models that you will be able to virtually and physically walk through, providing real-time simulation of a proposed or in-progress building design, including lighting effects, surround sound, and thermal modeling, among other senses.[37] Others are attempting to converge reality capture and other features into a single, accessible device. One such device integrates features to determine structural integrity of existing buildings and infrastructure.[38] The big idea behind such platforms as Magic Leap is that the technology will allow 3D virtual elements to appear in real life. As mentioned, HoloLens utilizes augmented reality (more accurately, mixed reality) to create 3D objects within an actual, physical space, thus creating a mixed-reality experience of both the digital and the real. The fact that HoloLens is untethered—requiring no mouse or keyboard, no wires, phones, or connection to a PC—makes that technology all the more accessible for the AEC industry. Although the technology is still emerging, AR and VR both enable you to step inside a CAD or BIM model, even on mobile handheld devices.[39]

The use of AR on mobile devices speaks to the opportunity to bring BIM and AR to the construction site. With the prevalence of inexpensive mobile devices and increasingly advanced software apps, design professionals now have the opportunity to merge their BIM models with actual site conditions. But AR doesn't have to take on such complex forms. We don't often think of QR codes as a form of augmented reality, but they are perhaps the most familiar example of the technology in use in the AEC industry today.

"QR codes are a vital component of one the largest implementations to date of augmented reality (AR) technology in the U.S. construction industry. At any given time, a project superintendent, subcontractor, architect, facilities team member, or other field personnel can scan one of the QR codes throughout the campus with a smartphone or tablet computer and instantly immerse themselves in the up-to-date, as-built 3D BIM model or 3D laser scan of that space."[40] Damon Hernandez's recap of his team's project at the first HoloLens-based Holographic Hackathon, held in Seattle in 2016, gives an indication of how far the various technologies and work processes are converging in the AEC space. Describing their effort to create a HoloLens version of a building application developed for VR and browser-based web3D using the Kinect, "this application uses digital fabrication ready 3D models of building components to 1) give the user/ general contractor the ability to place these items in a scene to build a structure and 2) provide them a price of our material and machine time costs for fabrication at our factory."[41] In the simplest terms, Microsoft's HoloLens projects holograms that people can interact with onto the real world. "Hence the term 'augmented' reality; you still interact with the real world in the HoloLens, but virtual elements can be integrated in various ways. No longer is there such a drastic separation between cyberspace and physical reality."[42] In addition to holograms, AR technology enables users to superimpose computer-generated images created in CAD or BIM software onto real-world spaces, creating a composite, combined, or even *converged* augmented view of the space.[43] Common challenges faced by AR tools—such as the potential for out-of-date or incorrect BIM model information, or the need to ensure accurate positioning—can be overcome with real-time access to cloud-based models.[44]

One way of thinking about AR apps is that they not only bring both architectural and construction concepts to life, but also, due to the virtual/actual convergence, help to reduce the possibility of project delays and cost overruns.[45] "It can sometimes take hours to address a question on the job site itself, mainly because of a lack of access to the information that's needed," explains Mani Golparvar-Fard, Associate Professor of Civil and Environmental and Computer Engineering at the University of Illinois UrbanaChampaign.[46] "Augmented-reality applications can cut the access problem down to less than a minute, saving developers, contractors, and ultimately clients time and money, while helping improve communications among the site personnel."[47] With handheld tablets increasingly present on site, AR may potentially have more application in construction than in the design process. "While virtual reality can help designers visualize a structure to see how everything will look, augmented reality plays a role in helping construction teams in the field understand how various systems and components fit together during production."[48] Enabling the convergence of BIM, virtual reality, and augmented reality are improvements to the technology, including faster conversion times and higher-quality graphics. "A major obstacle that building teams face when looking to implement VR gaming on projects is turnaround time. The process of converting a BIM file to a realistic gaming environment could take days, even weeks." One vendor's rendering process, depending on the level of service, can take between 3 hours (fast-track option) and 10 hours (standard service), representing a range that is among the industry's fastest turnaround times. These turnaround rates, given time, will inevitably diminish.[49]

LEVERAGING VIDEO GAMES IN AEC

One technology that virtual reality can be built on top of is gaming. The AEC industry has recently seen the worlds of gaming and virtual reality converge, as well as the worlds of gaming and spatial analysis. In 2016, USC School of Architecture Professor Jose Sanchez launched a neighborhood-building simulator game called Block'hood, which, while exploring ecology and urban planning, also sets out to solve intractable urban problems such as gentrification and other challenges of contemporary cities. Sanchez says that video games will be "new tools" to solve architecture's challenges.[50] Design professionals have been leveraging video games to make better decisions in design and construction.[51] This is gaming for better/faster/cheaper, where video games become a tool not only to solve architecture problems, but also to enable architects to look at multiple issues simultaneously. "Architects today start designing by thinking of form either through drawings or models," says Sanchez. "We don't often start from a study of ecological dependencies. Block'hood allows [us] to do both simultaneously, understand how form and ecology are interrelated."[52] From a convergence standpoint, Block'hood explores the relationship between architecture and gaming. Upon recently receiving a coveted award for his game, Sanchez acknowledged that "the jury recognized how the mechanics of the game are fundamentally defining its ecological narrative. It means a lot for someone like me coming from architecture to be recognized outside my field, validating all the effort in attempting interdisciplinary research."[53]

As we saw in Chapter 1, interdisciplinary research is a driver of converging tools. The convergence of virtual reality and architecture doesn't end with gaming. Emerging design professionals are blending gaming, virtual reality, and robotics together at AEC and VR hackathons.[54] Virtual reality has potential

beyond the world of gaming. "It could prove to be the next stage of computing interface, paving the way for a more integrated amalgam of our minds and computers, and possibly even leading to Ray Kurzweil's concept of the Singularity."[55]

IMPLEMENTING ENCAPSULATED KNOWLEDGE

"We live in a time of convergence, where programming languages, APIs and libraries encapsulate expert knowledge increasing cross-disciplinary interactions," explains Block'hood creator, Sanchez.[56] "Architects can access global data by remote sensors, implement structural optimization, rationalize fabrication or learn about [a] crowd's behavioral patterns without the need to study any of these subjects in depth, just by implementing the encapsulated knowledge in an interface." Sanchez continues: "In this landscape we have seen the emergence of new mediums that are able to take advantage of an ongoing digital infrastructure. Software can be considered the fundamental medium of a technological era, but such denomination is still too broad to address the issues of the current design landscape. Games, on the other hand, are a subgenre with a particular attitude in the interaction of humans and computers, allowing also for a bias that can engage audiences in a particular narrative. Games have become mass media products engaging audiences of all ages dealing with complex issues in often-simplified formats. The key here is to think of platforms of engagement at a large scale; that is why games, as opposed to specialized software, have an edge on breaking from niche users towards global audiences. A game is required to take responsibility over a player's experience, taking them from complete ignorance to mastery in just a few hours."

"Architecture and design have never before had tools to address communities in such an interactive and engaging way, sampling user behavior in a diverse set of scenarios," explains Sanchez. "This kind of platform has historically been in the hands of large companies where hundreds of engineers develop the experience players will find in the market. This is no longer the landscape in which games are developed; the democratization of gaming engines, such as Unity 3D and Unreal Engine, [has] contributed to the development of a vibrant and dynamic scene of independent developers, where small teams (even individuals) are able to develop and put in the market a potentially million-dollar product that can engage millions of users just via digital distribution. Platforms such as STEAM allow for indie developers to sell their games to a global audience without the need of retail copies or physical products. Games like Minecraft have become success stories of independent developers navigating this new marketplace. It is precisely in this landscape of fast iterative prototyping and innovation where individuals with different ideas can innovate and add novelty to the field, questioning the conventions and discovering new desires present among player communities. Minecraft is a game that did all this by proving how user-generated content could be a game, without the need to follow the conventions of narrative inherited from film that many early video games adopted. Some associate Minecraft more with a toy, where you can constantly tinker and play with the pieces of a system, but Minecraft has become much more than that. By allowing user creations to define interactions, the game has been able to develop a true digital culture, where the contribution of users is as important as the support from developers. Minecraft has become a medium in itself, as an entertainment and education tool to address a whole series of issues across disciplines."

"The digital culture generated by Minecraft has allowed games like Block'hood to exist," Sanchez adds. "The gamble here is to address urban and environmental issues assuming a vocabulary of discrete parts that interact with one another." Block'hood is a neighborhood simulator video game developed by Plethora Project, directed by Sanchez. "The game is an attempt to

15 Dan Stine Interior Design, law office, Duluth, Minnesota, 2015.
With its live markup tools, Revizto Issue Tracker allows collaboration on 2D drawings or 3D models with the project team in real time, on any device.

16 Dan Stine Interior Design, law office, Duluth, Minnesota, 2015.
Marking up on 3D in Revizto Viewer provides an extensive list of markup tools to help convey ideas and directives in a clear, comprehensive way when marking up on 3D.

16

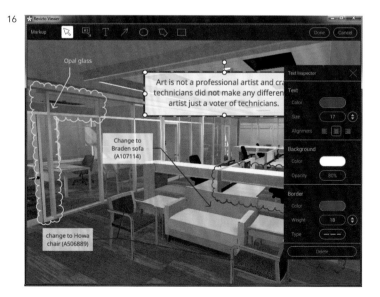

engage a global audience with notions of ecology, entropy and coexistence. The game uses an input/output paradigm to model the circularity of resources between a community, encouraging the player to think creatively of how to minimize the production of waste and the consequences of different players in an economy. The simulation needs to be maintained in a state of equilibrium, otherwise the creations will deteriorate and decay, generating a design space that is constantly making the player aware of the actions and decisions he or she takes."

"Games have enabled large crowds of players to intuitively explore all possible paths within digital systems, often discovering (and exploiting) the unexpected interactions in a simulation," says Sanchez. "This is often called a bug, a loophole, or a glitch, where players go beyond the expectation of the designer, forcing for an update, creating a true symbiosis between a player community and a development team. Games like Block'hood seek to engage such culture. The game was released in 2016 under an early access license, meaning that the game is still unfinished at the date of this publication. By releasing an unfinished product, the development team is able to use the players' feedback to improve the game and balance the simulation. Games are a form of communication and they require clear and intuitive interfaces that can communicate to players without lengthy manuals or tutorials. Players are relentless at the moment [to speculate as to] what could be improved and demand that every feature of the game works flawlessly, as they are customers that have paid for a product, and they feel empowered to request improvements. If done well, a game can really become an extension of a human mind, allowing a player to intuitively play and manage complex variables with ease."[57]

BIM AND GAMING

Looking briefly at the convergence of gaming technology and BIM, it appears there is a great deal of potential in the integration of these tools. "The marriage of the two technologies is changing the way construction professionals and designers do business with customers and with each other. And now, it seems the combination is on the verge of changing the industry as a whole."[58] Prior to the introduction of virtual reality tools, Amr Raafat, virtual construction planner at Shawmut Design and Construction, utilized multiple tools and platforms, including BIM, to achieve results. However, Raafat discovered, "with gaming engine software, you can do basically anything in one interface."[59]

Revizto is one such tool that merges virtual reality, gaming engines, and BIM. Merging gaming and BIM allows design and construction professionals to increase coordination of their projects, models, and documents while reducing the risks normally associated with designing and building large-scale, complex structures.[60] Built Environment Information Modeling Craft or BeIMCraft is a Minecraft "mod" or modification of the existing Minecraft platform reflecting "the interdisciplinary nature and requirement for collaboration with the built environment's supply chain by challenging young gamers to consider planning issues, health and safety risks, structural aspects, sustainability, and cost when creating their 3D world."[61] The game educates children about construction and BIM by mimicking "requirements expected of the modern interdisciplinary design team."[62] In convergence terms, it is only a small step from BIM tools to the virtual environment, due to the fact that the technology has become increasingly accessible to more users, as illustrated in such demonstrations as "Revit to Oculus Rift in One Click."[63]

ARTIFICIAL INTELLIGENCE, MACHINE LEARNING, AND MACHINE VISION FOR BIM

Like virtual reality, research is being conducted in computer vision, and related to—but distinct from—machine vision, especially as it integrates with BIM. "New software and hardware platforms are emerging that allow immersive environment representation … along with gestural modeling, or the translation of hand movements captured via computer vision into design information. Taken together, these two tools allow designers to visualize and virtually inhabit three-dimensional spatial conditions at 'full scale,' where we can do design work with intuitive hand and body motions."[64] This book does not venture far into perhaps the greatest convergence, that of man and machine, including such topics as transhumanism, and the widely anticipated Singularity, where humans transcend the human to achieve a superhuman status. Nevertheless, teaching machines to think, or *machine learning*, and machines teaching machines to think are topics that designers and the AEC industry will need to come to terms with in the near future.

"Convergence is quite a big term," notes Toru Hasegawa.[65] "I assume it has to do with tools and technology, and the process in which we make architecture at large." Hasegawa zeroes in on interoperability and speed as potential challenges to convergence. "The one thing that sticks in my head is how technologies are still firewalled from each other. Even though it is somewhat seamless now to go from Rhino to AutoCAD to whatever, it's still a cumbersome process. That means that it is still not converged. They are in their own domain. They may play well together but they're not seamless. The terms that are out there now on the technology side machine learning, artificial intelligence (AI), these are becoming the big buzzwords now. These largely have not yet entered the context of architecture. We—Morpholio—believe that these will be part of these design applications. Maybe it is not next year, but we are moving directly toward that direction. My personal guess is that is where it will go. How they are applied is the important question. Right now, Amazon or Google uses a sophisticated algorithm to get what you are searching. This is in conjunction with what I think design is. Design as a search problem: those two terms overlap. You might not think that what Google is doing as design. But to an extent, it is the mechanism that design relies on. What is the most advanced technology around that problem of search will quickly identify leaks in the territory of AI. Computers will capture our responses even better than we can capture ourselves," says Hasegawa. "Imagine what

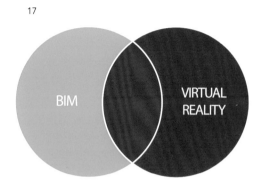

17

17 Deutsch Insights, Venn diagram, 2017.
Diagram representing the convergence of BIM and virtual reality.

18 Dan Stine Interior Design, law office, Duluth, Minnesota, 2015.
Marking up on 3D in Revizto Viewer provides an extensive list of markup tools to help convey ideas and directives in a clear, comprehensive way when marking up on 3D.

Google thinks in the world of hardware/software. What if they could capture what you are intending in a half a second before you think it? They could probably create a list of things you could look at. Instantaneously, the world is going to look as if your thoughts are just showing as you think it. When we are developing some of these drawing tools, we're collecting data in order to understand and find the environment in which we ideate."

NATURE ABHORS A CONVERGENCE

"Genetic algorithms build in disruption and have a property called mutation where—in a population of 100%—a certain percentage will mutate," explains Hasegawa. "It is a form of random generator. It is just shuffling so it can find solutions better. But at its core, you use it if you need that kind of randomization to seek out different territories. The reason designers want to destabilize in their practices is so they can seek out different territories. That's the whole intention of destabilization. Genetic algorithms contain that. The problem with genetic algorithms is that the fitness landscape is so fixated that it won't find a solution outside the fitness landscape. In other words, a solution space. The randomization will include other possible solution spaces. So it will only be a randomization within the solution space. It's not thinking outside the box. I'm sure someone working in GA has come to this problem and tried to identify that. But it is not such a sophisticated algorithm to begin with to consider."

"The only way for software to exist is for it to be public," said Hasegawa. "It is important for people to invent tools and make them available for others. On the software of everything, it's strange that some people are looking for salvation from their tools. Looking for a one-size-fits-all solution. That's very much an engineer mindset. I could see Autodesk thinking like that. Where they want to own everything. Does that really make people's lives better? How does it truly benefit us? That's the ultimate question. When you are writing software, you're standing on giants' shoulders. If you're an amateur programmer, you can think I wrote everything and here it is. They can't see that the plane they're standing on is the giant's shoulder. Millions of man-hours have been put into building programs. Take our program, Trace. We're writing on top of GO. Which is an open source graphic language. That has thousands upon thousands of man-hours under it. I'm just writing this extra bit standing on their shoulders."

"Architecture is a series of one-offs where you can calculate how much time was spent by how many humans to make something," continues Hasegawa. "If you start to include that glass was invented by this person, etc., it would encapsulate the whole human race. Software has not been around for that long. And yet it is accumulating so much knowledge. It's accelerating how you combine things. And how you add things. As you write software you start to think that those survived because they were open. Or became open. And kept evolving. Software—to use the evolution metaphor—may become just another branch and die out. If you want to live in the grand scheme of things and contribute to the social structure, you then have to consider the extendibility by others."

"Integration becomes a problem," adds Hasegawa. "Modularity is the best solution programmers have found so far. Don't integrate because then it becomes its own problem. Playing well (with others) is becoming the paradigm. API [Application programming interface] where you disclose a certain area of the program to play well with other areas. It's social. It's scary when someone says we should only have one software. We're social people. We live in a community of people. We can only define ourselves because there are people around us. The same goes for software. Software is a mirrored version of our manifestation. If you only have one software, it's a social structure that will die out. There are very few instances in history where such groups lasted. Convergence is how big companies develop. Autodesk spends hundreds of millions of dollars every year acquiring companies. What are the reasons they are buying up companies? They would want to say it is convergence when what it is is *consolidation*. Google was just a branch 20 years ago. Facebook was just a branch 10 years ago. It is crazy how these new branches are spawning out every day. If the world wanted to unify that to one case, it would almost be an example of anti-evolution."

"When you look at designs for evolutionary design, there is no such thing of convergence—for example, the image of the tree of life," states Hasegawa. "Name where an animal and an animal converged? There is no such thing. Nature, by definition, is branching. Thinking about the start-up culture, all I see is older companies acquiring small companies. Or small companies growing so fast they bypass the big companies. As a small company, you want to be that branch that grows so fast in a different direction that the big branch cannot come after you. From a business standpoint, you may want to be bought out. But from a survival standpoint, it would be suicide to converge all the time. The problem with branching all the time comes down to design.

19 Toru Hasegawa and Mark Collins, Columbia GSAPP's Cloud Lab with Van Alen Institute, DUMBO, 2014. Van Alen Institute joined Columbia GSAPP's Cloud Lab in DUMBO, Brooklyn, to gather 50 EEG datasets recording our brains' response to outdoor urban environments.

19

Design is branching ten things. But you have to choose one. You branch out again and you choose one. If you branch out on top of a branch on top of a branch you have a thousand options already. But if you do ten then choose one, ten then choose one, you're only at thirty. You've improved your energy efficiency. Even if it is not the best, it's good enough. Nature treats that good enough better than perfect. Convergence may be very human due to the fact that we never see it in nature."

Convergence is focused on how design professionals and others in the industry are leveraging technology and work processes today—especially where they are overlapping or combining—to help assure that projects are smarter, faster, cheaper, greener, or altogether better. The convergences in this book have business and practical antecedents; this isn't an academic exercise. A fascinating example of this is the research of Nels Long and M A Greenstein, of Gamer Lab and RotoLab, into the nexus of gaming, neuroscience, and architecture.[66] The industry is interested in learning about what it means to bring gaming, neuroscience, and architecture together. Gamer Lab is a curriculum under development for teaching architecture and design using games, game mechanics, game technology, and virtual reality. "We work very hard to think about the problem you are addressing, which is why anyone would want to do cross-sector or combined technology," explains Greenstein. There is an overlap of gaming, neuroscience, and architecture in the work of Gamer Lab and RotoLab. "My interest in gaming comes through my [studies] in architecture," explains Long. "I was fortunate as an undergraduate to spend some time with leading cognitive philosophy and neuroscience people. It began begging the question about the environment in which we work. What my time in architecture school taught me is that I enjoy making the tool more than I enjoy using the tool. Looking to the way the mind and brain works, you can create the perfect tool. It was archaic to me the number of programs that I used that worked the opposite way that my brain then worked. I found through things like virtual reality and game mechanics that we're actually able to get at the risk/reward mentality a lot faster, become a lot more productive, and have a lot more fun."

"When you think about convergence, it can come about naturally, because of people working in the world have connections," explains Greenstein. "They have colleagues that have worked together. Michael [Rotondi], Nels, and I—as colleagues—have a natural affinity for working together. But the actual fields that we are bringing together also bring with it the fact that within the George Greenstein Institute (GGI) that I developed, we were working specifically within the area of looking at spatial learning. Many of our members are spatial memory researchers. Many people in spatial memory and spatial learning are architects or work in architecture. We also work with game mechanics because we are working with kids. It adds to the value of teaching kids—high schoolers—about spatial memory. So the idea [is] that you can bring neuroscience research to understand the way the brain works with problems architects deal with everyday that

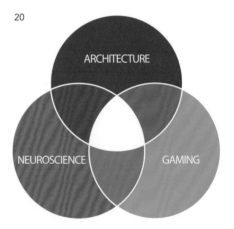

20 Deutsch Insights, Venn diagram, 2017.
Diagram representing the convergence of neuroscience, gaming, and architecture.

are spatial. And game mechanics could be the way in which the actual work process makes the mechanics fun. The kids don't know better. So there's the natural affinity that we have working together as colleagues—and our fields have an affinity for working together. And the fact that we have technologies now that speak directly to the question of working in more dimensions than a 3D rendering allows. Suddenly you recognize that it is easy to make a convergence. It's the perfect storm of opportunity."

"One of the most exciting things about virtual reality as a tool, and as an enterprise software, rather than as a content experience, is the ability to have convergence across [teleological] boundaries," adds Long. "In the same way that I can be teleported into virtual spaces of my own creation, I can also teleport other people into that space that augments my physical presence. This allows for the convergence of ideas in a virtual studio, in a virtual office, in a virtual classroom that allows for collaboration and teamwork to happen."

"Concerning being inside a representation as opposed to being outside of one, we are currently—I am actually looking at two people screens right now that are doing this—they are looking to create a working journal, a recipe book, for empathic responses in architecture using virtual reality as a tool to understand what is it about color, what is it about light, what is it about shape and form, that broaches a specific response in a different set of people?" asks Long. "We are open to creating virtual worlds in the same way that we are creating physical worlds moving forward. Each of these can be tied back to the human brain-centric response based in neuroscience. When something happens in a virtual environment that physically knocks you on your knees? It's pretty apparent that there is little distinguishing the virtual and physical."

We are still at the beginning of this enterprise. The convergence of the physical and virtual raises as many questions as it answers. "Do we need a new language of design to bridge the territory between the digital and physical worlds? If so, what might be its most salient characteristics? Where is the most obvious commercial value, and how can design unlock it?"[67] Perhaps the most important for design professionals, how should we design for a world where the virtual and physical are converging? The next chapter takes up these questions.

ENDNOTES

1 In John D. Sutter, "Why Games Will Take Over Our Lives," April 5, 2010, http://www.cnn.com/2010/TECH/04/05/games.schell/.
2 Howie Leibach, "Should You Buy the Hype? An Inside Look at the Virtual Reality Landscape," August 2, 2015, http://singularityhub.com/2015/08/02/should-you-buy-the-hype-an-inside-look-at-the-virtual-reality-landscape/.
3 Brandt Ranj, "Goldman Sachs Says VR Will Be Bigger than TV in 10 Years," January 13, 2016, http://uk.businessinsider.com/goldman-sachs-predicts-vr-will-be-

bigger-than-tv-in-10-years-2016-1?r=US&IR=T.

4 David Philp, "Compliance and Regulation—Building Information Modelling," July 7, 2016, https://www.linkedin. com/pulse/compliance-regulation-building-information-modelling-david-philp.

5 Phil Bernstein, "Top 10 AEC Trends for 2016," December 17, 2015, https://www.linkedin.com/pulse/top-10-aec-trends-2016-phil-bernstein?trk=hb_ntf_MEGAPHONE_ARTICLE_POST.

6 David Barista, "BIM Giants: Robotic Reality Capture, Gaming Systems, Virtual Reality," August 6, 2015, http:// www.bdcnetwork.com/giants-300-report-robotic-reality-capture-gaming-systems-virtual-reality-aec-giants-continue-tech?eid=216280757&bid=1156708#sthash.llUfMiuU.dpuf.

7 Jack Loughran, "3D Scanning Technology Coming to Smartphones," January 8, 2016, http://eandt.theiet.org/news/2016/jan/lenovo-google-project-tango.cfm.

8 Jack Loughran, "Entire Building Exterior 3D-Mapped with Tablet," January 14, 2016, http://eandt. theiet.org/news/2016/jan/3d-mapping-buildings. cfm#%2EVp6B6YCR4O8%2Elinkedin.

9 Kyle Maxey and Sharon Donovan, "Autodesk Releases ReMake, a Photogrammetry Program for Everyone," June 6, 2016, http://www.engineering.com/DesignSoftware/DesignSoftwareArticles/ArticleID/12318/Autodesk-Releases-ReMake-a-Photogrammetry-Program-for-Everyone.aspx?

10 Kathleen Maher, "Autodesk Launches Memento Gallery with New Build," October 22, 2015, http://gfxspeak. com/2015/10/22/autodesk-launches-gallery/.

11 Lee Mullin, "Photogrammetry for Construction?," August 5, 2015, http://beyonddesign.typepad.com/posts/2015/08/photogrammetry-for-construction.html.

12 "Site Logistics with BIM and Photos?," July 17, 2015, http://autodesk.typepad.com/bimtoolbox/2015/07/site-logistics-with-bim-and-photos.html.

13 Erin Green, "Mapping the World in 3D—with Drones?," October 26, 2015, http://www.engineering.com/BIM/ArticleID/10876/Mapping-the-World-in-3D-with-Drones. aspx.

14 Ibid.

15 Ibid.

16 Arne B. Jelland, "My Experience with the Trimble DPI-8," June 29, 2015, https://digitalstoryofanarchitect. wordpress.com/2015/06/29/my-experience-with-the-trimble-dpi-8/.

17 Ibid.

18 "Introduction to Reality Computing," April 28, 2015, https://www.augi.com/library/introduction-to-reality-computing.

19 Kyle Maxey, "Why Reality Computing May Be a New Reality for Designers," February 27, 2015, http://www. engineering.com/DesignerEdge/DesignerEdgeArticles/ArticleID/9685/Why-Reality-Computing-May-Be-a-New-

Reality-for-Designers.aspx.

20 Angel Say, "Virtual Reality for Architecture Predicts Patterns, Drives Business Decisions," March 17, 2016, http://www.archdaily.com/784008/virtual-reality-for-architecture-predicts-patterns-drives-business-decisions?utm_source=dlvr.it&utm_medium=twitter.

21 Ibid.

22 "The Many Magical Uses of Virtual Reality," November 7, 2014, http://www.builtr.io/the-many-magical-uses-of-virtual-reality/.

23 Diana Budds, "This Architecture Firm Is Turning VR into the Next Great Productivity Tool," April 28, 2016, http://www.fastcodesign.com/3059341/this-architecture-firm-is-turning-vr-into-the-next-great-productivity-tool.

24 Kym Porter, "Architectural & Design FAQ's about VR," January 23, 2016, https://www.linkedin.com/pulse/architectural-design-faqs-vr-kym-porter.

25 Budds, "This Architecture Firm."

26 Kalle Kahkonen, ed., "Virtual Reality Technology in Architecture and Construction," http://www.itcon.org/cgi-bin/special/Show?2003vr.

27 John Gaudiosi, "How This 150-Year-Old Company Uses Virtual Reality," August 25, 2015, http://fortune.com/2015/08/25/mccarthy-construction-vr/.

28 Terri Peters, "Autodesk University 2015 Bets on the Augmented Age," December 4, 2015, http://www.architectmagazine.com/technology/autodesk-university-2015-bets-on-the-augmented-age_o?utm_source=newsletter&utm_content=Article&utm_medium=email&utm_campaign=AN_120714%20(1)&he.

29 Kim Slowey, "Autodesk Partners with Microsoft on "Mixed Reality" Project, Unveils New BIM Doc Management Service," December 2, 2015, http://www.constructiondive.com/news/autodesk-partners-with-microsoft-on-mixed-reality-project-unveils-new-bi/410084/.

30 "Augment Reality with the DAQRI Smart Helmet," February 2, 2016, http://www.bimireland.ie/2016/02/02/augment-reality-with-the-daqri-smart-helmet/.

31 Lindsay, "VR or AR for AEC Professionals?," December 4, 2015, http://www.augment.com/blog/vr-or-ar-for-aec-professionals/.

32 "How Augmented and Virtual Reality Will Impact the AEC Industry," October 22, 2015, http://reports.builtr.io/2/.

33 Eric Johnson, "Choose Your Reality: Virtual, Augmented or Mixed," July 27, 2015, http://www.recode.net/2015/7/27/11615046/whats-the-difference-between-virtual-augmented-and-mixed-reality.

34 Ibid.

35 Lachmi Khemlani, "Augmented Reality in AEC," July 30, 2015, http://www.aecbytes.com/feature/2015/ARinAEC.html.

36 Jack Loughran, "3D Scanning Technology Coming to Smartphones," January 8, 2016, http://eandt.theiet.org/news/2016/jan/lenovo-google-project-tango.cfm.

37 Gaurang Trivedi, "Google Tango—Architect and Contractor's Next for Indoor Mapping," March 21, 2016, http://archinect.com/firms/release/67343028/google-tango-architect-and-contractor-s-next-for-indoor-mapping/149935737.

38 Jason Ford, "Spectral and 3D Imaging to Be Integrated into Single Device to Assess Structural Integrity," June 10, 2016, http://www.theengineer.co.uk/spectral-and-3d-imaging-to-be-integrated-into-single-device-to-assess-structural-integrity/.

39 Hallie Busta, "Augmented Reality in AEC," August 27, 2015, http://www.architectmagazine.com/technology/products/three-augmented-and-virtual-reality-apps-for-design-and-construction_o.

40 David Barista, "Augmented Reality Goes Mainstream: 12 Applications for Design and Construction Firms," September 4, 2013, http://www.bdcnetwork.com/augmented-reality-goes-mainstream-12-applications-design-and-construction-firms#sthash.SP9D92MJ.dpuf.

41 Damon Hernandez, "My Experience at the World's First Holographic Hackathon,", May 28, 2016, http://damonhernandez.blogspot.com/2016/05/my-experience-at-worlds-first.html.

42 "How Microsoft's Hololens Could Change the AEC Industry," January 30, 2015, http://www.builtr.io/insights/how-microsofts-hololens-could-change-the-aec-industry/

43 Jeffrey Heimgartner, "Augmented Reality for Architects and Civil Engineers," May 27, 2016, http://www.engineering.com/BIM/ArticleID/12233/Augmented-Reality-for-Architects-and-Civil-Engineers.aspx.

44 Ibid.

45 Monica Rozenfeld, "Virtual Blueprints for Construction Projects," July 21, 2014, http://theinstitute.ieee.org/technology-focus/technology-topic/virtual-blueprints-for-construction-projects.

46 Ibid.

47 Ibid.

48 Erin Green, "Using Augmented Reality for Construction," February 10, 2016, http://www.engineering.com/BIM/ArticleID/11473/Using-Augmented-Reality-for-Construction.aspx.

49 David Malone, "Latest Tech Devices Simplify the Leap from BIM to Virtual Reality," March 21, 2016, http://www.bdcnetwork.com/latest-tech-devices-simplify-leap-bim-virtual-reality

50 "Video Games Will Become 'New Tools' to Solve Architecture's Global Challenges," March 7, 2016, http://www.dezeen.com/2016/03/07/jose-sanchez-block-hood-video-game-tools-solve-global-challenges-architecture/

51 Tudor Van Hampton, Jeff Rubenstone, and Tom Sawyer, "How Video Games Became Design and Construction Tools," March 3, 2016, http://www.enr.com/articles/38932-how-video-games-became-design-and-construction-tools.

52 "Video Games Will Become 'New Tools.'"

53 Andrew Good, "Building Better Architecture Through Video Games Like Block'hood," June 27, 2016, https://news.usc.edu/103200/building-better-architecture-through-video-games-like-blockhood/.

54 Alexander Walter, "How Video Game Engines May Influence the Future of Architecture," March 5, 2015, http://archinect.com/news/article/122202906/how-video-game-engines-may-influence-the-future-of-architecture-and-everything-else.

55 Sarosh Mulla, "Future Thinking V: Virtual Reality," June 20, 2016, http://architecturenow.co.nz/articles/future-thinking-v-virtual-reality/.

56 Jose Sanchez, interview with author, July 5, 2016.

57 Ibid.

58 Slowey, "Autodesk Partners with Microsoft."

59 "New Player: How Gaming Technology Adds a "Wow Factor" to BIM," December 17, 2015, https://www.linkedin.com/pulse/new-player-how-gaming-technology-adds-wow-factor-bim-contractor-rap?forceNoSplash=true.

60 Danielle Dy Buncio, "Taking Control of the Game—An Exploration of Virtual Reality and Gaming Workflows," https://www.youtube.com/watch?v=N5OBUbtwfgl

61 Tom Ravenscroft, "Modified Game Adds BIM to Minecraft," June 17, 2016, http://www.bimplus.co.uk/technology/modi5fied-gam5e-add2s-bim-minecraft/.

62 Ibid.

63 "Revit to Oculus Rift in One Click" August 18, 2015, https://www.youtube.com/watch?v=ZIB-ydgg1-E.

64 Casey Mahon, "4 Ways Virtual and Augmented Reality Will Revolutionize the Way We Practice Architecture," March 12, 2016, http://www.archdaily.com/783677/4-ways-virtual-and-augmented-reality-will-revolutionize-the-way-we-practice-architecture.

65 Toru Hasegawa, interview with author, April 19, 2016.

66 Nels Long and M A Greenstein, interview with author, July 6, 2016.

67 DaeWha Kang, "How Should We Design for a Networked World?," July 4, 2016, http://thoughts.arup.com/post/details/559/how-should-we-design-for-a-networked-world.

IMAGES

Figures 1–3, 20 © Deutsch Insights; figures 4–8 © Yulio Technologies Inc.; figures 9–18 © Revizto; figure 19 © Toru Hasegawa/GSAPP Cloud Lab with the Van Alen Institute

1

2

CHAPTER 6 CONCEPTION AND CONSTRUCTION

This convergence brings both opportunity and concern for design and construction.—Blaine Brownell[1]

1 Deutsch Insights, Design and Fabrication Convergences, 2017.

Convergences in contemporary design practice occur at the meeting of two seemingly opposite forces.

2 Deutsch Insights, Convergence of Design and Fabrication, 2017.

Today, we are seeing the maturing and scaling of digital design-to-fabrication tools for the design professions and construction industry.

BIM Forum Chicago in 2011 focused on how BIM is shifting when the design phase ends and construction begins. The conference addressed questions such as: Are clients willing to pay for additional early design effort by nondesigners? Where does traditional design leave off and spatial coordination begin? When does spatial coordination morph into design? How can contractors and designers find common ground for design and coordination? As the BIM Forum Chair and Tocci Building Co. CEO John Tocci, Sr., clarified, "This is NOT the contractors coming to take over scope earlier. This is to, hopefully, help us work better together."[2]

WHEN DOES DESIGN END AND CONSTRUCTION BEGIN?

Robert Yori of SOM spoke at the BIM Forum in 2011 and sees where convergence in the industry is heading. "The best example is the level of conversation that you see at BIMForum, and how it's been formed over the years. There's a convergence there. Increase in specialization has gotten a bit segmented, but overall, BIMForum is a good example of why that dialogue needs to be maintained. It's great for providing a conduit, a thread of continuity, in the era of increasing specialization."[3] Yori continues: "If you take a look at their mission statement and the way they are organized, it's clear. Such a spread of disciplines are represented—designers, engineers, construction managers, fabricators, owners, the insurance industry, and more. It's truly a forum for each specialization to get together and understand the others' perspectives, and how each can contribute to the whole that is the project." Yori mentioned Christof Spieler's Chicago BIM Forum presentation, *The Fallacy of Design Intent*—a favorite of mine. Christof Spieler, PE, a trained engineer who at the time was director of technology and innovation at Houston architecture firm Morris Architects, gave a passionate presentation about both his experiences as an engineer working for architects and how further line-blurring and role-blurring would be needed to meet the efficiency demands of today's clients. "Fundamentally, architects have to take responsibility for constructability," Spieler said. "Contractors must take responsibility for the design implications of construction decisions. We've put an awful lot of work into separating design and construction, things that really are and should be inseparable."[4] Spieler added: "A century ago, the master builder gave way to the architect and the contractor, and the process of building a building split into design,

McNeel **Rhinoceros 3d**	Autodesk **Revit**	McNeel **Grasshopper**	McNeel **Rhinoscript "Monkey"**	Microsoft **Excel**
Geometry Setout	Rationalization	Panelization	Analysis	Statistical Breakdown

Single Type | One Per Row | Unique

Zones Of Panel Optimization
Eastern Facade

Open | Puched | Glazed | Screen | Metal

Zones Of Material Setout
Eastern Facade

2%
9%
18%
70%

Panel Optimization

Panel Optimization

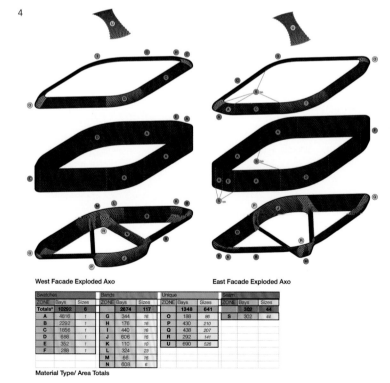

4 Woods Bagot, South Australian Health and Medical Research Institute (SAHMRI), Adelaide, Australia, 2010. SAHMRI panel schedule showing panel counts and size variations per façade zone. Each zone is color-coded to indicate panel variation relative to local geometric conditions.

West Facade Exploded Axo

East Facade Exploded Axo

Swatches			Bands			Unique			Seam		
ZONE	Bays	Sizes	ZONE	Bays	Sizes	ZONE	Bays	Sizes	ZONE	Bays	Sizes
Totals*	10292	6		2674	117		1348	641		302	44
A	4816	1	G	344	16	O	188	86	S	302	44
B	2292	1	H	176	16	P	430	210			
C	1656	1	I	440	16	Q	438	207			
D	688	1	J	606	16	R	292	141			
E	352	1	K	110	10	U	690	526			
F	288	1	L	324	23						
			M	66	16						
			N	608	6						

Material Type/ Area Totals

3 Woods Bagot, South Australian Health and Medical Research Institute (SAHMRI), Adelaide, Australia, 2010.
To rationalize the construction process, SAHMRI's building mass was divided into zones of primitive geometry sections, indicative of panel variation.

- One Type per Zone
- Zones (A-F)

Swatches

- One Type Per Row
- Zones (J-N)

Bands

- Every Panel Unique
- Zones (O-R,U)

Unique

- Single Columns
- Zones (S)

Seam

note:
* Totals per zone reflect number of unique sizes per that zone, overall totals reflect total unique sizes per type (ie swatches), and exclude duplicates which may exist between zones.
** Type counts based on triangle dimensions, (edge lengths), and do not take into account material differences.

documentation, detailing, and construction. BIM promises to bridge these divides."[5]

BIM is sometimes seen as a panacea for all that ails the AEC industry. However, it is more the mindset of those who use the technology than the technology itself that provides an opportunity to mend the ways of an industry built on miscommunication and antagonistic relations. *When does design end and construction begin?* is a question of line-blurring, phase-blurring, and role-blurring, asked at a time when lines, phases, and roles are merging. BIM, when used on even the least complex of projects, requires construction representation at the table earlier in the design process. The contractor isn't interested in designing the project—as John Tocci Sr. made clear.[6] If contractors understand the reasons for the design intent, perhaps they will have a better understanding of how to construct the project? Or, if a change is in order, the contractor could suggest a substitution that is more in line with the intention behind the design? BIM introduces a convergence driven by owners who are looking for a single source of responsibility. Clients would prefer to hire one architect for both design concept and technical resolution, but often aren't able to do so.[7] "The advantages of construction tech are numerous, and extend to every project stakeholder. Consequently, a collaborative approach will be required across the board, wherein clients, contractors, and consultants from all sectors and specialisations must put their best feet forward to make the industry safer and smarter."[8]

Markku Allison believes that BIM is a tool, but can also be a roadmap for required change.[9] "If you push it to its limits in every area of its practice, you're going to bump up against business and cultural boundaries, and you're going to want to remove them," explains Allison. "It'd be great if I could share this model with a mechanical contractor—I don't usually have a relationship with him so I can't. Effectiveness—eventually owners will understand the benefits that will accrue through the implementation of these technologies. Technology delivers lots of benefits within our individual silos. But those benefits are multiplied when they are supplied to a collaborative environment. As the technologies become more robust, they will require cultural change. That doesn't seem unlikely to me at all. It seems like something that can easily happen."

Allison continues: "Ten years ago I would have said [it will take] 510 years, but today [it will take] another 510 years. We are starting to understand that problems of business and culture today are complex problems. We are starting to see it in every business sector—collaborative models employed to greater benefit. You've heard the software engineering role of programming. One guy is driving, one guy is watching. That's spending twice the amount of money on that, all the benefits on the backside prove it out. I think that, as an example, is the direction of where we're going. The technology is pushing us in that direction and the construction industry is pushing us towards more transparent collaborative

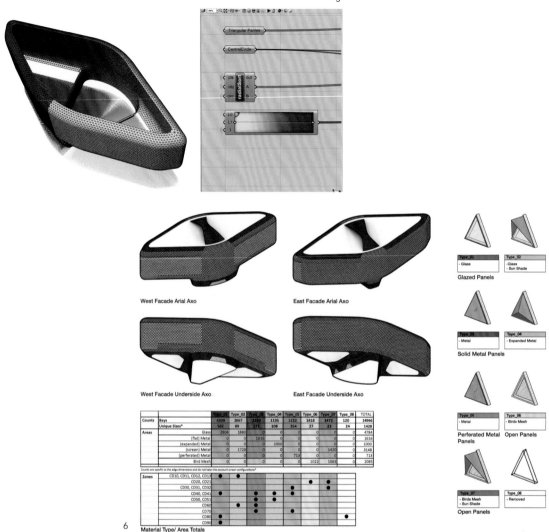

West Facade Arial Axo

East Facade Arial Axo

West Facade Underside Axo

East Facade Underside Axo

Type_01
- Glass

Type_02
-Glass
- Sun Shade

Glazed Panels

Type_03
- Metal

Type_04
- Expanded Metal

Solid Metal Panels

Type_05
- Metal

Type_06
- Birds Mesh

Perforated Metal Panels

Open Panels

Type_07
- Birds Mesh
- Sun Shade

Type_08
- Removed

Open Panels

		Type_01	Type_02	Type_03	Type_04	Type_05	Type_06	Type_07	Type_08	TOTAL
Counts	Bays	4339	2667	2583	1135	1222	1418	1472	120	14966
	Unique Sizes*	502	89	177	108	354	27	23	24	1428
Areas	Glass	2904	1880	0	0	0	0	0	0	4784
	(flat) Metal	0	0	1616	0	0	0	0	0	1616
	(expanded) Metal	0	0	0	1000	0	0	0	0	1000
	(screen) Metal	0	1728	0	0	0	0	1420	0	3148
	(perforated) Metal	0	0	0	0	713	0	0	0	713
	Bird Mesh	0	0	0	0	0	1022	1063	0	2085

Counts are specific to the edge dimensions and do not take into account screen configurations*

Zones	CD10, CD11, CD12, CD13									
	CD20, CD21						•	•		
	CD30, CD31, CD32					•				
	CD40, CD41	•			•	•				
	CD50, CD51				•					
	CD60		•	•						
	CD70			•		•				
	CD80	•							•	
	CD90									

Material Type/ Area Totals

7 Woods Bagot, South Australian Health and Medical Research Institute (SAHMRI), Adelaide, Australia, 2010. Grasshopper was used to identify and quantify sets of unique triangles for the panelization of the SAHMRI façade.

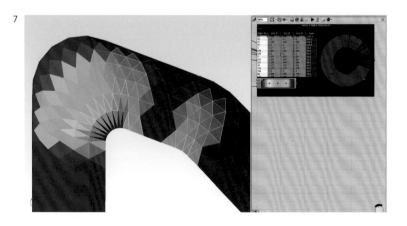

behaviors. That's going to be par for the course. People working together can leverage benefits more effectively than people working alone. That doesn't necessarily mean we are always working on the same thing, but just if we do it collaboratively where we know that our efforts are reinforcing one another. Rather that it's not a duplicative thing, it's a leveraging thing."

"Convergence only works in the social space," explains Brian Ringley, Design Technology Platform Specialist at Woods Bagot.[10] "Convergence only works if you have a multidisciplinary team. Convergence doesn't mean one person has access to this technology, therefore they can get everything themselves. This is what is so interesting to me about WeWork. WeWork seems like the first time that architecture has successfully prefabricated at mass fabrication. SHoP Architects is trying to do it with SHoP Construction (SC) Modular." Ringley continues, "It's hard to build a consistent product in architecture that lets you build upon a knowledge base. Everything is kind of a wash. Every time you start over. You can carry certain principles forward, but we're always doing something different, the team is something different, the state of the labor market, legalities, and the contract are always different. It's impossible for us to have a solid base to have that one might say other industries have a more solid footing on. Prior research that has been done. The legal industry may have more solid footing in terms of access to precedent cases as they approach new ones. It's very difficult for us to build a knowledge base. What that means is that we're slow and inefficient."

BIM means no longer working in silos, no longer tossing the design intent documents over the cubicle wall and hoping for the best. With BIM, design intent documents are informed by construction—because the contractor and other key members of the project team are at the table from day one. With BIM, there is no avoiding addressing means and methods. BIM means that design and construction are no longer an either/or proposition, but instead require a both/and approach. Does it ever make sense to design without construction in mind? Or, put otherwise, *when* does it make sense to design without construction in mind? In what situations? When there is no intent to build? If the intent is to build what you design, doesn't it make sense to design with construction in mind? To design with *constructability* in mind?

Why *conception*? BIM doesn't dictate when the idea arises in the process, nor from whom the idea will come. It can come from anyone and anywhere on the project team, at any time. Because conception is messy—iterative, informed, integrated—it is often the case that no one can pinpoint where the idea originated, where or when the design concept was *conceived*. With BIM, this is all the more the case, as the architect doesn't design alone in a cave. Instead, the idea is *informed* by experts at the table. The *team* conceives the idea. The architect's role then becomes to facilitate the process, and to refine the design until each stakeholder feels represented. Collaboration leads to the convergence of conception and construction. As Philip Bernstein,

8 Woods Bagot, South Australian Health and Medical Research Institute (SAHMRI), Adelaide, Australia, 2014.
SAHMRI as viewed from the entry plaza. Photograph by Peter Clarke.

9 Woods Bagot, South Australian Health and Medical Research Institute (SAHMRI), Adelaide, Australia, 2013.
SAHMRI façade under construction.

10 Woods Bagot, South Australian Health and Medical Research Institute (SAHMRI), Adelaide, Australia, 2013.
SAHMRI façade under construction. Photograph by Peter Fisher.

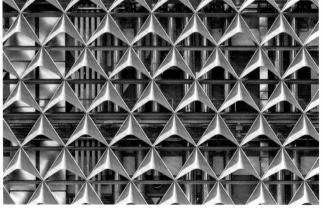

11

11 Woods Bagot, South Australian Health and
Medical Research Institute (SAHMRI), Adelaide,
Australia, 2013.
Close-up shot of SAHMRI façade showing
shaded screen panels with mechanical systems
behind. Photograph by David Sievers.

12 Woods Bagot, South
Australian Health and Medical
Research Institute (SAHMRI),
Adelaide, Australia, 2010.
Unique panel types being
identified and quantified in
Grasshopper and visualized in
Rhino for an early panelization
study of the SAHMRI façade.

13 Woods Bagot, South
Australian Health and Medical
Research Institute (SAHMRI),
Adelaide, Australia, 2010.
Unique panel types being
identified and quantified in
Grasshopper and visualized in
Rhino for an early panelization
study of the SAHMRI façade.

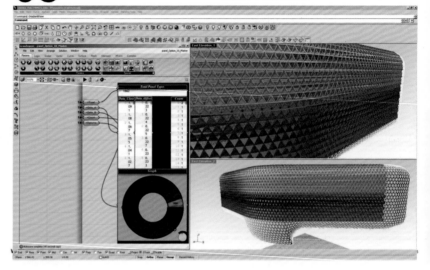

05

Parametric Transformation
East Facade

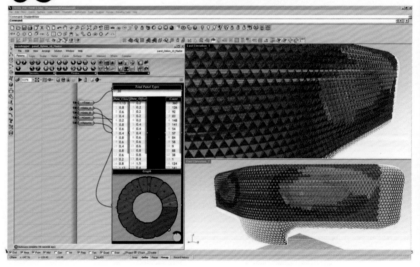

05

Parametric Transformation
East Facade

14 Woods Bagot, South Australian Health and
Medical Research Institute (SAHMRI), Adelaide,
Australia, 2010.
Solar radiation analysis in Ecotect being used
to drive façade panel aperture sizes in the
Grasshopper model.

15 Deutsch Insights, Venn diagram, 2017.
Diagram representing the convergence of
robotics, reality capture, photogrammetry, visual
sensing, and drones.

14

Solar Orientation

175	175	175	175
250	500	750	1000
350	350	350	350
250	500	750	1000
525	525	525	525
250	500	750	1000
700	700	700	700
250	500	750	1000
Panel Variation Parameters			
Offset			
Closure			

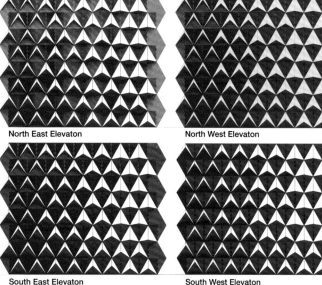

North East Elevaton **North West Elevaton**

South East Elevaton **South West Elevaton**

15

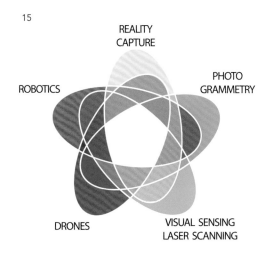

REALITY CAPTURE

PHOTO GRAMMETRY

ROBOTICS

VISUAL SENSING LASER SCANNING

DRONES

FAIA, suggested (see Chapter 4), in the near future "there will be a stronger connection between what's designed, built, and how it operates brought forth by the use of BIM at the onset of the design phase."[11] Part of that connection occurs in the front half of the building lifecycle, during the design and construction phases.

Where, then, is the line between design and construction? "In the past architects have faced at least two stopping points: between design and construction, and at a building's completion. Recent advances in computer software in architecture have removed these stopping points," explains architect and educator, Richard Garber.[12] "The dissolution of the conventional breaking points in the construction and completion phases of a building's delivery has blurred 'the distinction between the production of design intent and the transmission of information.'"[13] Construction firms with the resources and inclination to venture into research and development (including Skanska, Suffolk Construction, and Turner Construction) continue to experiment with tools, robotics, reality capture, gaming systems, and virtual reality.[14]

One merger between concept and construction is due to the fact that BIM mediates between the two poles. In one previously discussed example, an industry app such as Autodesk ReCap is able to make 3D models from photos of construction machinery and equipment taken at the site. Other apps are able to connect the BIM to the construction layout process, in essence connecting a digital model with the physical world. Much of this connection is due to what has been called *the digitization of construction*, leading to increased coordination, collaboration, and communication, while just as importantly, reducing waste; this is all part of upgrading an age-old industry—construction—and its ubiquitous equipment and tools for the digital age. Because most construction projects

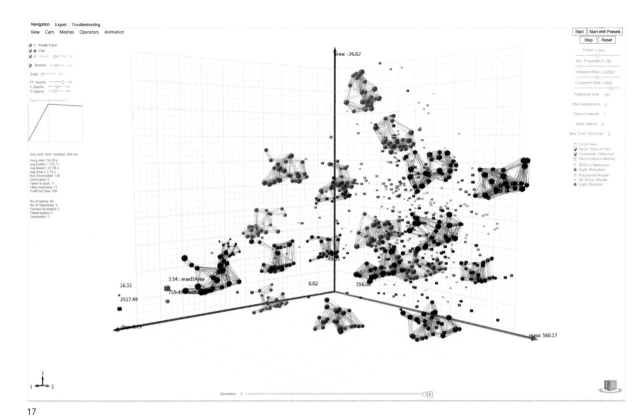

17

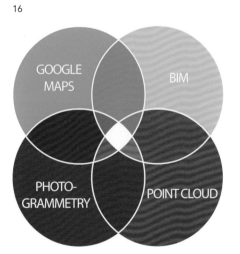

16

GOOGLE MAPS

BIM

PHOTO-GRAMMETRY

POINT CLOUD

18

are considered one-offs, where it's difficult to see the benefit of automation for a stand-alone project, and many construction sites are remote and not connected, "historically, construction has not had a good platform to automate work and predict tasks (and timing) accurately."[15] The convergence of work processes and tools such as BIM with the leveraging of available data in design and construction is not limited to the jobsite. In search of answers to questions concerning worker advocacy, for example, one exhibition project team asked, *How can architects ensure human rights protections extend to those who build architecture worldwide?* In other words, we may know who works on the conceptualization of a project, but how can we know who builds it? The team responded by interspersing "mapping of the convergence of global workforces on a building site with reports from sources such as Human Rights Watch and Amnesty International that document the issues facing migrant construction workers. Descriptions of steps in the migratory paths of workers as well as working processes in design and construction processes ended with questions speculating where solutions might intervene."[16]

"'The Bearable Lightness of Being' is a research pavilion designed and built at SmartGeometry 2014, in a workshop hosted by Klaas de Rycke, Kristjan Plagborg Nielsen, and Mathew Tam from Bollinger+Grohmann Engineers," says Robert Vierlinger, Design Researcher, University of Applied Arts Vienna & Bollinger+Grohmann.[17] "Its design, amongst many other versions, is proposed by search algorithms based on structural and spatial goals using Karamba3d and Octopus; Octopus visualizes the 3D models of solutions in the performance space for an intuitive association of form and function. Projects of smaller scale, like our installation 'The Bearable Lightness of Being' in Hong Kong, or the research pavilion with Zaha Hadid Architects in Beijing, allow us to narrow down, focus, and isolate specific parts of the design to exert a high level of control. For architecture, these provide ideal testing grounds for new developments and approaches, to ultimately bring state-of-the-art technology closer to the full-scale building site. Teaching activity further intensifies our understanding [of] how people would like to make use of technology and gives feedback on the design of user experience. It is satisfying if a project like 'The Bearable Lightness of Being' happens to merge technical and architectural ideas, rooted in the concept of bringing locality and tradition closer to technological advances, to use simple, open, and modular parts in both design tools and construction."

BUILDINGS AS DOCUMENTS
AECBytes founder, Lachmi Khemlani, recalls, during the "golden age of reprographics," taking a hard-hat tour of the new International Terminal at the San Francisco International Airport when still under construction. "Remember the pre-BIM era of the AEC industry when drawings were king?"[18] One of Khemlani's most vivid memories "was of the document room … stacked with shelves filled with binders of the drawings that were being used in the construction of the project. Multiply this by the number of active construction projects in every region, and it's not difficult to

16 Deutsch Insights, Venn diagram, 2017. Diagram representing the convergence of BIM, photogrammetry, point clouds, and Google Maps.

17 and 18 Robert Vierlinger, "The Bearable Lightness of Being," 2014. "The Bearable Lightness of Being" is a research pavilion designed and built at SmartGeometry 2014, in a workshop hosted by Klaas de Rycke, Kristjan Plagborg Nielsen, and Mathew Tam from Bollinger+Grohmann engineers. The design is proposed by search algorithms based on structural and spatial goals using Karamba3d and Octopus. Octopus visualizes the 3D models of solutions in the performance space for an intuitive association of form and function.

see why we had an entire industry focused on printing, copying, distributing, storing, and archiving drawings."[19] Architecture can be thought of in terms of buildings, documents, or data—and increasingly, a merger of all three. While documents remain the primary means for architects to communicate design intent, a greater emphasis is seen on the use of 3D building models in the continuum between conception and construction—and that spectrum continues to shrink with each passing year. We have already discussed many of the tools on the conceptual design end. Some of the technologies focus on the construction end of the spectrum, such as document management tools and reality-capture technologies.

Document management tools such as Autodesk BIM 360 can be thought of as convergence tools in that their main selling point is speed (*Less time fighting with files. More time building*), achieved by leveraging real-time/right-time access to information in the cloud. These tools also represent the further collapsing of design and construction in that they enable users to mark up documents for changes during construction (*Extract 2D sheets from 3D models; Create and share 2D and 3D markups*): reinforcing the notion that design, to the chagrin of building owners, doesn't end until the building is complete. At the project back-end, cloud-based building management platforms promise to integrate and aggregate building and metering systems data for analysis.

FUSING THE COMPUTATIONAL AND MATERIAL

A further development that has the potential to bridge the design/construction gap is a new conception of the material world that has recently emerged. According to philosopher Manuel DeLanda, this conception fuses the physical and computational world: a world of programmable building materials. "Gone is the Aristotelian view that matter is an inert receptacle for forms that come from the outside … as well as the Newtonian view in which an obedient materiality simply follows general laws and owes all of its powers to those transcendent laws."[20] A convergence in building materials—physical, virtual, programmable—opens up possibilities for designing in digital tools that have a more direct connection with project outcomes, including the built work itself. "Designers are no longer conceiving of the digital realm as separate from the physical world," explains Achim Menges.[21] "Instead computation is being regarded as the key interface for material exploration and vice versa. This represents a significant perceptual shift in which the materiality of architecture is no longer seen to be a fixed property and passive receptor of form, but is transformed into an active generator of design and an adaptive agent of architectural performance."[22]

CONVERGENCE OF TECHNOLOGY AND CONSTRUCTION

The tagline for *Constructech* magazine is: "Where Construction and Technology Converge." Technology is, of course, not new to construction. The construction industry was an early adopter of the mobile phone to improve onsite communication. And construction isn't technology-averse—just risk averse. Professor

19

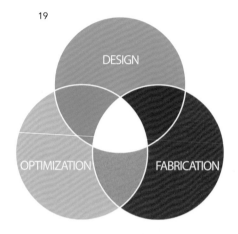

19 Deutsch Insights, Venn diagram, 2017.
Diagram representing the convergence of design, optimization, and fabrication.

Mani Golparvar-Fard PhD, Associate Professor in the Department of Civil and Environmental Engineering, an affiliate in the Department of Computer Science at the University of Illinois UrbanaChampaign, and Director of the Real-Time and Automated Monitoring and Control (Raamac) Lab,[23] brings lean construction principles together with virtual design and construction (VDC), offering a form of predictive analytics. "One element that I have always been looking at that hadn't advanced as fast as it should have has been 4D BIM," explains Golparvar-Fard. "It offers a lot of capability for constructability from preconstruction on. People cannot measure tangible benefits from constructability reviews via 4D BIM vs. conventional practices. There's also a premium associated with creating this 4D BIM—there's a cost associated with that. What is the exact dollar return you're getting from 4D BIM? It's hard to measure. Because of that, a lot of companies have not been proactive in doing 4D BIM. Or, if they do it, they pay a third party to create a 4D BIM for them, or maintain that model on a weekly or monthly basis. They don't have any workflow on how they can actually benefit from it. This is on the one side. On the other side, I have always been working on visual sensing, which is all about capturing reality from the jobsite. Now there is an opportunity to extend the application of the 4D BIM into something that could be used in every single aspect of the project lifecycle. We can use it as a platform on a daily basis, capturing productivity information. We can use it for coordination purposes. We can use it for contractor hand-offs. We can use it for pull planning sessions. So I thought, what if we brought these two elements together? This is how I got the idea."

Golparvar-Fard continues: "The practices that we have are retroactive. I started to look into what people do in the LinkedIn community. They just measure percent of plan complete. They feel like this is a great metric. What are the other metrics that people have offered? Looking into more progressive researchers, such as [Professor in Engineering and Project Management at University of California Berkeley] Iris Tommelein, she offers these task-anticipated, task-ready metrics that measure reliability of looking ahead at the schedule. But then I was thinking, these are great metrics, but these are academic works. Somebody needs to figure out how this can be embedded into a workflow. How can you benefit from the intelligence of task-ready or whatever metric it is? In a way that people can actually act on it. So I thought we should start working on predictive analytics. Instead of measuring retroactively, success or failure in the past, let's look into measuring readiness in the future. What if we tried to come up with statistical models that can predict when a contractor can notify you when they're moving to a location, and commit that this is the information I will be working off of on this date to that date? And present this information to them in a visual way that they can understand on a daily basis. Am I going to be ready to call John Doe and his entire crew to bring this to that location on tomorrow morning and actually start working? I want to present this information to them in a way that is dynamic, and also visual, so they can easily understand it."

20

DESIGN AUTHORING

AGGREGATED FABRICATION

ENERGY ANALYSIS

TRADE FABRICATION

EXISTING CONDITIONS

DESIGN DISCIPLINE

3D COORDINATION

AGGREGATED DESIGN MODEL

CONSTRUCTION RECORD

20 Deutsch Insights, Venn diagram, 2017.
Diagram representing the convergence of purpose-built BIM models.

21

DESIGN AUTHORING

ENERGY ANALYSIS

AGGREGATED FABRICATION

EXISTING CONDITIONS

DESIGN DISCIPLINE

3D COORDINATION

AGGREGATED DESIGN MODEL

CONSTRUCTION RECORD

TRADE FABRICATION

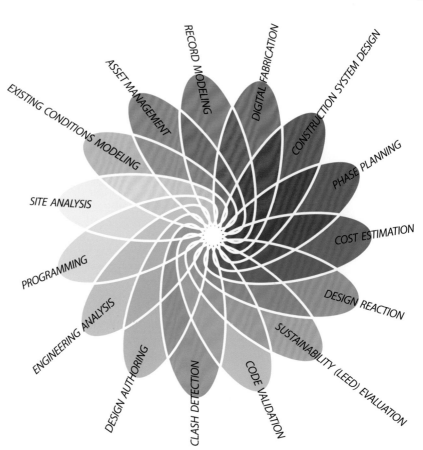

RECORD MODELING

DIGITAL FABRICATION

ASSET MANAGEMENT

CONSTRUCTION SYSTEM DESIGN

EXISTING CONDITIONS MODELING

PHASE PLANNING

SITE ANALYSIS

COST ESTIMATION

PROGRAMMING

DESIGN REACTION

ENGINEERING ANALYSIS

SUSTAINABILITY (LEED) EVALUATION

DESIGN AUTHORING

CLASH DETECTION

CODE VALIDATION

21 Deutsch Insights, Venn
diagram, 2017.
Diagram representing the
convergence of purpose-built
BIM models.

22 Deutsch Insights, Venn
diagram, 2017.
Diagram representing the
convergence of purpose-built
BIM models.

"What is the state-of-the-art planning tool? Primavera," notes Golparvar-Fard. "We started realizing that a lot of construction companies are not using P6 [Primavera P6 Professional Project Management], they're still using a spreadsheet to plan. So we need to explore forms that can more quickly and easily communicate that information to people. We started creating these new metrics. What we call a readiness index and readiness reliability, and something we call location stability index. These are all academic terms. What does it mean for a contractor? You walk into a coordination meeting. You get visuals that show you the locations of the at-risks. What does a location at-risk mean? That means I may not be able to move my crew into that location. If I was expecting something being done prior to my being there, that's not going to get done. Am I going to show up on the jobsite with seven guys and the owner has to pay the two hours for walking on the jobsite without having anything to do? Or can I plan for that? Maybe there's a way we can start bringing this intelligence to weekly coordination meetings to prepare companies on exactly what could be done on a daily basis. And present them with visuals that can guarantee that. Their expectation of readiness of these locations was met. So your contractor at the end of the day, you come back to the trailer, you're filling out your daily report, and you're telling us how many people you have. Why don't you also review what you want to be doing tomorrow visually? You don't need to open up plans. You just click on the screen to see the elements. There's going to be a color associated with that location. Am I going to be able to move my crew into it? If not, will I have some alternatives to it? This is something we've been doing and carefully documented for Clark Construction to show them that 4D BIM is a great planning tool. It can now become a live model that can serve as the basis of communication. It can also serve as a basis for capturing reality on the jobsite. That's something that we've never had. Planning is significantly improved, but we've never had the capability of closing this loop in a systematic way. The other element I wanted to achieve with it is I wanted to make sure there's also the visual images and videos to go with it. It's a liability tool. Due to billing. If you want to pay your subs, how do you pay them? Most contractors pay them based on the hours or days these guys put into the work. As opposed to tracking their physical progress. Contractors want to pay based on actual physical progress that these guys make. If you present these visuals to them, then there's something that they can go back and verify. 'You guys were supposed to do this much work, this is what the image shows you.' Initially it was a [superintendent] drone, but we don't want this to be made into any specific platform."

"When Turner Construction and DPR Construction first approached us with the idea of a ground robot, we started building that. We want to remain completely agnostic as to how visual data is being captured. To remain flexible for those companies that may not have the drone, that may not have the robot. At least they may be able to rely on pictures from the subcontractors. The form-figure visual capture is going to change over the next few years. Depth cameras, for example, will be on commodity phones. What that would do for

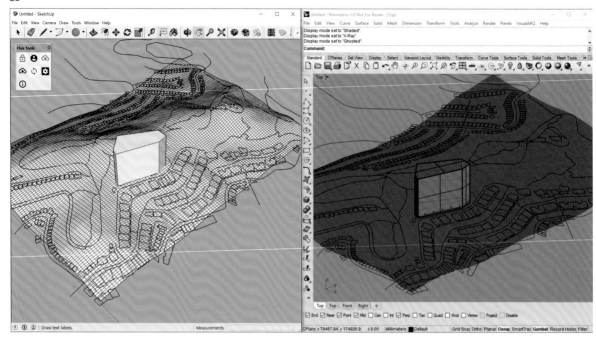

us is, when a subcontractor would be taking pictures, they could also provide us with depth information. That means we don't have to worry about providing image data analytics by generating a 3D point cloud model. That would come as a commodity. We've been trying to bring these elements together and offer them as a visual production management tool. One thing that has always been missing is: *This is great, you've been showing me problematic areas. How will I be able to make a decision on it? How can I make an action such that I can prove the reliability of my plan?* We need to document root causes. There are a number of common reasons why things get behind schedule. The fact that we are now visualizing—who is going to do what work in what location—as an example, solved 20% of DPR Construction's problems. Another is underestimated effort. They thought they were going to be able to do some scope of work, but weren't able to achieve it. We started thinking about this as a productivity problem, with an input and an output. We can capture output—the physical output that happens. What about input? What do companies do today? Every company without exception has daily logs that capture how many hours people put into an effort. These daily logs have never been associated with production rates. Some companies do post-assessments, but there's no way of getting this intelligence in real time or even near real time in a way that would be meaningful. Until now. We thought, what if we used a visual production management system as a daily reporting tool as well? The contractor returns to the trailer, or logs into the web-based system, they see the elements that they're expected to finish that day. They click on the elements that they've completed, or to note the percentage completed on those elements, by uploading a photo.

They'll note how many people were involved, while identifying each, by just selecting their photos on a screen. Now we know how many worker-hours were actually involved in that activity. We can create this big productivity data that provides us with measures of reliability on how subcontractors perform on the jobsites."

"What, besides the technology, was missing ten years ago to enable all of this to happen?" asks Golparvar-Fard. "Lean construction wasn't as accepted in the industry as it is now. The culture is changing. People are more receptive today that the foreman can sit in the meeting and help with the planning process. I'd like to think that technology is helping with that. Because now, someone who might otherwise not be a savvy planner, and can see stuff visually that can help make decisions. Technology has advanced in recent years. We can now do better 3D construction. We can do it more frequently, at a speed that supports daily coordination. The science is also advanced. We can do predictive analytics."

One potential impediment to convergence is a designer's ability to anticipate outcomes: to speculate on, and even predict, the future. To the extent that a tool or app can predict consequences of and for architectural acts, then (in the form of a feedback loop) inform design decisions before they are committed to, the more likely these predictions will be of use to designers in the early stages of projects. Golparvar-Fard mentioned that, instead of looking back and doing a post-mortem, he could look forward using predictive analytics. But can't predictive analytics be considered looking back? "Yes, we are looking back. We track performance in previous tasks on that job," says Golparvar-Fard. "We also track reliability of suppliers, subcontractors, architects, and engineers. Instead of informally capturing commitments in meeting minutes, which every company does now, when you go into a meeting—there are no meeting minutes. Everything is being electronically captured as part of the plan. If you are waiting on a piece of equipment to come into the site, if you are waiting for this RFI to be addressed, this is a task that is going to be on my list, something that someone has to commit to. And now we can track reliability, from a productivity perspective, so we can use that. It's just shifting the way we've been doing the measurements to be proactive as opposed to being retroactive. Using the same sources of data."

"One opportunity that is on the horizon is bringing in the knowledge of controls into construction planning," adds Golparvar-Fard. "By controls, I mean to automatically be able to provide feedback to a plan. You walk into a meeting and the system has already told you here are your five alternatives you can suggest to your subcontractor. It's algorithms. This is a rather advanced, science-based, electrical engineering, in the robotics community, people who do controls. They use it for a real-time system, and embedded system, a machine that does this control. They have data and sensors they can use to train these controls algorithms. The construction community has never had this. Now, with this data—real data vs. plan data—now we can start thinking

23 Flux, Site context extractor app, San Francisco, 2016.
A Flux app built using the Flux JavaScript SDK runs in a web browser environment. Flux connects to the Open Street Map Database via its API and seamlessly delivers the area of interest as geometry directly into the user's preferred design tool.

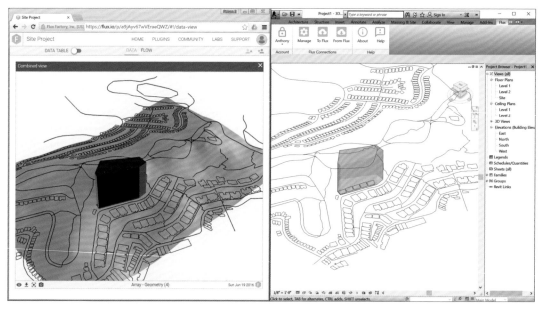

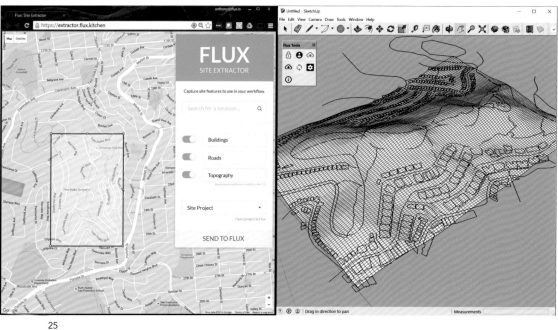

24 Flux, Site context extractor
app, San Francisco, 2016.
A Flux app built using the Flux
JavaScript SDK runs in a web
browser environment.

25 Flux, Site context extractor
app, San Francisco, 2016.
A Flux app built using the Flux
JavaScript SDK runs in a web
browser environment.

about this as a control problem. What are the ways we can start offering feedback to the plans? That's the most exciting part of the next ten years."

To help bridge the conception/construction divide, how can this data inform the earlier project phases? "Martin Fischer suggested years ago that I start thinking about how this can improve the basis of design in engineering. In fusing constructability knowledge into design, in fusing safety knowledge into design. Google's planning division is doing this. They're looking to capture information from their occupancy of hundreds of facilities that they have around the world and use that as the basis for improving the design."[24]

Just as there's a tendency for contractors to focus on the project's back end, there's an equal tendency for architects to focus primarily on the early stages of the building lifecycle. What design tools are looking to have an impact on the later stages of projects? "We fully intend to address the whole building lifecycle, including operations," says Anthony Buckley-Thorp, Application Engineer at Flux Factory."[25] "We have to start somewhere. Just to give focus, not only to ourselves, but to the users of our tools by providing entry points. If we were doing something about the layout of space, but also ways to space cranes on a construction site, it would not be so disparate that you couldn't get that traction for the users of the tools. Nothing in our tools should influence how people design."

Buckley-Thorp continues: "I worry sometimes: a lot of buildings that have been completed in the last few years use voronoi patterns, not because there is a voronoi button in Grasshopper— there are other patterns out that just might not exist as buttons— wouldn't it be a tragedy if an architect designed a building knowing subliminally that they are going to make their lives easier to draw and document that building if they do it in a certain way? Paper certainly never had that impact on them. Paper lets you draw anything on it. Paper doesn't care if you're using a pen or pencil. Or finger paints. Paper is just paper. If you get to the edge of the paper, you just stick another piece of paper next to it, attach it with tape, and keep drawing your line. We don't have that in the digital world. If Flux can be that agnostic digital paper—you can put any data through Flux, you can put just 1s and 0s, you can put native Revit data, you can output IFC data—Flux doesn't care. It will just transport it. It's highly agnostic in that regard. Also, it will connect to anything. There are no limits. If that old piece of software has an entry point, then you can connect Flux to it. You can connect Flux up to Microsoft Word if you wanted to. That feels to me like the new paper."

"Architecture has been dogged by insurance and financial concerns, instruments that have nothing to do with the fundamentals of architecture," explained PARTISANS co-founder, Alexander Josephson.[26] "One of our goals on a project is to remain in charge of overseeing the design and build alongside the contractor so that the process remains transparent throughout. We

26

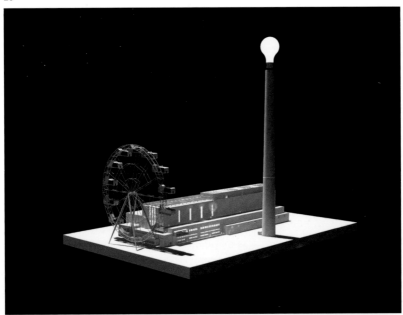

27

make 3D digital construction documents, which are the equivalent of a shop drawing. It's about eliminating the middleperson approach to building buildings, an approach that became popular due to the risk management culture that has come to plague architecture and the construction industry. Technology has allowed us to take back control and reestablish the dignity of architecture. Architects and designers have great intelligence and insights into how something complex can be built, but also know how to make that process efficient and economical. It's not about whether the technology is the tail that wags the dog. It's about using technology to actually redesign the processes that dictate the industry, to give birth to the DNA needed to build buildings. What's happened in the past is that the process has been driven by aesthetic concerns. Architects would use technology to achieve a particular aesthetic at all costs, or to meet a budget, but not necessarily to reinvent the way things are done."

LMN partner Sam Miller explained why the architect's design renderings are frequently pinned up at their construction sites. "One of the things I try to do when we're transitioning from design into construction, or when we're starting to engage a contractor, is to inspire contractors to want to do great work all the way down into the trades," says Miller.[27] "Because it's one thing if this guy comes off a job site, 'Yeah, it's another job and I'm getting paid to work my eight hours and I'm going to do my thing and go home.' But if they appreciate that they are working on a really amazing building, that their work is going to be on display, and valued, that starts with the design team. That brings a different level of attention to their work, and the craft, and the outcome can be stronger. The renderings are helpful to convey to the trades and to the contractors and the people doing the work that there is a vision of what this thing is going to be. It's going to be really amazing and remarkable and powerful, and you're part of making this happen. It is important and something I have tried to do. In fact, on one job that I was on, I gave a talk in the beginning of a job to a bunch of MEP subcontractors about how important this building was, and that there were going to be people travelling from around the world to see this building. About halfway through construction, when things were getting tough, when we're battling it out a little bit, one of the superintendents said, 'I think it's time for you to give your pep talk again.' Because you have to just step back. Sometimes you get so into the weeds it's important to step back and look at what it is we're trying all together to accomplish. The renderings are a great opportunity to do that, because they're about an outcome, and we want to inspire people to work toward that outcome."

26 PARTISANS, Trove, Luminato Festival, Hern Lightbult, Toronto, Canada, 2016.
The shipping containers that PARTISANS used to build out the space within the Hearn Generating Station for Luminato 2016 are the phenotypic antecedents to the pods the team designed to house Trove, the world's largest virtual art gallery.

27 PARTISANS, Trove, Luminato Festival, Interior, 2016.
Trove is a photographic collection of iconic objects and artworks from both private and public collections across Toronto.

ENDNOTES
1 Blaine Brownell, "The Architect as the Orchestrator of Information," October 29, 2015, http://www.architectmagazine.com/technology/the-architect-as-the-orchestrator-of-information_o.
2 Jeff Yoders, "When Does Design End and Construction

Begin?," BIM Forum Chicago in 2011, June 20, 2011, http://bimforum.org/2011/06/20/bim-forum-chicago-where-does-design-end-and-construction-begin/

3 Robert Yori, interview with author, April 19, 2016.

4 Yoders, "When Does Design End and Construction Begin?"

5 Christof Spieler, "The Fallacy of Design Intent," July 19, 2011, http://proposalspace.com/p/57/s?key=wVzqbp9B8NNr8hkY.

6 Yoders, "When Does Design End and Construction Begin?"

7 Elizabeth Hopkirk, "Clients 'Forced to Replace Concept Architects Because They Lose Interest,'" September 1, 2015, http://www.building.co.uk/news/clients-forced-to-replace-concept-architects-because-they-lose-interest/5077324.article.

8 Neha Bhatia, "GCC Construction Needs a Tech Transformation," August 29, 2015, http://www.constructionweekonline.com/article-35102-gcc-construction-needs-a-tech-transformation/.

9 Markku Allison, interview with author, May 11, 2016.

10 Brian Ringley, interview with author, January 5, 2016.

11 Stephanie McDonald, "Philip Bernstein," October 21, 2015, http://www.architectureanddesign.com.au/features/comment/in-profile-autodesk-s-philip-bernstein.

12 Richard Garber, "No More Stopping," Architecture Timed: Designing With Time in Mind 86, no. 1 (January/February 2016), 120–127; http://gluckplus.com/sites/default/files/press_item/files/Garber-2016-Architectural_Design.pdf.

13 Ibid.

14 David Barista, "BIM GIANTS: Robotic Reality Capture, Gaming Systems, Virtual Reality—AEC Giants Continue Tech Frenzy," August 6, 2015, http://www.bdcnetwork.com/giants-300-report-robotic-reality-capture-gaming-systems-virtual-reality-aec-giants-continue-tech.

15 Amar Hanspal, "Latest Construction Technology: Hello Profit, Goodbye Waste," July 23, 2015, http://lineshapespace.com/latest-construction-technology/.

16 Kadambari Baxi, Jordan Carver, and Mabel Wilson, Who Builds Your Architecture?: An Advocacy Report, 2015, http://www.e-flux.com/journal/who-builds-your-architecture-an-advocacy-report/.

17 Robert Vierlinger, interview with author, April 21, 2016.

18 Lachmi Khemlani, "SKYSITE: Cloud-Based Document Management for Construction," July 7, 2015, http://www.aecbytes.com/review/2015/Skysite.html.

19 Ibid.

20 Manuel DeLanda, "The New Materiality: Towards a Novel Material Culture," in Material Synthesis: Fusing the Physical and the Computational, September 1, 2015, http://onlinelibrary.wiley.com/doi/10.1002/ad.1948/abstract.

21 Achim Menges, Material Synthesis: Fusing the Physical and the Computational, September 1, 2015, http://www.

wiley.com/WileyCDA/WileyTitle/productCd-111887837X. html.

22 Ibid.

23 Mani Golparvar-Fard, interview with author, May 4, 2016.

24 Ibid.

25 Anthony Buckley-Thorp, interview with author, May 16, 2016.

26 PARTISANS, interview with author, April 29, 2016.

27 Sam Miller, interview with author, April 12, 2016.

IMAGES

Figure 1, 2, 15, 16, 19–22 © Deutsch Insights; figures 3–14 © Woods Bagot 2017; figures 17, 18 © Robert Vierlinger; figures 23–25 © Flux Factory Inc.; figures 26 and 27 © PARTISANS

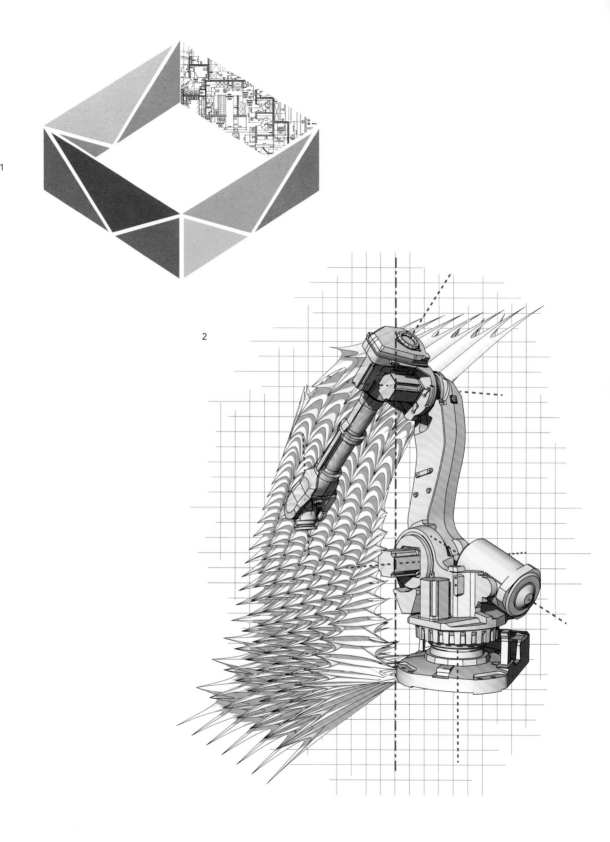

1

2

CHAPTER 7
DESIGN AND FABRICATION

Today, the building engineering industry is experiencing a convergence of critical needs where engineers, fabricators and builders expect greater levels of collaboration to keep pace with demanding project complexity and faster construction schedules. The forces driving this set of needs collectively is something we call "BIM to Fabrication."—Michael Gustafson[1]

As with conception and construction, design and fabrication are converging. Today, we are seeing the maturing and scaling of digital design-to-fabrication tools. Until now, in piecemeal fashion design professionals output digital designs for laser cutting, 3D printing, or computer numerical control (CNC) production by combining 2D-to-3D workflows. The historical separation of design and construction means and methods—for liability, legal, and insurance reasons—is starting to blur, and the industry is moving closer to a unified workflow, moving one big step away from the limitations of 2D CAD.[2] Design and fabrication convergence puts the power of *making* in the hands of design professionals.

YOUR NEXT BUILDING WILL BE MANUFACTURED

Prefabrication and assembly of architecture, including building parts, components, and systems—on site, with no need for a factory, reducing transportation and handling costs; or produced off-site in controlled conditions—is admittedly not new. At least one software manufacturer espouses the idea that we are entering the age of the mass-manufactured building: this holds that the future of construction is manufacturing buildings,[3] where "there will be a stronger connection between what's designed, built, and how it operates."[4] This trend has gradually built up, "but now that surge is really taking off and going beyond the typical stuff: metal, curtain wall panels, cabinetry. There's a huge rush to prefabrication—from whole bathrooms 'plopped' into place to hospitals with entire floors built in days rather than weeks."[5] As Lachmi Khemlani points out, "it was also informative to learn about Autodesk developments in the Manufacturing and M&E fields, especially given the fact that Autodesk, at least, sees a growing convergence between all of them.[6] Philip Bernstein explains the factors driving prefabrication for buildings today, including the effects of the recent financial crisis, reduction in computer manufacturing costs, and how today's graduates are exposed to technologies such as 3D printing tools earlier in their tutelage: "Your next building won't be built—it will be manufactured."[7] LMN Architects partner Stephen Van Dyck adds that "the worlds of architecture and manufacturing continue on their collision course."[8]

1 Deutsch Insights, Conception and Construction Convergences, 2017.
A further example indicating convergences in contemporary design practice that now occur at the meeting of two seemingly opposite forces.

2 Deutsch Insights, Convergence of Conception and Construction, 2017.
"Where does design end and construction begin?"

3

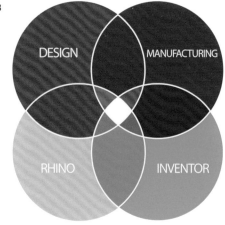

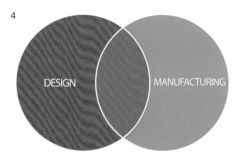

4

REASONS FOR A DESIGN/FABRICATION CONVERGENCE

The reasons for design/fabrication convergence are many. Construction companies that are trying to do more with less look to design-to-fabrication workflows to speed up the construction process, for faster modeling and assembly. Prefabrication means potentially better, faster, less expensive, greener, and even smarter buildings.[9] Firms are using BIM to increase quality and reduce mistakes, premanufacturing and delivering pre-installed wall panels. In places where tax calculations are based on labor on site, builders get a tax credit for building offsite. There is a movement toward preassembled components and away from building in place. A potential challenge to leveraging prefabrication, beyond finding talent, is potential opposition from organized labor unions.[10]

Design-to-fabrication is not limited to three dimensions. Skylar Tibbits, Director of the Self-Assembly Lab at Massachusetts Institute of Technology (MIT), focuses on what he calls 4D printing. His interest in 4D printing, where objects that are 4D printed have the capability to transform themselves over time, came about due to a frustration with the laborious construction process.[11] Additionally, laser scanners are used in manufacturing, architecture, engineering, construction—and merging these, manufacturing in AEC. Using laser beams to measure the distance points in space, a laser scanner's point and distance data can be used to construct 3D models. In doing so, the distance between design and fabrication decreases. One such workflow using milling is Rhinoceros (Rhino) and Grasshopper (gh3d) to a CNC machine.[12]

3 Deutsch Insights, Venn diagram, 2017. Diagram representing the convergence of design, Rhino, Inventor, and manufacturing.

4 Deutsch Insights, Venn diagram, 2017. Diagram representing the convergence of design and manufacturing.

When manufacturing is connected with IT, sometimes referred to as *Industry 4.0*, a convergence of advanced manufacturing techniques with information technology, data, and analytics forms.[13] There has also been talk of a "Third Industrial Revolution," an architecture that appropriates technology—digitization—and computation for the collective good.[14]

Leveraging machine learning and computer vision, Stanford University researchers are making progress in automatically turning laser scanning point clouds into usable BIM files.[15] The purpose of creating such an automated process is to create better buildings, and reduce the amount of repetitive work, freeing up designers to spend more time working creatively. Part of the shrinking of the design-to-fabrication continuum can be explained by the fact that increasingly larger structures[16] can be 3D printed, as printers are getting larger.[17] Modular assembly and 3D printing, which often occur off site, are increasingly taking place on site, where "construction sites look more like open-air factories with automation, modular assembly, and 3D printing."[18]

DRONES AND ROBOTS

Drones are changing construction for the better even as they raise questions concerning privacy and security. Drones are more accurate and can provide more variety in terms of types of modeling, including 3D modeling, contour line maps, 3D volumetric analysis, and progress forecasting models. In addition to the high amount of detail drones can provide, they also reduce risk, in that they can provide constant progress updates, and do so in a way that is safer.[19] Drones can map a construction site in a fraction of the time it would take people to do the same task. "Using drones for mapping and analysis of construction sites does more than save time and money, it enables builders to see details that were previously unattainable."[20]

Nevertheless, drone use in the AEC industry is still in its nascent stage. As of 2016, only 1% of all UK architecture firms reported extensive use of drones in their projects, whereas approximately a quarter of firms claim they make moderate use of drones, and 68% report no drone use.[21] Drones are already proving their worth at the construction site, especially in the areas of aerial photography, where drones can access hard-to-reach places; in site observation, construction administration and oversight; and in reality capture and site data-gathering. But how drones can be of use during the design phases is still an area for inquiry and experimentation. Most drones that have entered the AEC space have been used for construction, especially wall-building. In terms of convergence, can drones be used to collapse the design-to-fabrication workflow?

This is where robotics comes in. Skanska plans on using advanced robotics to help prefabricate a portion of construction of its Battersea development. Based on a simulation using a BIM model, they anticipate saving time, money, and increasing accuracy while reducing potential defects. "It has been used in Norway, and proved cost effective, providing speed and accuracy and

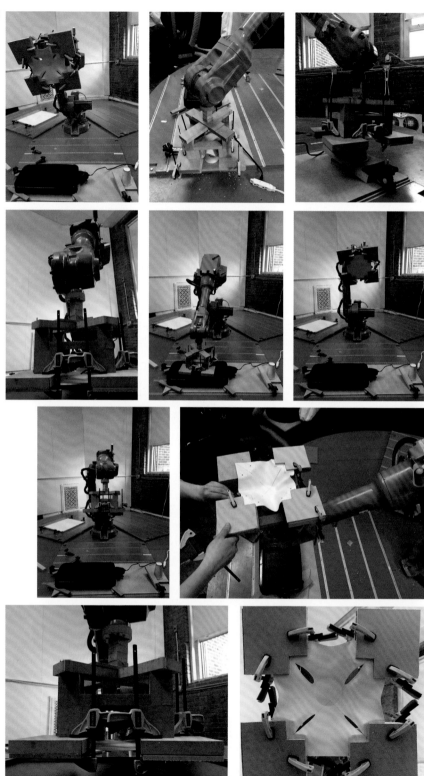

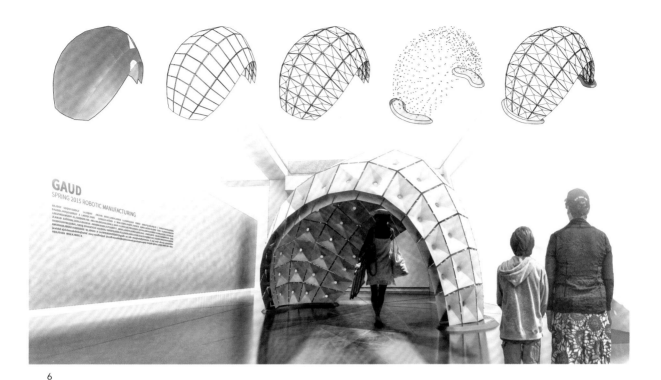

6

5 Brian Ringley, Pratt GAUD, with students
Nada Asadullah, Changbum Park, Cansu
Demiral, Maria Echeverry, and Ricardo
Diaz, New York, NY, 2016.
Pratt GAUD students' robotic
manufacturing process wherein polystyrene
sheets are heated and then pressed
over forms to create panels with conical
extrusions for a double-skin shell assembly.

6 Brian Ringley, Pratt GAUD, with students
Rawan Yassin, Brigitte Ngo, Erika Cañas,
and Wayne Erb, New York, NY, 2015.
Pratt GAUD students' proposal for double-
skin shell structure with diagram showing
panelization, connection details, and base.

safety gains. We are currently analyzing its potential productivity
benefits."[22] Robotics and laser scanning today are considered
technologies "that make it easier to close the gap between the
real world and digital design."[23]

There is today an increasing skepticism about 3D printing.
According to Brian Ringley, "3D printing is arguably the most
hyped technology of the decade." Importantly, though, Ringley
points out that "what started the hype wasn't necessarily the
technology itself (the first functional 3D printer was made in 1984)
but rather its affordability, and in particular the democratization
of use and understanding that comes with a low price point."[24]
In other words, the accessibility of the technology is what helped
spur its use in the industry. The wide-scale use of industrial
robotic arms has helped to assure the ubiquity of 3D printing and
repetitive prefabrication in architecture and other industries.[25]

As with drones, robots have been used in the AEC industry to
construct walls—in some cases, faster than masons.[26] Architect
and researcher at the Institute for Computational Design at the
University of Stuttgart, Achim Menges, claims that robots could
be programmed to build stadium roofs using carbon fiber as an
exposed building material.[27] Menges has also researched how
robots could fill the design/prefabrication gap using materials such
as bioplastic and laminated wood. Other architects, including Coop
Himmelb(l)au's Wolf D Prix and BIG's Kai-Uwe Bergmann, believe
that robots are the future of the construction industry.[28]

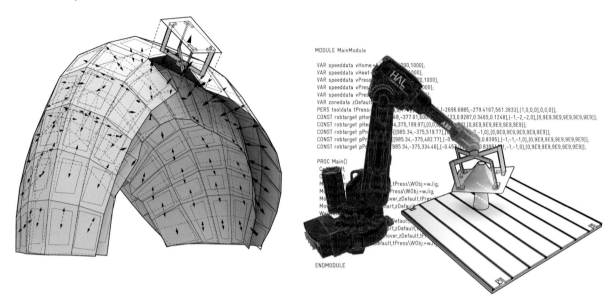

```
MODULE MainModule

  VAR speeddata vHome:=        00,1000];
  VAR speeddata vHeat=        1000];
  VAR speeddata vPress        0,1000];
  VAR speeddata vPres         000];
  VAR speeddata vPres
  VAR zonedata zDefault
  PERS tooldata tPress:            [-2696.6885,-279.4167,561.3833],[1,0,0,0],0,0,0]];
  CONST robtarget pHor     48,-377.01,600      [23,0.9287,0.3465,0.1248],[-1,-2,-2,0],[0,9E9,9E9,9E9,9E9,9E9]];
  CONST robtarget pHe     4,375,199.97],[0,0,      ],[0,9E9,9E9,9E9,9E9,9E9]];
  CONST robtarget pPr       [985.34,-375,519.77],        -1,0],[0,9E9,9E9,9E9,9E9,9E9]];
  CONST robtarget pPr      985.34,-375,482.77],[-0.         ,0.8395],[-1,-1,-1,0],[0,9E9,9E9,9E9,9E9,9E9]];
  CONST robtarget pP      985.34,-375,334.46],[-0.45        0.8365  1,-1,-1,0],[0,9E9,9E9,9E9,9E9,9E9]];

  PROC Main()
    C         ff;
    C         t;
    M           t,tPress\WObj:=wJig;
    M           Press\WObj:=wJig;
    Mo           over,zDefault,tPress
    Mo           art,zDefault,tPress
    W
                 rt,zDefault,tP
                 over,zDefault,tP
                 efault,tPress\WObj:=wJ

  ENDMODULE
```

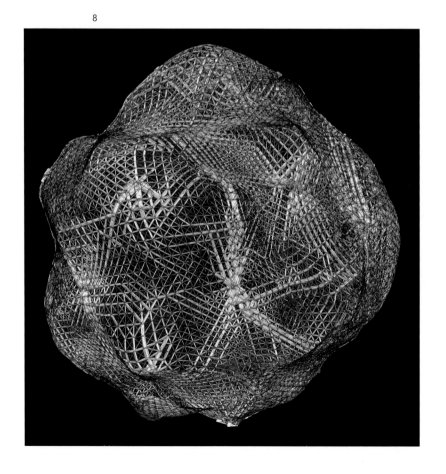

8 Robert Vierlinger, Geometric
Study using Karamba3d, 2016.
Geometric study using
structural member sizing of
Karamba3d.

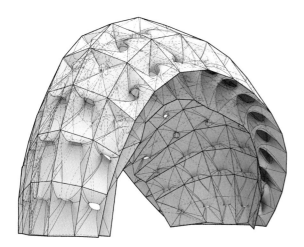

7 Brian Ringley, Pratt GAUD, New York, NY, 2016.
To connect and stiffen the two shell layers, each plastic panel is robotically heated and pressed over a conical form. The data inherent to each panel, such as its identification, tooling, press vector, and press depth, is passed downstream to routines that automate their post-processing into machine code (ABB RAPID) and motion via Thibault Schwartz's HAL, establishing a design-driven relationship between design intent and architectural manufacturing.

Amsterdam's UNStudio is one firm that is looking into how they can use robots to streamline design-to-fabrication. "Robotic fabrication can make it possible to produce a structurally and aesthetically complex design within a very short time period— and with minimal labour and costs."[29] UNStudio recently collaborated with Studio RAP of Rotterdam to identify key advantages of robotic fabrication for the architectural design and construction process, "including minimising time, labour, materials and costs."[30] Autodesk CEO Carl Bass also spoke recently on the transitioning of Autodesk from a software company to a making company.[31] One can expect that other organizations will follow suit as the design-to-fabrication workflow becomes increasingly accessible.

CROSS-DISCIPLINE KNOWLEDGE OF ENGINEERING, ARCHITECTURE, COMPUTER SCIENCE, AND MANAGEMENT

To be able to rise to the challenges of the convergence, superusers will need to acquire the ability to think like those in other disciplines. "In an AEC company, the position to interface between the disciplines needs an educated understanding for artistic priorities while maintaining an overview of the technically thinkable, to negotiate interests and conflicts," explains Robert Vierlinger, with Bollinger+Grohmann Engineers.[32] "Growing knowledge separated engineering from architecture a hundred years ago, and since then many have been pledging for improvement of collaborations for better designs in both perspectives. Ever more knowledge has been accumulated and separated into new professions, such that project managers today are facing a highly complex design-and build-process even for simple projects. The digital revolution brought new possibilities in planning, and unprecedented interconnectivity makes them develop in unprecedented speed. The evolution of a classical interface position is now sometimes called a technology consultant, a twenty-first-century version of the architectural engineer: cross-linking analogue and digital platforms, ideas, and approaches within a virtually open environment of digital planning. Cross-discipline knowledge of engineering, architecture, computer science, and management are skills of a new breed of experts, a new glue of the future's building industry."

How does the new breed of superuser describe what they do? "We design, teach, and develop," says Vierlinger. "We make ideas buildable on the one hand and create tools on the other. Both involve holistic thinking around purpose, context, and complex technology at the core. Creating good solutions for clients is a challenge, a trade in the alchemy of design to balance economy, quality, and innovation. We work in different scales and in different environments. A positive attitude towards new and unusual ideas is one of the great drivers of built innovation in our office." Vierlinger continues: "A hard task in algorithmic design is to produce novel solutions, ones which have not been expected by the user. Creativity can only happen within the human-designed space of possibilities, and the so-called 'curse of dimensionality' describes a core problem to this: the more open a problem is

9 Robert Vierlinger with Bollinger+Grohmann Engineers and Zaha Hadid Architects (ZHA), 3D print of the Pavilion for the CIAB, 2013.
The project development of expressive structural logics with Karamba3d demanded an extraordinary level of interdisciplinary collaboration in the design and development of the structure, working closely with the Co|De team at ZHA.

10 LMN Architects in association with Neumann Monson Architects, University of Iowa Voxman Music Building, Iowa City, IA, 2016.
The 700-seat concert hall will be one of Iowa City's prime performance venues, occupying a prominent volume in a 6-floor architectural composition.

9

10

defined, exponentially more solutions are possible and the harder a search algorithm has to work to find good ones. On the other hand, the more a search space is defined, the less diversity is possible. This mapping between parameters and solutions is called *representation*, and is important to a successful search. Biology richly inspires ideas of representations with principles of Darwinian evolution and neural learning."[33]

"Genetic algorithms are great tools for problem solving, and have been used in engineering for a long time," explains Vierlinger. "For instance, if the algorithm can shift the positions of a bridge's pillars along its length, it can propose the safest and cheapest ones. Or, it changes the positions of diagonals of a structural truss from chaotic configurations into stiffer ones. Step by step it will come up with more informed versions of the initial chaos, but probably the solutions will still look random in the beginning. Eventually, after the algorithm has run for long enough, a placement has evolved which resembles patterns of repetition, symmetry, or variation that a human designer also would have drawn. If the algorithm is given no hints to those patterns, this can take a lot of time. Another example for this is the production of drawings: Imagine one should come up with patterns for a façade by randomly altering the greyscale values of each pixel: the degrees of freedom are so many that it would take a long time to find good solutions. Again, without any hint on patterns, any idea of what an edge or a gradient

 11 LMN Architects in association with Neumann Monson Architects, University of Iowa Voxman Music Building, Iowa City, IA, 2016.
The sculpted form appears to be a unified visual expression, but in fact integrates five technical systems (acoustics, stage lighting, house lighting, audio-visual, and fire protection) designed and coordinated in close collaboration with several specialists and builders.

11

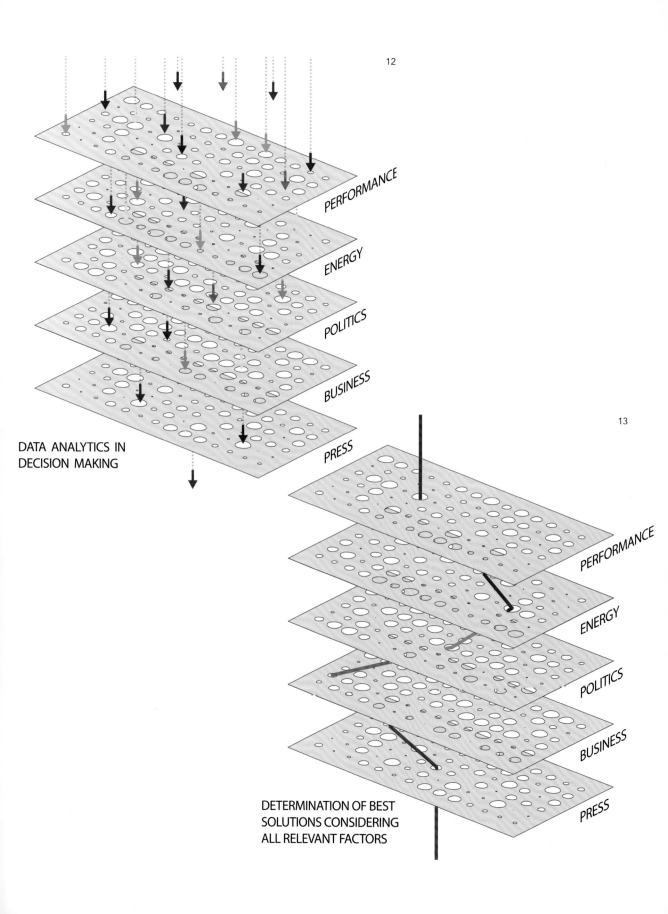

PERFORMANCE

ENERGY

POLITICS

BUSINESS

DATA ANALYTICS IN
DECISION MAKING

PRESS

PERFORMANCE

ENERGY

POLITICS

BUSINESS

DETERMINATION OF BEST
SOLUTIONS CONSIDERING
ALL RELEVANT FACTORS

PRESS

is, it will take a long time for good solutions to come up. Form can be inspired by information of different kinds. One kind of information is about function, and another is about aesthetics. The latter one is the harder one to be synthesized, and can hardly be made understood by a computer. Questions of optimization, but also tasks of describing and synthesizing new formal languages and methods of design, are using state-of-the-art scientific methods. The interfaces between experts in the respective fields are key to an effective integration."[34]

TOWARD AN ARCHITECTURE OF EVERYTHING

The term *Total Architecture* comes from Walter Gropius's book, *Total Architecture*—but today a firm that leverages technology doesn't care if it uses an awl to shape wood or a robot to shape wood. If they think it will result in excellent architecture, the wood can even be programmed to shape itself.[35] Total Architecture firms represent a form of convergence because they don't hold back on anything. They're *tributary firms*.

Evolution implies diverging branches—the opposite of convergence. And yet, several architects discuss their work in evolutionary terms. Architect Bjarke Ingels explained, "I like the idea of architectural evolution in a Darwinian sense; that the forms and shapes (designs if you like) of the biosphere have evolved through millennia-long selection processes—various lifeforms (design attempts) have encountered the forces of the nature (society) and have been edited to become what they are today."[36]

Proving Ground's Nathan Miller works with a handful of artisan architects, including the Snøhettas and the UNStudios.[37] "They push the boundaries of design in extraordinary and visually provocative ways that require new technologies, materials, and processes. But a lot of the work that I do, and a lot of the collaborators that I have, are with the big firms. Big organizations that are shaping the world around us whether we know their names or not." Miller continues, "When I think of Total Architecture, I think of aesthetics, I think of performance, politics, business, relationships across the board, research and innovation. Snøhetta and KieranTimberlake, two firms that do well because they understand those aspects. KieranTimberlake especially is doing some great stuff marrying research and practice in a way many firms aren't able to do."

Many have said there is a convergence in our industry. In doing so, they may be referring to *consolidation*: to mergers and acquisitions of software companies or AEC firms. They could also mean that everything is digitized, where everything is either a zero or a one, where convergence is no different in AEC than any other industry. There may be something more to it, where someone behind a closed door might be working on a Software of Everything or a Master Algorithm.

Another firm that is creating what can only be considered Total Architecture is PARTISANS. "It sounds like exactly what is going

12 and 13 Deutsch Insights, Decision Process, 2016.
Total Architecture considers multiple criteria: aesthetic, performance, politics, business, relationships across the board, research, and innovation.

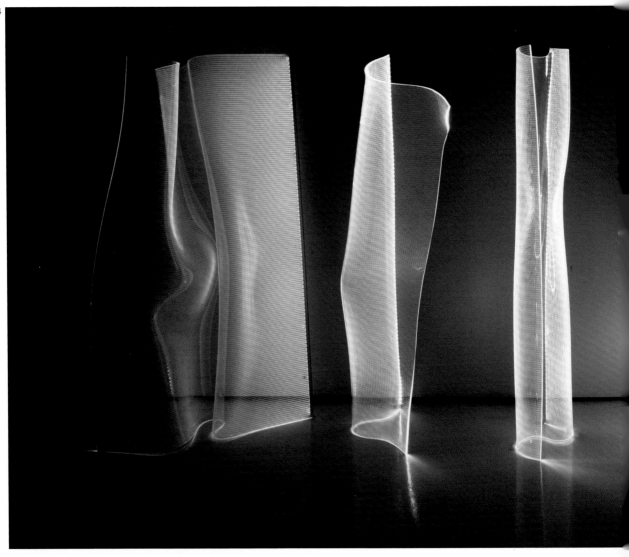

14 and 15 PARTISANS, Gweilo Light, 2016.
Gweilo is a new type of visual LED lighting that
transforms the light source itself. Thin sheets of
LED bulbs are carefully molded into a beautiful
and dynamic sculpture. Each light is hand-
sculpted by an artist in its hot plastic state,
allowing for infinite possibility in the shape, size,
and detail of the finished object.

15

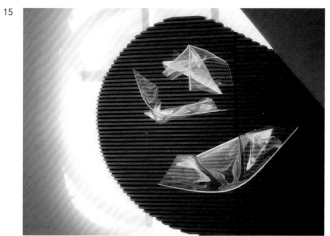

16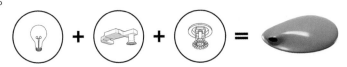

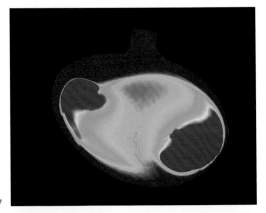
17

18

16 - 18 PARTISANS, Union
Station, 2016.
Images illustrate integrated
services in ceiling fixture;
Aerocado heat map; and view
of the market interior.

on in our office at PARTISANS," says Alex Josephson.[38] "I like this word 'convergence.' It definitely describes our practice and our ethos. Architecture for us is a surprise. Only through a willingness to engage in a problem or technology or subject you're not necessarily familiar with can you discover something. We believe that 'beauty emerges when design misbehaves.' By *misbehaving* we mean using processes and design thinking that hack conventional methods to produce something unexpected."

Josephson continues: "By calling ourselves PARTISANS, we acknowledged the reality that architecture is not just about building buildings. We were never interested in the title 'architect.' Architecture is this kind of dreamscape that on every level incorporates the interests of so many different people and ideas. That includes technologies. It includes politics. It includes art. This idea that we were more than willing to disengage from the tendency toward specialization that is occurring and rather go toward complexity, toward convergence. That is how we operate. A lot of people ask architects: *What do you specialize in?* Do you think as an architect you can just do one thing? I'm not sure you can. At least, I'm not sure you'd be practicing architecture. You'd be practicing airport design. With many of our projects we're creating new languages. Not just with software, but also aesthetically. Convergence is a willingness to have conversations, to collaborate, to innovate. This is what we do on a daily basis. Architecture has tended to be risk averse because of tendencies toward litigation. Convergence requires a willingness to engage in the unknown and take risks. That's what it means to us."

PARTISANS started as fabricators, then ventured into R&D, and has realized that the type of convergence found in their projects is scalable. "We work on everything from smaller projects and objects to others the scale of Toronto's Union Station, which occupies an entire city block, and the Hearn Generating Station, which sprawls over several acres," says PARTISANS partner Jonathan Freidman. What does that convergence actually look like? "That's exactly what we're exploring and figuring out," Freidman says. "The smaller projects, like the Grotto Sauna and Bar Raval, have taught us strategies we are now employing on residential and office projects, like the value of 3D laser scanning, for example. All of our projects influence and inform one another. Convergence is ultimately about deepening the learning process and forging partnerships with people in other disciplines to help you continue to learn."

"The Union Station revitalization project is 800,000 square feet, but we're in charge of the interior fit-out of 250,000 square feet of retail space," explains PARTISANS partner Pooya Baktash. "Not only are we designing a 70,000-square-foot ceiling featuring a series of sculptural pods that integrate and conceal all the systems—sprinklers, HVAC, and lights—we are also designing the furniture—the benches, the tables, even the garbage bins! We love to work at all scales, from macro to micro, from the larger scale of a dropped ceiling to the smallest furniture details. We are very excited

19

20

about the sculptural ceiling pods, which are a perfect example of convergence. Coming up with a design that would bring all the systems together also meant bringing together all the different tradespeople. It was a really gratifying and unusual process."

PARTISANS has been of late working on the largest of scales. "I started school right after September 11, 2001," explains Josephson. "Like everyone, it had an impact on me, as did the ensuing war between secular culture and radical religion, and Islam in particular. I became interested in how architecture could be deployed as an intervention in the Abrahamic religions. Pooya and I met while we were doing our masters degrees. I was working on a project about Islam and Mecca, and Pooya was working on one about Los Angeles. We realized that we were working on inverse projects: whereas Mecca is the city of God, LA is the city of the self! From the beginning we've been intrigued by the possibility of designing for cultures, religions, cities, and questioning what architects can aspire to design. In other words, we didn't start with buildings. Buildings are just one of the ways that cultures manifest themselves. But basically, before we even started our practice, we were asking ourselves: Why are architects just building museums and airports? Why did architects stop redefining the very foundations of civilization?"

"Union Station is a huge infrastructure project," notes Baktash. "Using parametric software like BIM was the only way a small studio like ours could compete and deliver on a project of such immense scale. We are in some kind of renaissance if you think about how it's possible for young firms like ours to leverage technology to punch above our weight. You don't have to be a 200-person firm to pull it off. Technology is one of the foundations of our office."

"But one of the things we are very conscious of is not letting the technology drive the design," adds Freidman. "You see that now in a lot of buildings. You can tell whether it is a SketchUp building or a Revit building. We have made a very conscious decision to treat technology as a toolkit and not be bound by any one particular kind of software. If we have an idea for something, we will research which technology best allows us to visualize, implement, or fabricate it. Or in some cases maybe we work with the software developer to develop software patches that allow us to fabricate what we imagine. Even though we prioritize technologies, drawing and hand-sketching are fundamental techniques in our office. There's a convergence between manual craft and technology. One summer we had an artist come in once a week and work with the staff on their hand-sketching. So we go back and forth between technology and hand-drawing, keeping freedom and organic-ness fundamental in our design. We don't want the technology alone to be pulling us along. We like to think that we're bringing back the role of the architect, not as a master builder, but as a visionary and as a doer. Someone who can facilitate things. Most of the time architects are relegated to being permit pushers, where owners go to architects to get a permit. We resist that and fight that daily."

19 and 20 PARTISANS, Grotto Sauna, 2016.
The curved interior emulates Lake Huron's waves and mirrors the Precambrian shield—a soft, undulating rock surface that has been worn over billions of years. PARTISANS collaborated directly with our fabrication partners to develop new prototyping and milling methods.

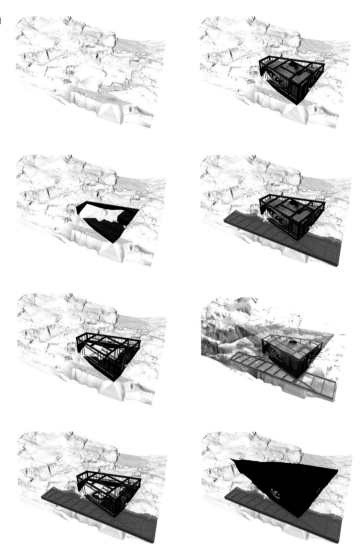

"Union Station is a perfect example of this," says Josephson. "The developer wanted someone young and with a voice. What they were really interested in was what our vision was for Union Station. They came to us with the project, but didn't know exactly what they were doing with it yet. We met with them first to sketch, in a sense, to tease out the words for what we wanted to accomplish with the station. We helped them design and articulate a vision: Union Station would become one of the world's most incredible civic experiences—a place where Toronto's best independent culinary, cultural, and retail offerings could call home and help create a neighborhood. This was a huge stretch; train stations are normally transit hubs that move people in and out. We said, it needs to be more than a station, which meant going beyond the brief. Ultimately, we drew on the architectural components and the vision to establish a graphic identity for Union. This creative visioning process has become a cornerstone of how we practice and work with many of our clients. In addition, we implemented state-of-the-art BIM technology to turn what would have been a daunting task for our office (i.e., 5 to 10 people) into a completely manageable one. On top of that was the struggle to implement design rigor on a project that is fundamentally utilitarian. At its core, Union Station must serve civic and infrastructural purposes. We had to deal with lots of columns, lots of hallways, lots of pipes, lots of HVAC. We had to learn to love the systems and got to thinking: how could we turn those utilitarian components into poetic architecture? How could we make the HVAC technology, life-safety elements like sprinklers, and lighting all converge into one beautiful yet functional object? We ended up consulting with all the different tradespeople and working with RWDI to innovate a new line of sculptural ceiling pods that marry all the systems. At the same time, the pods create spaciousness and bring architectural dignity to the dropped ceilings in the train station. Out of troubleshooting systems for a civic infrastructure project we generated a new family of products that other architects and builders can use in their projects. It's a perfect example of convergence."

"All the things we learned from our earliest projects—the Grotto Sauna and Bar Raval—have fed into the projects we are working on now," Josephson notes. "Those early projects were the first ones in our three-year-old start-up. You don't even know what you're getting into when you're starting out. If we had stayed with the status quo, in terms of fabrication and technological approaches, we would not be working on the projects we are now. The practice certainly wouldn't look the way it does now. It comes back to risk. Beauty emerges when design misbehaves. It was *misbehavior* to do the kinds of things we were doing at that stage of our practice. When you start you may just want to do a good job and be safe versus literally putting everything on the table. We put it all on the table!"

"When we show something to a client, it's always a bit of a risk because we have to be able to back it up," adds Freidman. "We

21 and 22 PARTISANS, Grotto Sauna, 2016.
Perched on an island's edge in Georgian Bay, Ontario, the Grotto Sauna is a feat of old-world craftsmanship and new-world sustainability made possible by cutting-edge software and fabrication technology. A sculpted space, a sensual experience, and a sophisticated exercise in building science.

23 PARTISANS, Bar Raval, 2016.
Carefully hewn from what look like unbroken Mobius strips of sinuous mahogany, Bar Raval is a twenty-first-century reinterpretation of Spanish Art Nouveau.

24 PARTISANS, Bar Raval,
2016.
In a stand-up-only
environment, the rippled—and
rippling—surfaces encourage
patrons to get comfortable,
lean into their soft edges,
and become a part of the
woodwork.

don't necessarily immediately know how we're going to execute
or achieve it, but we take on the challenge of figuring out how
to do it."

"I don't like that word 'renaissance,' admits Josephson. "I prefer
'revolution.' People are saying there's an evolution toward
convergence because they can couch big change in a digestible
term. It is sort of like we are at a dinner with our parents and we are
avoiding the conversation about politics that we all secretly really
want to have. People are too afraid to stand up and say that actually
what we are experiencing is full-scale revolution. The ground is
shifting beneath everyone's feet in every profession—people are
losing their jobs to machines. To characterize the technological
and resource shifts on the horizon as evolutionary in nature is to

ignore the gravity of them entirely. I think that that's irresponsible. The term *evolution* has become popular because architects like Bjarke Ingles and his firm BIG, as well as many others, are selling it. Everyone's using this word because it is so much easier to sell. Evolution is a bunch of diverging branches. Convergence is a revolution. We call ourselves PARTISANS. We challenge anyone to question our authenticity and the validity of our approach, of believing in the possibility of revolution. We have to change the way architectural practice works. We essentially built buildings the same way for thousands of years. We have to change the way people are employed in our industry. And we have to change the way people think about architects. I don't think evolution is fast enough. I don't think what we're doing is evolutionary at all. We're talking about this from the perspective of speed. Look how quickly things are moving! Evolution is a slow crawl. Revolutions per minute is the actual true pace of the world we live in."

"I don't think the world has time for evolution. Or for evolutionary architecture," Freidman continues.

"How can you use the word *evolution* in a world that's basically evolving on a second-to-minute basis?" responds Josephson. "You're talking about a world that doesn't go through incremental change. From a technological perspective, we're already looking at what the next technology is. It's not enough to say things are evolving. If things are evolving, it's on fast-forward."

ENDNOTES
1 Michael Gustafson, "Autodesk Launches Tech Preview of Structural Analysis Platform Called React Structures," October 2, 2015, http://inthefold.autodesk.com/in_the_fold/2015/10/autodesk-launches-tech-preview-of-future-structural-analysis-platform-called-react-structures.html.
2 Randy Deutsch, quoted in Wanda Lau, "The Tech to Expect in 2016," January 12, 2016, http://www.architectmagazine.com/technology/the-tech-to-expect-in-architecture-in-2016_o.
3 Philip Bernstein, "Future of Construction: Your Next Building Won't Be Built—It Will Be Manufactured," August 26, 2015, https://lineshapespace.com/future-of-construction/.
4 Stephanie McDonald, "Profile: Philip Bernstein," October 21, 2015, http://www.architectureanddesign.com.au/features/comment/in-profile-autodesk-s-philip-bernstein
5 Bernstein, "Future of Construction."
6 Lachmi Khemlani, "Autodesk University 2015," December 17, 2015, http://www.aecbytes.com/newsletter/2015/issue_78.html.
7 Ibid.
8 Stephen Van Dyck, quoted in Lau, "The Tech to Expect in 2016."
9 Rory Stott, "MIT Researchers Develop 10-Material 3D Printer Capable of 'Smart' Printing," September 1, 2015,

http://www.archdaily.com/772838/mit-researchers-develop-10-material-3d-printer-capable-of-smart-printing

10 Carlos Rico, "Executive Roundtable: New Waves in Construction: Prefabrication, Modeling," August 25, 2015, http://www.sddt.com/News/article.cfm?SourceCode=20150824czb&_t=New+waves+in+construction+Prefabrication+modeling#.VedgJempR0s.

11 Wanda Lau, "MIT's Skylar Tibbits Explores the Next Dimension," December 30, 2013, http://www.architectmagazine.com/design/mits-skylar-tibbits-explores-the-next-dimension_o.

12 John Stoughton, "Nested, CNC-Milled Fins Produce Moire Effects," February 26, 2016, http://blog.archpaper.com/2016/02/nested-cnc-milled-fins-produce-moire-effects/#.VtBcd9WDnCQ.

13 Brenna Sniderman, Monika Mahto, and Mark J. Cotteleer, "Industry 4.0 and Manufacturing Ecosystems," February 22, 2016, http://dupress.com/articles/industry-4-0-manufacturing-ecosystems-exploring-world-connected-enterprises/?id=us:2pm:3tp:xmfg:awa:pip:051016:deloittemfg

14 Eric Oh, "7 Futuristic Fabrications Leading Us Towards a Newer Architecture," March 26, 2016, http://www.archdaily.com/783309/7-futuristic-fabrications-leading-us-towards-a-newer-architecture?utm_source=ArchDaily+List&utm_campaign=94ce973c96-RSS_EMAIL_CAMPAIGN&utm_medium=email&utm_term=0_b5a382da72-94ce973c96-408550377

15 Shara Tonn, "Stanford Researchers Automate Process for Acquiring Detailed Building Information," July 1, 2016, https://www.ecnmag.com/news/2016/07/stanford-researchers-automate-process-acquiring-detailed-building-information.

16 Madeleine Wedesweiler, "Pod Home by SOM Architects Is 'World's Largest 3D Printed Structure,'" February 7, 2016, http://www.domain.com.au/news/3d-printed-pod-is-powered-by-a-car-20160204-gmli1e/

17 Ian Wright, "Voxeljet Announces Arrival of Largest Industrial 3D Printer in North America," April 28, 2016, http://www.engineering.com/AdvancedManufacturing/ArticleID/11967/voxeljet-Announces-Arrival-of-Largest-Industrial-3D-Printer-in-North-America.aspx?ENGCOM.

18 Julie Jacobson, "Top 10 AEC Trends for 2016," January 14, 2016, http://beyonddesign.typepad.com/posts/2016/01/top-10-aec-trends-for-2016.html

19 John Boitnott, "4 Reasons Why Construction Companies Can't Get Enough of Drones," July 2, 2016, http://www.inc.com/john-boitnott/4-reasons-why-construction-companies-cant-get-enough-of-drones.html.

20 Ibid.

21 Richard Waite, "Drone Use by AJ100 Practices Takes Off," June 7, 2016, http://www.architectsjournal.co.uk/news/drone-use-by-aj100-practices-takes-off/10007273.fullarticle.

22 "Skanska Plans Robots for Next Phase of Battersea,"

July 1, 2016, http://www.constructionmanagermagazine.com/news/skanska-plans-rob2ots-next-p3hase-bat4tersea-power/

23 Bernstein, "Future of Construction."

24 Brian Ringley, "Out of Our Hands: Robotic #D Printing and Autonomous Construction," July 7, 2015, https://3dprinting.microsolresources.com/2015/07/07/out-of-our-hands-robotic-3d-printing-and-autonomous-construction/.

25 Ibid.

26 Julia Sklar, "Robots Lay Three Times as Many Bricks as Construction Workers," September 2, 2015, http://www.technologyreview.com/news/540916/robots-lay-three-times-as-many-bricks-as-construction-workers/.

27 Jessica Mairs, "Carbon Fibre and Robots Could Create a 'Fourth Industrial Revolution,' Says Expert," May 9, 2016, http://www.dezeen.com/2016/05/09/carbon-fibre-robotic-production-fourth-industrial-revolution-university-stuttgart-achim-menges/.

28 Amy Frearson, "10 Projects Paving the Way to a Future of Robot-Built Architecture," May 10, 2016, http://www.dezeen.com/2016/05/10/10-projects-that-look-future-robotic-construction-robots-architecture/.

29 "Robotics with Studio Rap," http://www.unstudio.com/research/spp/robotics-with-studio-rap.

30 Ibid.

31 "The Blueprint Talks with Carl Bass," October 8, 2014, https://theblueprint.com/stories/carl-bass/.

32 Robert Vierlinger, interview with author, April 21, 2016.

33 Ibid.

34 Ibid.

35 Self-Assembly Lab, "Programmable Materials," http://www.selfassemblylab.net/ProgrammableMaterials.php

36 AoN, "Interview with Bjarke Ingels," http://www.archi-ninja.com/interview-with-bjarke-ingels/.

37 Nathan Miller, interview with author, February 23, 2016.

38 PARTISANS, interview with author, April 29, 2016.

IMAGES

Figures 1–4, 12, 13 © Deutsch Insights; figures 5–7 © Brian Ringley, Pratt GAUD; figures 8 and 9 © Robert Vierlinger; figures 10 and 11 © LMN Architects; figures 14–24 © PARTISANS

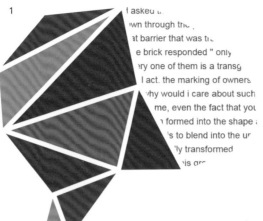

1

I asked t...
wn through the ...
at barrier that was t...
e brick responded " only
ery one of them is a transg
I act. the marking of owners
why would i care about such
me, even the fact that you
formed into the shape
's to blend into the ur
'ly transformed
is or

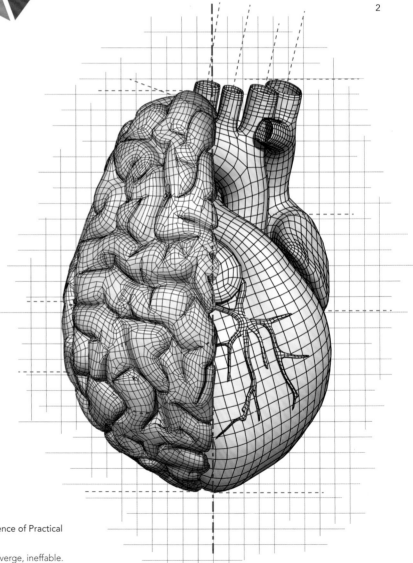

2

1 Deutsch Insights,
Practical and the Ineffable
Convergences, 2017.
This book has explored
convergences in contemporary
design practice that now
occur at the meeting of two
seemingly opposite forces.

2 Deutsch Insights, Convergence of Practical
and the Ineffable, 2017.
To converge is practical; to diverge, ineffable.
Do the two ever overlap?

CHAPTER 8
PRACTICAL AND INEFFABLE

It's not just the element of place, but also each moment in time presents a convergence of potentials and challenges, and these specifics are translated through concepts and tectonics into a unique architecture.—Chris McVoy, Senior Partner at Steven Holl Architects, on their design approach[1]

Starting with both divergence and convergence, divergent thinking is associated with evolution, ideation, and creativity, whereas convergent thinking comes into play when one is required to make a decision, or choose a course of action. In the world of creativity, "convergence is most important during the stage when ideas are being ironed out and made tenable."[2] Convergence takes the novel and impractical and makes it practical and useful. According to the authors of *Wired to Create*, "convergence refers to the ability to conform, put in the hard effort necessary to exercise practicality, and make ideas tenable. Convergence consists of high conscientiousness, precision, persistence, critical sense, and sensitivity to the audience."[3]

To converge is practical; to diverge, ineffable. The two seldom overlap. When we first learn to brainstorm, we're told to hold back our judgment (convergence) until we're done ideating (divergence). For example, Autodesk's structured brainstorming methodology for innovating, the Innovation Genome, helps illustrate both divergent and convergent thinking in the creative process to generate multiple ideas in a short period of time.[4] Yet, the same thinking that believes the right brain is associated with creativity misses the nuanced reality that creative thinking requires both the right and left sides of the brain. Even with these seemingly polar opposites, we're increasingly seeing a melding, a blurring, a *convergence*.

IDEATION IS ALMOST ANTITHETICAL TO AUTOMATION
The word *practical* is trending in the AEC industry. The 2016 USC BIM Symposium was entitled "Effective, Productive, Profitable Workflows." Many of the sold-out Autodesk University 2015 classes featured the word "Practical" in their titles.[5] Nevertheless, the 2016 AIA convention in Philadelphia Day 2 keynote was delivered by the American-Israeli designer, architect, and professor Neri Oxman. Described as "using computational algorithms, 3D printing, robotics, and cutting-edge fields such as synthetic biology, Neri Oxman's work is nothing short of breathtaking and inspiring."[6] While Oxman's research is "at the

intersection of computation design, additive manufacturing, materials engineering and synthetic biology,"[7] she nonetheless told a crowd estimated at 8,000 architects that she was not interested in giving practical advice to professionals. Her research and designs landed squarely on the side of the ineffable. More typically, a recent symposium at the University of Minnesota explored the convergence of the three fields of architecture, art, and biology that results in works for the built environment. Points of intersection between the speakers and panelists included "the measurable benefits that such work can deliver, despite its inherent difficulties."[8] Their solutions—applied research—were largely practical.

Today, humans and robots are learning how to collaborate and work together so that they don't have to be an either/or choice, but rather a both/and proposition.[9] In the digital age, especially for architects and postdigital artisans, the notion of craftsmanship is still very much evolving.[10] Recent books have attempted to close the robot/human and algorithm/gut instinct divide. Author Brian Christian not only holds degrees in, but also works at the intersection of, science, philosophy, and poetry. In his co-authored book, *Algorithms to Live By*, he explained "how simple, precise algorithms used by computers can also untangle very human questions."[11] On navigating the robot/human spectrum, there's a recent addition to the literature, *Machines of Loving Grace: The Quest for Common Ground Between Humans and Robots,* that looks for "common ground between humans and robots," at a time when "we have seen some impressive demonstrations of artificial intelligence, including Watson, IBM's 'Jeopardy' champion; Siri, Apple's personal assistant; and Google's self-driving car."[12] Another recent book, *Art and Science,* covers the ongoing convergence of—as opposed to the more expected opposition of—art and technology in the digital age.[13]

Markku Allison got his start in architecture as a building designer. "Within our profession we have all the different breeds: project manager, project architect, project designer. Because I'm at the designer end of that spectrum, I'm really interested in the data and intuition and the practical and ineffable. That is where my passion is." Allison continues, "You can go to Louis Kahn, the difference between the architecture of the little 'a' and the architecture of the capital 'A,' or beauty with a little 'b' or capital 'B.' If it didn't have the *ineffable,* we would lose the heart and soul of what architecture is. That ineffable piece is the life-giving spark that really makes the building sing."[14] Many architects have a similar sentiment: that the aesthetic component—Vitruvius's *delight*—distinguishes architecture from mere building, and that architecture wouldn't be worth the trouble to practice without that distinguishing element.

Toru Hasegawa sides with the thinking that computers cannot replicate creativity. "As every day goes by, I'm less inclined to make this statement: Design is the last thing that technology will roll over," said Hasegawa.[15] "Let's throw out all of the possible

3 Deutsch Insights, Venn diagram, 2017. Diagram representing the convergence of art and science.

4 Deutsch Insights, Venn diagram, 2017. Diagram representing the convergence of firmness, commodity, and delight.

3

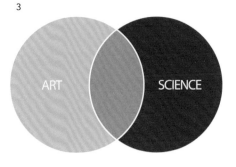

behaviors humans have. Throw out the garbage. Do our own laundry. Wash the dishes. Clean the house. You can classify these tasks as functions. If you list all of these functions, and compare what has been replaced by machines, the majority has or will be. There's a world in which a lot of this can be automated. The stuff that doesn't resonate well with automation is ideation. Ideation is almost antithetical to automation. If you don't have functions to automate, there is no automation. Or machine inquiry. Creation comes before automation can possibly happen. Machines have not been well-crafted to make things up. If an alien were to come down to earth and saw what humans could be consolidated to—it would be creation or creativity. We create stuff. Instead of repeatedly doing some task. That's where we are in terms of human-machine relationship. If a machine has no drive or necessity to create, there is no intent. Machines will always be in support of the creator."

Falling squarely in a camp holding that creativity is something that has evolved for millennia, and will continue to evolve in the age of computers, algorithms, and robots, works are appearing that explore assisted creation and generative creation, and the role AI plays in replicating, approximating, or replacing human creativity.[16] Recent research argues that beauty is *not* in eye of the beholder (personal preference), but instead is part of our biology (neurological).[17] The field of neuroaesthetics uses neurology to understand human response to art.[18]

BETWEEN FIRMNESS, COMMODITY, AND DELIGHT

It can be said that architecture is nothing more than the masterful, correct, and magnificent convergence of firmness, commodity, and delight. Architecture throughout history has always mediated between the practical (commodity) and ineffable (delight). Recent attempts at architecture serve to make this tendency more explicit. It's too late for architects to turn their backs on technology. As Norman Foster has stated, "Since Stonehenge, architects have always been at the cutting edge of technology. And you can't separate technology from the humanistic and spiritual content of a building."[19] As one example, AADRL Spyropoulos Design Lab explores an architecture that is self-aware, self-structured, and self-assembles. "The research explores high population of mobility agents that evolve an architecture that moves beyond the fixed and finite towards a behavioural model of interactive human and machine ecologies."[20]

Recent industry literature, such as *The Death of Drawing: Architecture in the Age of Simulation*,[21] bemoans the loss of meaning in architecture due to the rise of such technologies as BIM. However, others, such as MIT Architecture's Design and Computation Group, don't let the rise of technology curtail their pursuit of meaning in architecture, as it exists to inquire "into the varied nature and practice of computation in architectural design, and the ways in which design meaning, intentions, and knowledge are constructed through computational thinking, representing, sensing, and making."[22] The practical and ineffable, and the

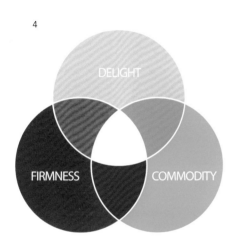

4

4

5

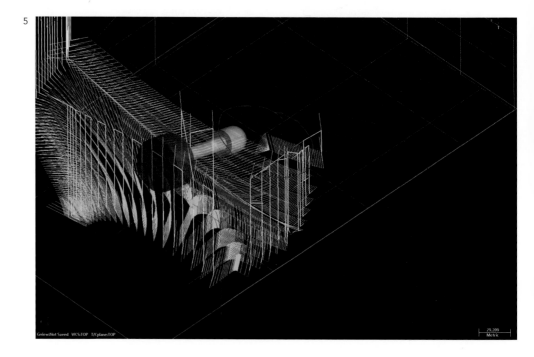

Gview:Not Saved   WCS:TOP   UCSplane:TOP

29.209
Metric

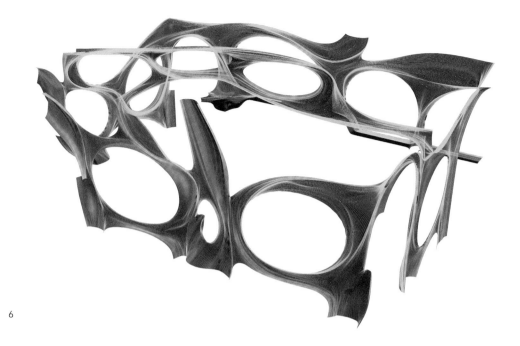

6

technological and mystical, not only can coexist, but *must* coexist in order for a complete work of architecture to be realized.

In reference to the work of PARTISANS, perhaps no assessment of the work of a design firm captures the range of mastering the practical and ineffable in architecture better than this assessment of their work: "What impressed me most—beyond the material palette and use of advanced technology—is how they make me *feel*."[23] While recent advances in robot art may raise questions concerning the monopoly humans hold on creativity, it is in the collaboration between robots or machines and humans where the greatest opportunities reside for advances in the fields of architecture, engineering, and construction.[24] The consensus so far is that robots can't achieve the creative solutions normally expected of humans, and that their function ought to be to supplement human efforts by taking over automated tasks. "If there's any comfort offered during the current debate around robots, automation and the future of work, it's that robots can't do creativity. Machines are great for automated, precise, repetitive work; not so great for creative, expressive work, robots can't do creativity."[25]

Projects need experts as well as generalists; the latter serve as glue for the project team, and are able to see the big picture. "Without the Architect the specialists are lost, fragmented, caught in their reductive view. The Architect brings to the activity that which the specialists cannot, sees the whole, and looks towards costs, utility, as well as aesthetics."[26] A firm such as the Turner Prize-winning interdisciplinary London-based Assemble collective, working across the disciplines of art, architecture, and design, is able in their work to bridge the divide between the practical and ineffable.

5 - 7 PARTISANS, Bar Raval, 2016.
PARTISANS worked closely with fabrication partner, MCM Inc., and the software engineers at Mastercam to innovate the milling process. Note the 3D tool path map.

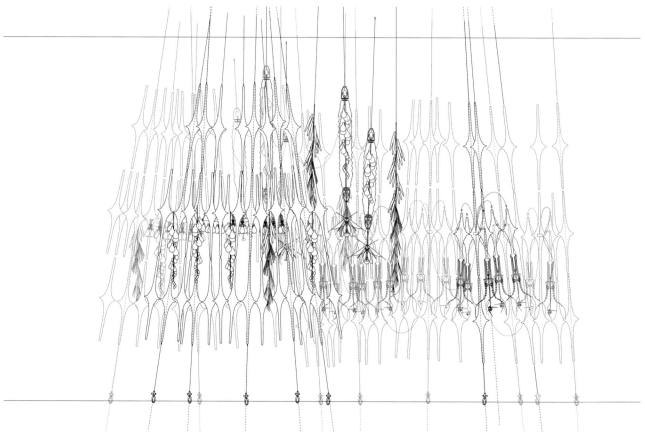

8 Philip Beesley/LASG/PBAI Epiphyte
Chamber, Museum of Contemporary and
Modern Art, Seoul, 2014.
Elevation illustration of an immersive
environment mounted for the inauguration of
the Museum of Contemporary and Modern Art,
demonstrating key organizations employed
by Living Architecture Systems Group
constructions, including lightweight resilient
scaffolds, distributed interactive computational
controls, and integrated protocell chemical
metabolisms.

One architectural critic has found affinities between Assemble and other individuals or firms with similar goals, including Theaster Gates in Chicago, and Alejandro Aravena's Elemental in Chile.[27] Neri Oxman, mentioned earlier, combines four disciplines—art, science, engineering, and design—in the "Age of Entanglement."[28] "The role of Science is to explain and predict the world around us; it 'converts' information into knowledge. The role of Engineering is to apply scientific knowledge to the development of solutions for empirical problems; it 'converts' knowledge into utility. The role of Design is to produce embodiments of solutions that maximize function and augment human experience; it 'converts' utility into behavior. The role of Art is to … create awareness of the world around us."[29]

Philip Beesley is a practicing visual artist, architect, and professor in architecture at the University of Waterloo who leads an interdisciplinary design collective in Toronto, Canada. His Living Architecture Systems Group undertakes collaborations with architects, engineers, artists, and scientists. Beesley himself is a convergence of architect, artist, and professor. What does the resulting work process look like? "Thinking of how we need to work in our unstable, constantly shifting environment, it is interesting to think about the way agile, flexible approaches are needed. I realize I'm working in a rather curious hybrid practice," offers Beesley.[30] "Through the generations of this past century, we've moved through an extraordinary turbulence with massive apprehension about the scale of nations and institutions. My own world has tended to gravitate to increments, with small group conversations and neighbourhood-level organization. My parents were deeply affected by the Second World War and responded with an activism rooted in local ethics and in immersion in nature. I have tended to respond with urban scales and with strong interest in artificial technologies."

Beesley continues: "Seen as multiple cycles, perhaps this makes a personal narrative of overlapping, stuttering movements, in which wholes are progressively sought. One can think of more systematically engineered living systems and other examples of movements that have a tremendous optimism about unification. Conversely, there are some fertile examples that resist whole-systems thinking and insist on decoupled, granular divisions. A good example might be our recent focus on emergence in computational design. This might resonate with a social model of agency rooted in individual action. In a hopeful sense it results in highly resilient, complex, extremely interesting assemblies. I savor the kind of churn that happens from the intersection of those different scales. That leads me to think optimistically about the kind of fertility that can come from classical disciplines working strongly, while at the same time alteric hybrids work experimentally, creating productive annoyance and friction."

"We can see a national and global trauma of homogenization coming out of the world wars of the past century," explains Beesley. "It is hard to speak of the sickeningly polarized politics

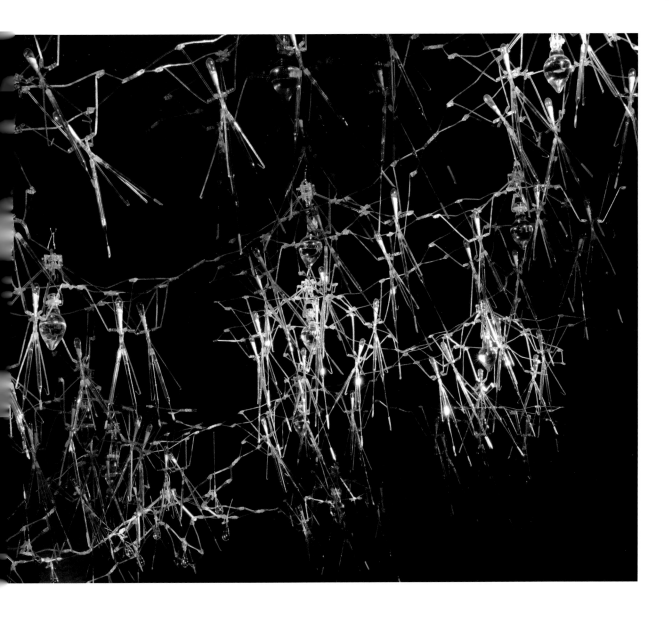

9 Philip Beesley/LASG/PBAI Epiphyte
Membrane, Opernwerkstätten, Berlin, 2014.
Sound designer Salvador Breed collaborated
with Beesley and the Hylozoic Series group to
create a synthetic forest of sound surrounded
by hovering membranes. Organic power
cells using vinegar, copper, and aluminum
created currents that triggered an array of
microprocessors, producing fluctuating fields of
machine-made whispers.

10 Philip Beesley/LASG/PBAI Detail of
epiphyte membrane, Opernwerkstätten, Berlin,
2014.
Detail image of *Epiphyte Membrane's* lower
membrane composed of interlinking, thermally
expanded meshwork acrylic spars and
hexagonal skeletons. The membrane supports
densely massed glass vessels that encircle
a central grotto-like area housing Breed's
soundwork.

11

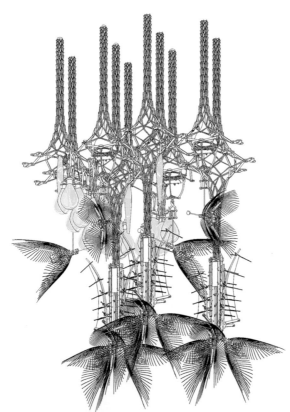

12

11 Philip Beesley/LASG/PBAI Fin Node Digital
Model. Curiosity Based Learning Algorithm
Testbed, 2015.
A detailed illustration of a "fin model." Recent
LASG projects have an increased density
of glass vessels, sensor and actuator arrays
that are organized within chains. Each array
is individually controlled by nested sets of
microprocessors that communicate via the
Internet with central computers, allowing for
ongoing interaction and adjustment.

12 Philip Beesley/LASG/PBAI
Detail of Grove, Waterloo
Architecture Nest Studio,
Waterloo, 2014.
Waterloo Architecture students
worked with Beesley to
develop the Grove pavilion.
A segmented structure with
central spine and radial kinetic
ribs enclosed a suspended,
foam-like lighting canopy.

of the Cold War. Fully engaging those polarized qualities might risk despair about working at public scales. At the same time as those pointed true movements in our culture, there were other kinds of sensibilities seen as unification of something deeply fulfilling, where a common state of existence could be acutely felt. The emerging understanding of the dynamics of systems, and the physics of systems in many cases, allowed a sense of stewardship of the world as a whole to emerge. We can readily see, along with polarization, an increasing ability to conceive and engineer self-sustaining environments with their own boundaries. I think of these as tremendously satisfying."

In Philip Beesley Architect's projects, does everybody work all together in an integrated way at one time, or on an as-needed basis? "A model like integrated project delivery [IPD] would instruct us to ensure that all parties have conversations from the earliest possible point in launching a design project in order to foster integration," says Beesley. "I appreciate the spirit of that, but the circumstance of my own work and relationships means that the model is far more one of a hiccupping, punctuated mongrel of multiple convergences combined with a great deal of work that is decoupled as well. So it's far from a model of utter harmonic communication. Plato would really disapprove of the way we work. It does not have a purity to it. My work goes through a multitude of cycles of development. There are five streams happening in my projects right now. That is lightweight resilient scaffolding and mechanisms requiring distributed computation and algorithmic development as well as electronics and synthetic biology, psychology and neurology working with synthetic responses. How can we put these things together and how might we verify things and how might we turn this into design models?"

Beesley sees the aforementioned impatience in the current generation that might lead to some of the solutions brought about by convergence. "I do see impatience, and we could have an interesting debate about whether that quality is an affliction or a virtue. Both would be true in their ways. It's very hard and challenging to find oneself in conversation with such distraction and short attention span. It's hard to have confidence in working with deeply complex and nuanced things when things are raised to the level of the paragraph at best. That doesn't seem compatible with the kind of integrated viability of whole systems my studio is dedicated to. On the other hand, to bring it home, I accuse my daughter of being completely obsessed with texting, turning herself into the most superficial machine. That was a cruel judgment of what she was doing to herself. Looking again, and treating her with respect, one could detect a radical poly-consciousness of multiple literacies, of being able to weave together 50 different conversations simultaneously. It's worth not being so quick to erect a moral judgment before the radical facilities and agility of that way of approaching things [are] also grasped. It would be true to say that the radical fragmentation and fluidity of individual increments of conception is not simply decay, but it does create some different scales which have a pretty

13 Philip Beesley/LASG/PBAI Detail of Grove,
Waterloo Architecture Nest Studio, Waterloo,
2014.
Repeating systems of cells are based on
tetrahedral cores, supporting interactive LED
lighting. Diffusive fronds expand the boundaries
of the canopy.

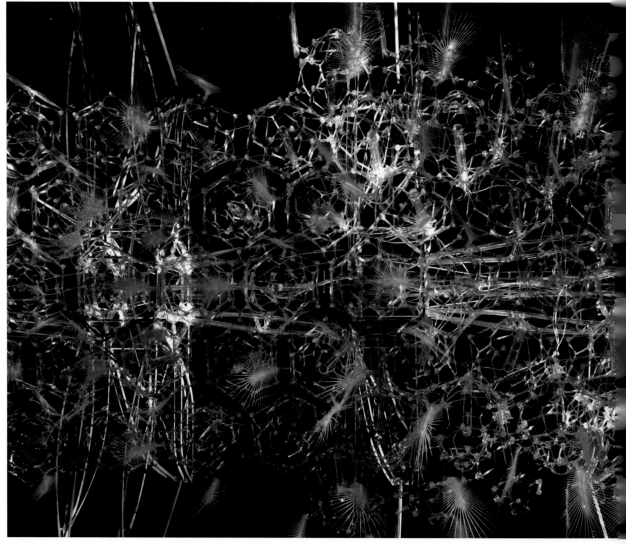

14

14 Philip Beesley/LASG/PBAI Detail of Grove, Waterloo Architecture Nest Studio, Waterloo, 2014.
Laser-cut wood and polymer sheets are combined with thermally expanded acrylic skeletons.

15 Philip Beesley/LASG/PBAI Hylozoic Ground, Venice Architecture Biennale, Venice, 2010.
Beesley worked with a collaborative team of designers, scientists, and engineers to present *Hylozoic Ground*, Canada's entry to the 2010 Venice Architecture Biennale. Densely massed, lightweight, digitally fabricated components were fitted with microprocessors and proximity sensors that reacted to human presence. Prototype chemical cells emitted liquid chemical skins and transformed carbon dioxide from the environment into harmless deposits akin to limestone and chalk.

ferocious liability in their own right. Moreover, [it may be that] this symptom is not simply apocalyptic, from one thing falling apart to the other, but rather is one of cyclical churn in which that kind of sensibility radiates itself intact back into a monolithic kind of consciousness that is dedicated long term into the deep whole. Then it is possible for it to have a refreshing kind of effect. Whether those things crash and cancel each other out is a very fraught question indeed, and depends on the emotions of the day as well. I'm becoming rather optimistic about it. I'm finding that kind of cycling is renewing. It makes it way more intense to navigate. But it can offer a tremendous contribution to resilience."

"The ingredients do need to have a certain richness to them," continues Beesley. "If you only drink Coke exclusively, it's going to get pretty thin. But the profound mixture of small increments can have a certain viability. Personally, I enjoy some periods that are almost monastic in their longevity. A long arc of just dwelling rather quietly, allowing multiple ingredients to rest and to be present. To wait for them to somehow condense into something that's much subtler and finer. That would be a model of something like a petri dish in which solutions are present and given enough peace and sanctuary to crystallize, for formation to occur. That's something that is very dependent upon boundaries. What are those ingredients? And how does that boundary work? There's great liability in it as well. Because that kind of model of creating sanctuary with a vital life inside it in unfortunate hands could be one of fascism, where the boundary is total. Where homogenization happens as opposed to fertility. It is no guarantee, but some period of contemplative or quieter practice does seem to be important in thinking about how disciplines can work together."

"How might the environments that this studio develops—what's the working method for generating?" Beesley asks. "A portion of the work is spent in classical rigor. Dwelling in the clearest, simplest possible idioms and fragments, building up a family of language, components, and systems which are thoroughly understood. Not, however, as a reductive objective. Not to clear away complexity,

15

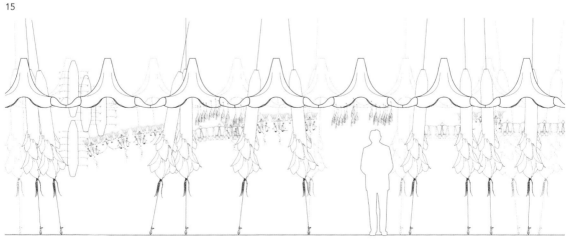

but quite the reverse. In order to enable a composer with a very strong and rich palette, that creates wilderness, requires much greater intensity. I'm very concerned with the rather abortive attempts to create density and richness that we've seen through the 20th century. I've become rather attached to the idea of building up component systems that have local integrity, then combining that in multiple loops of development. Then follow a couple fundamental vectors of physics. One pursuing maximum reaction, the other pursuing destruction, resistance, and consolidation. The first would be to pursue relations akin to a snowflake, flowers, or the gills of a fish. There's a risk that this will result in a saturation where things become homogenous and stuck again. The countering movement of mortality becomes a very effective one, to clear, destabilize by introducing division, and to intensify. I am trying to give anatomy to Le Corbusier's lovely saying, 'Creation is a patient search.' Because a lot is happening in the creation of the sanctuary of patience. You don't just sit still. While at the same time the arcs of generation can be rather long. It does seem very helpful for them to go through multiple cycles."

16 Philip Beesley/LASG/PBAI Hylozoic Soil, Laboratorio Arte Alameda, Festival de Mexico, Mexico City, 2010.
Hylozoic Soil was installed within the Laboratorio Arte Alameda. The detail shows a liquid system based on "protocells": prototype cells that use inorganic ingredients that combine into cell-like forms. The protocells are housed within digitally fabricated nest-like structures fitted with LEDs that stimulate chemical reaction.

17 Philip Beesley/LASG/PBAI Structural axonometric drawing of Sentient Chamber, National Academy of Sciences, Washington D.C., 2015-16.
The freestanding *Sentient Chamber* pavilion included an innovative structure employing a highly efficient three-dimensional truss system composed of thermally expanded acrylic and mechanically expanded stainless steel. The structure framed the upper entry to the main auditorium of the National Academy of Sciences, Washington, D.C.

17

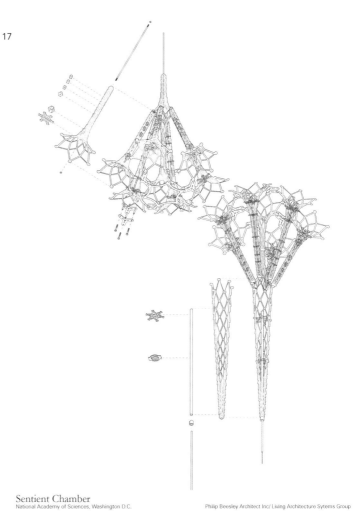

Sentient Chamber
National Academy of Sciences, Washington D.C.   Philip Beesley Architect Inc/ Living Architecture Sytems Group

18 Philip Beesley/LASG/PBAI breathing pore assembly diagram.

LASG designs components to form mechanical assemblies of controlled movement through the incorporation of sensors and kinetic "actuator" elements. Resilient, flexible materials—acrylic, copolyester, silicone, high-temper metal sheet stocks—are used. Kinetic components include fissured, frond-like surfaces that stir surrounding air and directly respond to human stimulus.

19 Philip Beesley/LASG/PBAI Chevron assembly diagrams.

A resilient structural scaffold forms the core of each LASG installation. This illustration details individual chevrons that are assembled into flexible diagrid scaffolding systems. Chevron units act as a basic building block from which a diverse set of resilient structures form. Chevrons provide force-shedding qualities, allowing elements under stress to transfer weight to neighboring supports in chained responses.

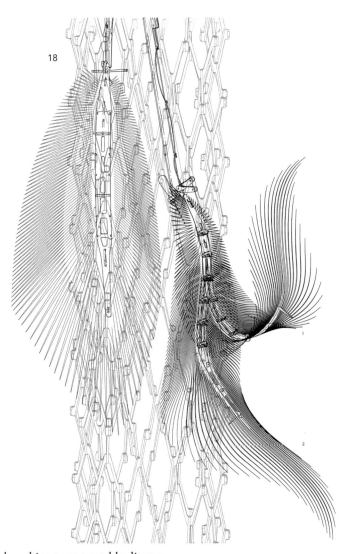

18

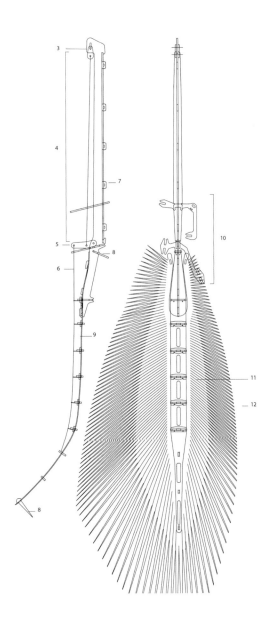

breathing pore assembly diagram

1 Breathing pore assembly actuated position 2 Breathing pore assembly rest position 3 Adjustable SMA clip 4 SMA
5 Lever 6 Tensioned tendon 7 Strengthening gusset for main spine 8 Gland clip
9 Copolyester tongue 10 Tongue clip 11 Arm units for attachment to mesh 12 Tongue struts 13 Feather

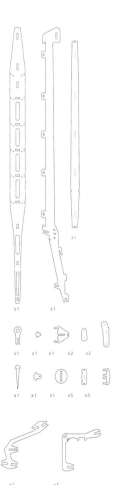

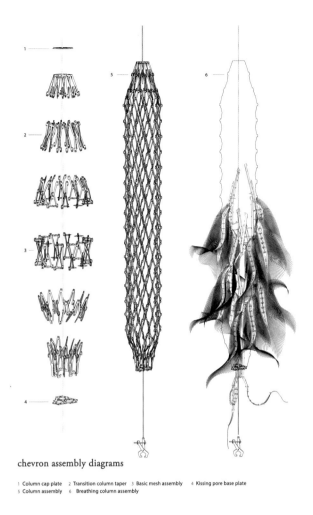

chevron assembly diagrams

1 Column cap plate   2 Transition column taper   3 Basic mesh assembly   4 Kissing pore base plate
5 Column assembly   6 Breathing column assembly

START WITH UTTER PRACTICALITY

To achieve both the practical and the ineffable, where does one begin? "If one were to stand amidst a very large forest, and for imagining strategies for building something of that complexity, it would be easy to be utterly swamped with the challenge," notes Beesley. "A cruel question would be to be asked to clean a battleship with a toothbrush. However, a satisfying involvement is of course possible. Our work tends to begin with utter practicality. Each joint is fashioned so that it fits in the next, and is developed to have a satisfying click—and if the forces for each component are worked on thoroughly so that they are balanced, they become capable of interlinking, and making a highly competent matrix where all the forces can be dynamically shed effectively, to create well-performing, resilient structures. If the assembly of these things is tuned so that your hands can push these elements together, using tools and jigs, out of that initial harmonization—which exists at a highly incremental scale— it becomes possible to orchestrate collective assembly systems and design systems, where things are not only done efficiently and expedited, it becomes possible to put them together and to work cooperatively in small tribes. The systems at that point start to get really interesting. A cadence can emerge, handing things off and assembling them. A stride emerges which tends to be amplified in a really extraordinary way, when you experience the rhythms of those assembled systems."

"That kind of meta-organization becomes a very significant thing. You might be helped by some enabling technologies. Digital fabrication in my case is a very significant tool. The significance of the cadences that combine at scale into rhythms that emerge are the most significant thing of all. Rather than simply making a complex environment by blowing your way through it, or having the money to make it happen, it's much more an experience of collective agency, of a deeply organized group of people. Not working individually but in multiple tribal clusters. A lot of energy gets generated with those interactions. Also in the agency of those quite small groups working together, there's a sense of stewardship that emerges that tends to flow outwards. This is very much a kind of a collective activity that produces the rather satisfying emergence that results. It couldn't possibly be achieved as a frozen music model."

On their way to the ineffable, Beesley's installations are described in almost human terms. "Lightweight interlinking systems are interwoven with next-generation chemistry that supports exchanges within the environment, in pursuit of an environment that 'cares.'" How important in the end is it that there is a practical side to the work that has been described as *an environment that cares*? "If I imagined being part of a community in the 13th century in a European town, coming up to the cathedral that would deeply guide my life," explains Beesley. "The hall and the framing of the space would be a religious act requiring the utmost of organization. The collective imagination of where the world is going in that kind of operation would be a central quality of a thing. In terms of my own practice, both utterly pragmatic function and unapologetic fiction and poetics are inevitably intermixed, and serve as reflections for each other. This sense of how very productive it is, inhabited fictions, is something I find entirely tantalizing. And is a very helpful way to understand architecture. I've tried to emphasize utter practicality as a kind of grounding. Looking locally, and having very deliberate conversations how much it weighs, how much waste, and how much it costs, and will it break as it ages? And yet at the same time the accompanying qualities are ones of consciousness, and the emotion that comes by imagining possibility. I simply don't know how to separate those things. Nor do I want to. Rather than seeing those as a polarity, where you have to choose between form and function, they work in multiple cycles. Stuttering, hiccupping cycles. Where you absolutely ground yourself. The consequences, as soon as you look at the impact of anything, you see it having ripples and objects around it. Those ripple out into the future as well. This to me almost qualifies as an internal question about how architecture works. As intermixing fact and fiction."

In *Design through Making,* Beesley said that his work mediates between craft and manufacturing; meaning and behavior; physicality and psychology.[31] It was almost that he was thinking in terms of convergence of these opposite poles. "I think of terms that affect me emotionally: one relates to past, the other relates to future," explains Beesley.[32] "The past or historical one would be a sense of coming culturally out of deep divisions. The utter cruelty of the Cold War. The yearning for harmonization is one that is a pretty acute and highly motivating state. I refer to Pierre Teilhard de Chardin with such lovely work as both a geologist and theologian, trying to reconcile those worlds in *The Phenomenon of Man.* In hoping that through the inter-combination of multiple technologies and geologies and cultures that the noosphere, the next stage of evolution, might be possible."

In conclusion, Beesley sees the convergence of the practical and ineffable in the opportunity to work collectively with living systems. "Looking to the future, on a practical level the achievements of the Human Genome Project (HGP) and the apparent completion of the General Theory of Relativity, the more recent work in gravitational waves, coupled to the wholesale agency that comes with this current generation in the widening and deepening of design tools, and enabling of fabrication methods, makes it possible to speak quite assertively about the possibility of working with life. Life as a genetic quality. A living system. Moving beyond analogies of a previous generation. Speaking quite literally about living systems. That calls on a harmonization of multiple disciplines. It invites a vision of convergence that is far from homogenizing or totalizing, but rather involves weed-like hybrids. Mongrels. Which produce tremendous vitality. So it is a stuttering, hiccupping, compulsive kind of convergence that I'm feasting on. Which has turned into a sense of commitment to a collective project."

ENDNOTES
1 Patrick Lynch, "Breaking Ground: Steven Holl Architects Celebrates 8 Projects Currently Under Construction," October 19, 2015, http://www.archdaily.com/775210/breaking-ground-steven-holl-architects-celebrates-8-projects-currently-under-construction.
2 Scott Barry Kaufman and Carolyn Gregoire, *Wired to Create: Unraveling the Mysteries of the Creative Mind* (New York: Penguin Publishing Group, Kindle ed.), xxv.
3 Ibid.
4 Scott Sheppard, "Autodesk Innovation Genome Example: How to Make Visualization Obsolete," February 19, 2016, http://labs.blogs.com/its_alive_in_the_lab/2016/02/autodesk-innovation-genome-example-how-to-make-visualization-obsolete.html.
5 Zach Kron, "Dynamo at Autodesk University 2015," December 8, 2015, http://dynamobim.org/dynamo-at-autodesk-university-2015/.
6 Anthony Frausto-Robledo, in "Brief: Highlights from AIA 2016 Philly," May 21, 2016, http://architosh.com/2016/05/

in-brief-highlights-from-aia-2016-philly/.

7 Pete Evans, "Perspectives on BEST of SHOW 2016: From Edge of Market to Maturing BIM, Framing a New Lens," June 3, 2016, http://architosh.com/2016/06/perspectives-on-best-of-show-2016-from-edge-of-market-to-maturing-bim-framing-a-new-lens/.

8 Blaine Brownell, "When Architecture, Art, and Biology Collide," May 24, 2016, http://www.architectmagazine.com/technology/when-architecture-art-and-biology-collide_o?utm_source=newsletter&utm_content=Opinion&utm_medium=email&utm_campaign=AN_052516%20.

9 Madeline Gannon, "Madeline the Robot Tamer," January 2016, https://vimeo.com/148982525.

10 Jeff Link, "Ways Architects and Postdigital Artisans Are Modernizing Craftsmanship," January 18, 2016, https://lineshapespace.com/postdigital-artisans/.

11 Brian Christian and Tom Griffiths, *Algorithms to Live By: The Computer Science of Human Decisions* (New York: Henry Holt, 2016) [audiobook].

12 David Alan Grier, "*Machines of Loving Grace,* by John Markoff," August 21, 2015, http://www.nytimes.com/2015/08/23/books/review/machines-of-loving-grace-by-john-markoff.html.

13 Abbeville Press website blurb for Eliane Strosberg, *Art and Science* (2d ed.), http://www.abbeville.com/bookpage.asp?isbn=9780789212191.

14 Markku Allison, interview with author, May 11, 2016.

15 Toru Hasegawa, interview with author, April 19, 2016.

16 Samim Winiger and Roelof Pieters, "CreativeAI: On the Democratisation & Escalation of Creativity," March 7, 2016, https://medium.com/@ArtificialExperience/creativeai-9d4b2346faf3#.gun5063a8.

17 Klaus Philipsen, "Beauty—Not in the Eye of the Beholder," March 25, 2016, http://archplanbaltimore.blogspot.com/2016/03/beauty-not-in-eye-of-beholder.html.

18 Stephanie Hughes, "Beauty and the Brain: Understanding Our Responses to Art," March 6, 2015, http://www.sciencefriday.com/articles/beauty-and-the-brain-understanding-our-responses-to-art/.

19 Norman Foster, "Building the Future," April 29, 1999, http://news.bbc.co.uk/2/hi/uk_news/330624.stm.

20 Theodore Spyropoulos, AADRL Spyropoulos Design Lab, 2015, https://vimeo.com/131823232.

21 http://deathofdrawing.com.

22 MIT Architecture, "Overview," https://architecture.mit.edu/computation/program/overview.

23 David Dick-Agnew, "Toronto's Partisans Is on a Winning Streak," November 23, 2015, http://www.azuremagazine.com/article/update-on-partisans/.

24 Martin Gayford, "Robot Art Raises Questions about Human Creativity," February 15, 2016, https://www.technologyreview.com/s/600762/robot-art-raises-https://

www.technologyreview.com/s/600762/robot-art-raises-questions-about-human-creativity/#/set/id/600857/.

25 Alexandra Spring, "Can Machines Come up with More Creative Solutions to Our Problems than We Can?" March 29, 2016, http://www.theguardian.com/sustainable-business/2016/mar/29/can-machines-come-up-with-more-creative-solutions-to-our-problems-than-we-can?linkId=23041602

26 *Journal of Design and Science,* "Discussion: Age of Entanglement," January 20, 2016, http://jods.mitpress.mit.edu/pub/AgeOfEntanglement/discussions.

27 Christopher Hawthorne, "Assemble Might Have a Turner Prize, But the London Collective Continues to Defy Categorization," April 28, 2016, http://www.latimes.com/entertainment/arts/la-ca-cm-assemble-architecture-20160501-column.html.

28 Neri Oxman, "Age of Entanglement," *Journal of Design and Science,* January 20, 2016, http://jods.mitpress.mit.edu/pub/AgeOfEntanglement?version=2.

29 Ibid.

30 Philip Beesley, interview with author, March 18, 2016.

31 Philip Beesley, "Orgone Reef," in *Design through Making,* ed. Bob Scheil (Hoboken, NJ: John Wiley & Sons, 2005).

32 Philip Beesley, interview with author, March 18, 2016.

IMAGES

Figures 1–4 © Deutsch Insights; figures 5–7 © PARTISANS; figures 8–19 © PBAI, Philip Beesley photographer

1

USER INTERFACE (UI)
EASE OF USE
STREAMLINING INFORMATION
PROJECT WORKFLOW
INTEGRATED DESIGN
COLLABORATION
INTEROPERAB
SENSORS
BECOMING AGILE
ACCESSIB
INTERNET OF THINGS
COMPLEXITY
INTERDISCIPLINA
OPEN SOURCE
BLUR
CONNECTI
CON
UBIQUITOUS DATA
ALGORITHMS
SUPERINTEGRA
IMPATIE
MILLENNIAL MINDSET
PARAMETRIC TOOLS
SIMULTAN
USER EMPOWERMENT
FEEDB
SOFTWARE-AS-A-SERVICE (SAAS)
DOWNSTREAM CONSEQUENCES
CLOUD COMPUTING
COMPUTATIONAL DESIGN

2

EPILOGUE:
AN IMPENDING PERIOD
OF INTENSE CHANGE

INTEROPERABILITY & ACCESSIBILITY
INTERDISCIPLINARITY & BLURRING
CONNECTIVITY & CONTEXT
SUPERINTEGRATION & IMPATIENCE
SIMULTANEITY & FEEDBACK

Announced in December 2015 at Autodesk University, construction document management beta Project Alexandria became Autodesk BIM 360 Docs. Usable on iPhones and iPads, working through a web browser, BIM 360 Docs, a cloud-based document management system developed in-house at Autodesk for reviewing and collaborating on project files, enables work to happen faster by providing project teams with the right information when they need it, and by enabling the project team to publish, manage, review, and approve project documents and models in the cloud.[1] BIM 360 Docs advertises itself as "One app. Period. Using different apps for blueprint viewing, PDF markups, issue management, and file sharing leaves teams out of sync. Get everything in one place—and accessible on the Web, tablets and phones—to always stay current and connected."[2]

Today, we're seeing convergences everywhere, not just in the AEC industry. Car maker Local Motors recently partnered with IBM to create "Olli," the world's first self-driving, electric minibus whose chassis is manufactured using 3D printing. Olli "makes use of IBM's 'Watson' cognitive learning technology."[3] But many questions for architects remain: What are the implications of the convergence for practice? Knowing how technologies and work processes are converging, how will architects be educated? How can design professionals leverage the convergence for competitive advantage? What are implications of convergence for design and aesthetics? For how we design buildings and cities, and how we fabricate and construct? For how we work with one another, to the greatest benefit of others?

1 Deutsch Insights, Converging Sankey Factors, 2017.
The factors or drivers that lead to convergence place it into a larger context, helping us to see where the industry is headed.

2 Deutsch Insights, Apps to Platforms, 2017.
The focus today is less on the individual software tools than on the project data and platform within which the tools are designed to run.

For those in academia, the design professions and industry are experiencing a tectonic shift approaching a real-time/right-time meeting point marked by multidisciplinary integration, intersections, interactions—and, we dare say, collisions. Because areas of professional expertise are converging on transdisciplinary teams increasingly made up of data scientists, computer scientists, mathematicians, sociologists, statisticians, strategists, scripters, and economists working alongside design professionals, it is no longer adequate for students of architecture, engineering, and construction management, or for design and industry professionals, to strive to learn and master segmented, individualized skills. Being proficient in any one domain—whether skill, technology, or tool—is no longer sufficient. *Being proficient is no longer sufficient.*[4] Adapting to the new world of work requires learning to think simultaneously on several fronts, and from several points of view. This is the world of convergence

SketchUp model of
room geometry for
acoustic analysis

Stage lighting and
catwalk criteria, ideal
lighting angles to achieve

Acoustic transparency
diagrams, analysis
results, and material
criteria

JHA
Acoustics

FDA
Theater

DWG containing
lighting locations,
with cone of light for
position analysis

3D DWG model of
ceiling with openings
for speakers and
screen rigging

JHA
Audio/Visual

LMN
Architects

ACM
Material

Connection details,
feasibility studies,
mockups

3D DWG model
containing speaker
and screen locations

Revit model with
openings for house
lighting positions
highlighted

HLB
Lighting

SFP
Fire

DWG or Inventor file
containing panel face
geometry laid out for
cutting

Sprinkler criteria
related to required
spacing and area of
coverage

2D DWG containing
the ideal lighting
locations in plan

PDF documenting
the location of the
sprinkler openings

3

4

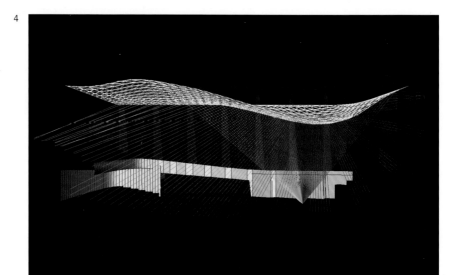

thinking that we have explored in this book. As we have seen, the convergence of sensors, networks, artificial intelligence, and robotics, among many other technologies and work processes, is making amazing things possible.[5]

THE SOFTWARE OF EVERYTHING

The superintegration of apps that address design professionals' tasks leads to what we are calling here the Software of Everything. It's the desire to have one tool do everything: the Swiss Army knife of architectural tools. Think of it as the single-model approach to design. It is a compelling idea, but is it possible to achieve? If so, is it even desirable? As much as we say we prefer a single source of responsibility, do we want one tool to do it all? "Within our industry is a new direction that goes way beyond integration that I've never heard anybody talk about: the end game of integration," said Markku Allison. "The Software of Everything is a compelling output in the mix."[6]

Allison continues: "I have no idea if we lose something significant with the Software of Everything—maybe that is outside of the purview. Maybe that will always be the human addition to the conversation, the ineffable, and the Software of Everything can't do it. A Software of Everything—we can give it rule sets to follow and points of comparison, and it can give us a judgment whether or not we hit all these data points and all the different points of comparison. In terms of some ineffable quality, I don't think the Software of Everything could pick that up. That's our age-old challenge as a profession. If I say that the real heart and soul of architecture is this *ineffable* thing, then you can't really measure it in some respects. How do you sell that value to the owner? I don't have a good answer for that. We can devise a system: this is the thing in the middle but we can't talk about the thing. But we can talk about this and this and this, etc. We can talk about all these things in such ways now that suddenly we've implied the thing. We can come at it from that respect, but we can still never talk about the thing. The computer or the Software of Everything can do a good job of hitting all these perimeter data points, but whether it actually captures the thing … ?"

The polarities presented in this book—for instance, the practical and the ineffable—are too often thought of as either/or propositions, when the convergence between them is what we need to focus on. "In the conscious mind, we typically divide activity into intuitive thinking (emotions and subjective truth) and rational thinking (logic and objective truth)." Psychologist Scott Barry Kaufman calls this distinction "a false one," where instead "we need to embrace what he calls 'the middle way.'"[7]

"Leveraging the input of multiple people may take more time or may take more money, but the richness and robustness of the outcomes may outweigh those restrictions," Allison reflects. "As these transformations move through business and culture, the things which we value and appreciate might change also. I've not spent much time in Nordic countries or Scandinavia, but it

3 LMN Architects in association with Neumann Monson.
Consultants in acoustics, structures, material science, theatrical systems, lighting design, mechanical design, audio/visual design, and fire protection looped into progressive design iterations.

4 LMN Architects in association with Neumann Monson.
Sound can be analyzed with raytracing even though it actually moves in a wave.

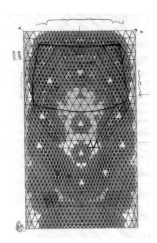  

5

6

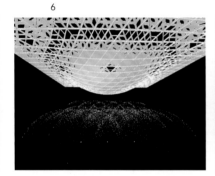 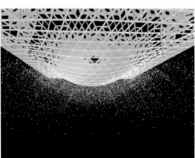 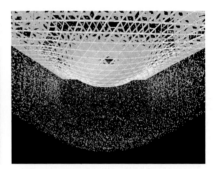

7

7 LMN Architects in association with Neumann Monson.

The design team made prototypes to support the design process. The physical and digital models informed the overall shaping, drove refinement of the opening geometry, and have been useful in exploring potential fabrication strategies. All of the cut files for generating the models were produced by the Grasshopper definition, allowing the cut files to be constantly updated as the design was being developed.

5 LMN Architects in association with Neumann Monson.
Hand drawings were provided by the acoustical consultant depicting the opaque and transparent areas of the proposed reflector geometry. These were translated by the architect and mapped to the parametric model to control how open or closed a given area could become.

6 LMN Architects in association with Neumann Monson.
Custom simulation visualizations were developed to aid in the design team's understanding of how the reflector would shape acoustic reflections.

seems they value a much broader range of things than we do here. It's not measured only by the dollar, but there's this ineffable quality that they're willing to invest in. Scandinavia and Nordic countries alone out of all Western culture came out of the modern movement better. If you look at Europe and the U.S., the modern movement ended up meaning less. Somehow the Scandinavian and Nordic countries kept a level of romance and humanism about their work. A richness—there's an acknowledgement of a richness of experience. One of the fringe benefits of the convergence of everything might be that we become more aware of this opportunity for richness. With the Software of Everything and convergence, more and more people will be able to do more and more of this stuff. What is the quality that will separate one outcome from another? It's probably going to start to zero in on those ineffable things."

"One thing is the happy accident," continues Allison. "Somebody on your team was on vacation in 1982 in the remote plains of Scotland and they had an experience that for whatever reason comes to the front of their brain when we are tackling this particular problem, and it completely changes the nature of the answer. IBM's Watson will never give us that answer. I'm sure we will be able to have serendipitous experiences with Watson where it pulls some whacky thing because it thought I said tomatoes instead of architecture. And that answer about tomatoes completely changes my thinking about the project. So that's not out of the realm of possibility. In a collaborative environment you multiply that opportunity. You have ten Watsons instead of one Watson."

"The Software of Everything? What it really means is that I have the opportunity to interface with a system. It's not apps, it's a whole platform, it's an environment—an operating environment. The idea that the tool will address the problem in any way I want the tool to address that problem in that moment in time. I might be sketching the way the sun strikes a window trim detail and think, wow, I wonder about the impact on BTUs? Let's look at our energy counts. Maybe it changes the quantity or material on a spreadsheet. It makes me think about particular pattern generation I might have thought of. *The ability to just—if I can think it, it can do it. In real time.* Right now we have that capability. Largely, if I can think it, there's something out there that can probably do it. I have to find the tool and drive the tool to make it do it. If I'm in an operating environment that lets me think it and the tool does it in one seamless movement. *Will made manifest.* That feels a little almost fascist. It's a little Nietzsche. It feels a little strong, but just the idea that if I imagine a drawing I make a drawing. If I imagine writing, it's writing. It's my magic pencil that will allow me to create. The Software of Everything allows me to create in any mode I want to create in that moment in time. To express, to solve, to explore, to do it all." While the public release of such a platform may still be a ways off, one intriguing instance of the Software of Everything is Project Quantum, Autodesk's next-generation BIM initiative announced at Autodesk University in both 2015 and,

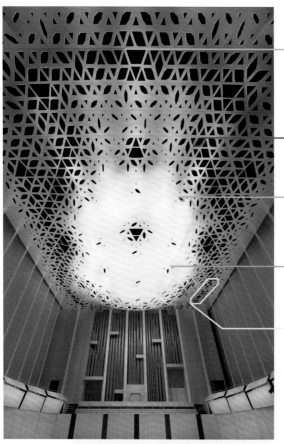

Audio Speakers - Large openings allowing sound profile of each speaker to pass through unimpeded. Two of the speaker openings must be large enough for the speaker arrays to be lowered through the reflector into the audience portion of the hall. Speaker locations provided by A/V Consultant.

Stage Lighting - Medium openings allowing light cone to pass through unimpeded. Stage lights are loosely arranged along contours of the reflector to ease layout of catwalks. Layout criteria provided by Theater Consultant

House Lighting - Small openings allowing light cone to pass through unimpeded. House lights are distributed throughout the reflector. Lighting locations provided by Lighting Consultant.

Fire Protection - Small openings allowing sprinkling from below ceiling in areas where openness is less than 70%

Acoustic Transparency- Inserted into areas where increased acoustic transparency is needed. Size of openings is determined based upon a combination of acoustic transparency and size of surrounding openings.

8

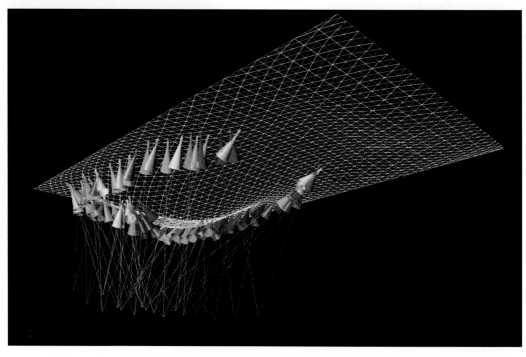

9

8 LMN Architects in association with Neumann Monson.
From the initial concept stage, a nimble and robust parametric model became the central generative tool, enabling coordination among disciplines to a high level of precision.

9 LMN Architects in association with Neumann Monson.
Theater consultant provides a set of rules for finding the locations of the stage lighting, which are encoded into the Grasshopper definition to find the initial layout of the lights.

10 LMN Architects in association with Neumann Monson.
The agility of the parametric model further engaged the architects in producing direct-to-fabrication data for construction. The design team used a three-axis CNC mill to prototype full-scale components and connections for testing. Construction managers and fabricators gave critical feedback affecting system detailing, componentry, and construction sequencing.

10

in more detail in 2016, that aims to deliver architectural design, engineering, structural analysis, fabrication, and construction in the cloud.

In contrast, Nathan Miller takes exception to the idea of the Software of Everything. "We're always looking for a new product or new software, something that's going to replace everything," explained Miller. "Why can't it just be what we have on our phones? Why can't it just be the web? One of the things we're doing at Proving Ground that intrigues me the most is building connections via API to anything that's going to improve or inform the building process. There are websites that track all of the APIs that are available on the Internet—all of the possible connections one can make to various data sources. There is a lot of hype around the 'Internet of Things' for a reason, and there are real-world practical applications to put this concept into practice, and access to sensors and weather data. Live, real-time—it's all there. It's just not connected. It's not necessarily funneled into the tool we're using desktop-side. I have heard people refer to IFC as the 'HTML for buildings' … but why not just use HTML, or the other languages of the web itself? Why can't HTML be the HTML for buildings? Autodesk is on this path with tools like Fusion 360. Tools like Onshape are taking these ideas to another level, with integrated product design and management all happing through the web browser. To me, the Software of Everything is the stuff that's staring us right in the face."[8]

"Think about the various data sources that are out there," continues Miller. "The APIs that are available on the web. They are all slices. If you look at any one slice individually, you see all the things that that slice is forgetting, neglecting, or not considering in their dataset. Inevitably it looks incomplete—there are a lot of holes. If you're looking at horizontal slices, like floor plates in a building, and each floor plate has its own pockets or holes. Then, when you go to plan view, they're all covered up. So how do you thread the needle between all the floor plates to where you have the data that you need to make decisions? Threading the needle is about connecting the relevant APIs for the design problem you're in. Potentially, you're building your own contribution to that. When I go to a client who has a specific problem, they're like 'if we only had the data.' I'm like, it's right there. They say they can't get to it. Sure you can—it has an API or it's publically available. But it's not something designers and architects are trained to think about." "Think about it as a socket," advises Miller. "How do you get to the electricity running through a wall? We need an interface to get to electricity. That interface is a power outlet. That's what an API is: An access point into the data stream."

Architecture is a complex undertaking requiring the input of many individuals with varying interests, backgrounds, and expertise. This has not changed, and will not change. As we have seen throughout this book, what is changing is the way these individuals are working, communicating, and collaborating: their individual contributions are converging. In response, they are integrating

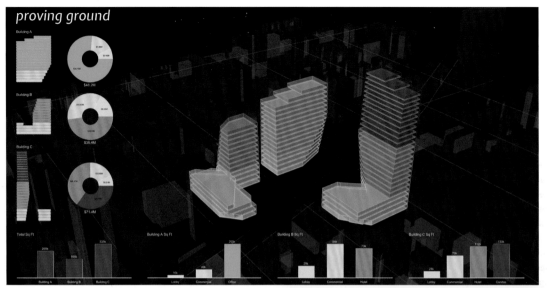

proving ground

Building A

Building B

Building C

$48.2M

$38.4M

$71.4M

Total Sq Ft

Building A Sq Ft

Building B Sq Ft

Building C Sq Ft

Building A   Building B   Building C

Lobby   Commercial   Office

Lobby   Commercial   Hotel

Lobby   Commercial   Hotel   Condos

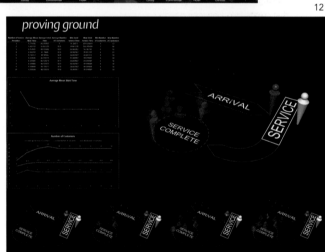

proving ground

Average Mean Wait Time

Number of Customers

ARRIVAL   SERVICE   SERVICE

SERVICE COMPLETE

ARRIVAL   SERVICE   SERVICE COMPLETE   ARRIVAL   SERVICE   SERVICE COMPLETE   ARRIVAL   SERVICE   SERVICE COMPLETE   ARRIVAL   SERVICE

13

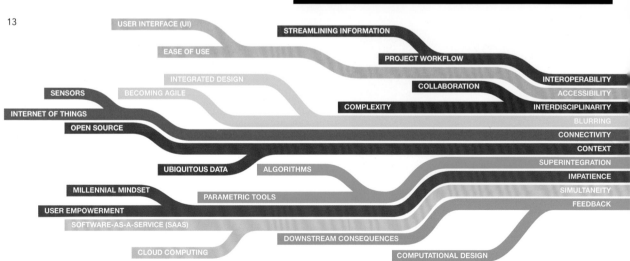

USER INTERFACE (UI)

STREAMLINING INFORMATION

EASE OF USE

PROJECT WORKFLOW

INTEGRATED DESIGN

INTEROPERABILITY

SENSORS   BECOMING AGILE

COLLABORATION

ACCESSIBILITY

INTERNET OF THINGS

COMPLEXITY

INTERDISCIPLINARITY

OPEN SOURCE

BLURRING

CONNECTIVITY

CONTEXT

UBIQUITOUS DATA   ALGORITHMS

SUPERINTEGRATION

IMPATIENCE

MILLENNIAL MINDSET

PARAMETRIC TOOLS

SIMULTANEITY

USER EMPOWERMENT

FEEDBACK

SOFTWARE-AS-A-SERVICE (SAAS)

CLOUD COMPUTING

DOWNSTREAM CONSEQUENCES

COMPUTATIONAL DESIGN

their efforts, not multitasking. To meet today's demands for speed, affordability, and quality, they are taking and making smart cuts, not shortcuts. They are currently learning to do this at conferences, at hackathons, at informal meet-ups, in online forums, via gaming, and in social media.

It is my hope, with this book, that the learning and exploration will continue, to the greatest benefit to those who are most in need of what convergence has to offer.

11 Proving Ground, Parametric Massing Tool and Dashboard, 2016. When combined with parametric models, dashboards provide intuitive, real-time feedback on design decisions.

12 Proving Ground, Parametric Massing Tool and Dashboard, 2016.
Proving Ground is working on new tools that create links between operational data, simulation, and parametric iteration.

13 Deutsch Insights, Convergence Futures, 2017.
The factors or drivers that lead to convergence place it into a larger context, but where this all leads is largely up to you: the industry's innovators, educators, and technologists.

ENDNOTES

1 http://bim360.com/docs.
2 Erin Green, "Behind the Scenes with BIM 360 Docs," January 13, 2016, http://www.engineering.com/BIM/ArticleID/11295/Behind-the-Scenes-with-BIM-360-Docs.aspx.
3 Joe Quirke, "Olli the Printed Self-Driving Minibus Hits the Road in the US," June 23, 2016, http://www.bimplus.co.uk/technology/olii-print5ed-self-driv5ing-min4ibus-hits-road-us/.
4 "Why Being Proficient Is Not Sufficient," November 27, 2013, https://bimandintegrateddesign.com/2013/11/27/why-being-proficient-is-not-sufficient/.
5 Vivek Wadhwa, "These 6 Technologies Will Define 2016—and Make the Impossible Possible," January 18, 2016, https://www.linkedin.com/pulse/6-technologies-define-2016and-make-impossible-possible-vivek-wadhwa?trk=hp-feed-article-title-comment.
6 Markku Allison, interview with author, May 11, 2016.
7 Scott Barry Kaufman, "True Creativity Is the Subconscious Mind Combined with Intuition and Rationality," May 1, 2016, http://bigthink.com/videos/scott-barry-kaufman-on-intuition-and-rationality?utm_medium=Social&utm_source=Twitter&utm_campaign=Echobox&utm_term=Autofeed
8 Nathan Miller, interview with author, February 23, 2016.

IMAGES

Figures 1, 2, 13 © Deutsch Insights; figures 3–10 © LMN Architects; figures 11 and 12 © Proving Ground

INTEROPERABILITY & ACCESSIBILITY
INTERDISCIPLINARITY & BLURRING
CONNECTIVITY & CONTEXT
SUPERINTEGRATION & IMPATIENCE
SIMULTANEITY & FEEDBACK
?

INDEX